Religions of the World

Ronald J. Wilkins

BROWN-ROA

Dubuque, Iowa

Book Team

Publisher

Matthew J. Thibeau

Production Coordinator

Phil Niles

Editor

Marilyn Bowers Gorun

Production Services Manager

Marilyn Rothenberger

Marketing Manager

Ginny Schumacher

Art Director

Cathy Frantz

Acknowledgments

From *Understanding Zen* by Amy and Benjamin Radcliff. Copyright in 1993 by Benjamin and Amy Radcliff. First published by Charles E. Tuttle Co., Inc. in 1993. Used by permission of Charles E. Tuttle Co., Inc. All rights reserved.

From *Shinto: The Kami Way* by Dr. Sokyo Ono, copyright 1962. Used by permission of Charles E. Tuttle Co., Inc., Tokyo, Japan.

Hermann Hesse: *Siddhartha*. Copyright 1951 by New Directions Publishing Corp. Reprinted by permission of New Directions Publishing Corp.

From *The Heart of the Buddha* by Chögyam Trungpa. © 1991 by Diana J. Mukpo. Reprinted by arrangement with Shambhala Publications, Inc., 300 Massachusetts Avenue, Boston, MA 02115.

Passages from the Jewish Bible in chapter 4 are taken from TANAKH: The New JPS According to the Traditional Hebrew Text. Copyright © 1985. Reprinted by permission of the Jewish Publication Society, Philadelphia.

Excerpt from "I Was An Atheist In a Foxhole," by Philip K. Paulsen, Sept/Oct '89, *The Humanist*. Reprinted with permission of the American Humanist Association, Copyright © 1989.

Excerpts from *Exploring Religion*, 2nd ed., by Roger Schmidt, Copyright © 1988 by Wadsworth Publishing Company. Reprinted by permission of Wadsworth Publishing Company.

Passages from the Christian Bible in chapter 5 are from the *New Revised Standard Version of the Bible*, copyright © 1989 by the Division of Christian Education of the National Council of Churches of Christ in the USA. Used by permission. All rights reserved.

SELECTED EXCERPTS FROM PAGES 1–2, 224–225, 267, 310–311 from THE WORLD'S RELIGIONS by HUSTON SMITH. Copyright © 1991 by Huston Smith. Reprinted by permission of HarperCollins Publishers, Inc.

EXCERPT from "CHRISTIANITY" FROM RELIGIOUS TRADITIONS OF THE WORLD by SANDRA SIZER FRANKIEL. Copyright © 1985 by Sandra Sizer Frankiel. Reprinted by permission of HarperCollins Publishers, Inc.

EXCERPT from "ISLAM AND THE MUSLIM COMMUNITY" FROM RELIGIOUS TRADITIONS OF THE WORLD by FREDERICK M. DENNY. Copyright © 1988 by Frederick M. Denny. Reprinted by permission of HarperCollins Publishers, Inc.

EXCERPT from "HINDUISM" FROM RELIGIOUS TRADITIONS OF THE WORLD by DAVID M. KNIPE. Copyright © 1991 by David M. Knipe. Reprinted by permission of HarperCollins Publishers, Inc.

Photo credits

Photo credits appear on page 200.

ISBN   0-697-17796-3

10   9   8

Contents

Part Three: The Question of Atheism

Chapter 10

Preface

economic system

The network of services by which a group of people obtain food, water, shelter, and other material necessities.

political system

The network of government to ensure the provision of necessities in an orderly and equitable manner.

human society

The organization of people into political and social groups to provide the necessities of life.

culture

A people's expression of who they are and what they believe about themselves and the world in which they live, the sum of their art, literature, music, dance, folklore, and religion.

Civilization developed over the course of many centuries. When primitive people discovered that their survival depended on mutual cooperation, they developed ways to live in peace with each other. They created an **economic system** that would provide food, water, and shelter, and a **political system** that would enable them to provide these necessities in an orderly and relatively equitable manner. The organization of people into political and social groups to provide the necessities of life is called **human society.** As time went on, people's economic and political systems became more sophisticated, but the purpose of those systems remained the same.

As people organize into political and social groups to provide life's necessities, they express who they are and what they believe about themselves and the world in which they live. This expression is called their **culture**—the sum of their art, literature, music, dance, folklore, and religion. It is this last element—religion—that is the subject matter of this book.

The historical reality of religion cannot be denied. It has been a part of the human experience since the dawn of civilization and has had a significant impact on the way civilization has developed. Its beliefs and practices have played a major role in shaping human culture. "Through their symbol system," said Gregory Baum, an authority on the sociology of religion, "the religions have provided [humans] with a vision of life, an orientation of their energies, and a hierarchy of values that eventually produced various forms of culture and society. And through its own institutions, the religions have affected the style of life of vast numbers of people, and have created attitudes and practices that eventually had a profound influence on culture and society." To see what this influence has been and is, *Religions of the World* examines these religions. It looks at their origins, their beliefs, their practices, and their current status in the world.

It is not enough, however, to look at the religions that have shaped, and are shaping, the cultures of the world. It is necessary, also, to look at the origin of religion, and to define and describe religion as a human phenomenon. Only in this way can we understand why religion has so profoundly influenced the shape of human culture and the expression of human needs.

Any human institution or expression of culture is a product of its own past. Like human beings and their institutions and culture, religion has experienced change. It is different from the way it was, but its roots are buried deep in the soil of human development. To know its origin and its expressions in the past is to understand its expressions at the present time. *Religions of the World* discusses the origin of religion and proposes a definition of religion that can serve as a hub around which discussions of religion, religious awareness, and the role of religion in modern society can revolve.

The goal of *Religions of the World* is not simply to define religion and its expressions as they are found in the world today. Its goal is to help you better understand **people.** In our multicultural society and in this age of global interaction, it is imperative that we better understand other people. We can do so if we understand their religious orientations—which, to a large extent, determine their vision of life, their moral values, their motivations, their hopes and fears, their joys and sorrows, their individuality and complexity.

Your study of the religions of the world will not only increase your knowledge and enable you to understand other people better, however—it will also enrich your life.

Word list

culture
economic system
human society
political system

Part One
The Origin of Religion

1 What Is Religion?

Sooner or later, all people face the question of the relevancy of religion in their lives. Whether they have been raised in a religiously oriented culture or in a **secular** or atheistic atmosphere, they ask themselves about religion. They wonder what religion is, why it is, whether it is necessary, whether it is natural to people, and whether it is for them. Eventually, everyone takes a stance concerning religion.

Why is this so?

Perhaps the first reason is that people experience religion around them. They see it in action and wonder why religion is part of human experience. Depending on what they see, they have a favorable or unfavorable impression of religion. They decide that it is for them, or they decide that it is not for them.

The second reason seems to be that people who have been brought up in a particular religion wonder about it. They ask what their religion really means, where it came from, why they belong to this religious community rather than that, how their religion compares with other religions, whether it is "true," and whether they should seek another or abandon the practice of any religion.

Some people also wonder about religion because of the influence some religious people have or have had on the world scene, for example, a pope, an evangelist, a missioner, a political-religious leader. Conversely, there are those who wonder about religion because they see many influential people around them practicing no religion or expressing a kind of disdain for or amused tolerance of religion. They wonder whether religion should affect their lives at all.

Still others, because they are unable to answer serious religious questions, wonder if religion really is a psychological crutch, an invention, a racket, or a superstition left over from "unenlightened" days.

Perhaps the most common reason for people asking themselves about religion and its role in their lives, however, is that, at some point in their lives, they have asked themselves about the meaning of life. They have searched for answers to questions about life that go beyond the obvious, the measurable, the observable, or the scientific. They have searched for answers to the *mystery of life*. They wonder where life came from, where it is going, and what its purpose is.

secular

Nonreligious; worldly or temporal.

Hindu dieties, Monkey God Temple, Singapore.

mystery

The unknown and unknowable dimension of reality that lies behind and beyond ordinary human experience.

Encounter with mystery

Behind humanity's questions about life's meaning and purpose lies an encounter with mystery. **Mystery** is the unknown and unknowable dimension of reality that lies behind and beyond ordinary human experience. It is "an area of incomprehensibility that cannot, even in principle, be mastered by scientific expertise."[1]

The mystery of life confronts people at various times in their lives. When they experience the power, the beauty, or the magnitude of the universe, they wonder where it came from, what its purpose is, what it means, and where it is going.

When a man and a woman experience the joy of true love, they wonder about its source, its meaning, its purpose, and its uniqueness.

When a husband and wife experience the journey of pregnancy and the wonder of birth, they ask themselves where life comes from.

The mystery of life confronts people most of all, however, when they are in the presence of death. For most people, death is the great mystery: the unexpected, the unknown, the point where mystery is master. Death raises the ultimate question: What is life? And that question demands an answer.

People's response to mystery

In response to their experience of the mystery of life, especially in its sacred or transcendent dimension, people have, in various places and at various times, formulated different answers. Whatever the answer, however, it contained a response to the decisive question: Where did life come from?

Some have found an explanation for the origin of life in the idea of many gods, each fulfilling a separate function and arranged in order of importance and power. Some believe in one God, explaining that their God is a Person, while others explain their God in impersonal terms.

Some have found their answer without God. They explain life in terms of the harmonious unfolding of material possibilities into more complex forms with even greater possibilities. They simply leave the question of the origin of these possibilities unanswered. They conclude that since the existence of God cannot be proved, God does not exist.

---

1. John F. Haught, *What Is Religion?* (New York and New Jersey: Paulist Press, 1990), 165.

Some people respond to the question, "Where did life come from?" by saying that there is no answer to the question. Others believe that life always was. They say it had no beginning. They believe that life is lived in a series of reincarnations—successive lives for a single person.

A sixth response to the question of life's origins comes from those who believe that people's role and purpose in life is meaningless. They believe that life is a tragic mistake, a trick of fate, a barbarous cruelty, a stroke of bad luck. They believe that death is a merciful release from an unwanted existence.

Whatever answer people have formulated, however, it is a response to the mystery of life.

What religion is

One way to define **religion** is to say that it is the response a person gives to the mystery of life. It is the attempt on the part of each individual to express a relationship to the mystery of life. In this sense, therefore, it includes the many different ways people have of expressing what they think life is all about. It encompasses both those whose response is found in a God answer and those whose response is found in a no-God answer, because both responses are based on faith.

Another way to define religion is to say that it is a response to the mystery of life that is organized, **ritualized,** and agreed upon by a group of people, whether that group gives a God answer or a no-God answer to the mystery of life. This is religion as it is ordinarily understood. When most people hear the word *religion,* this is what they think of. So Judaism, Christianity, Islam, Buddhism, Hinduism, and so on are all religions in this sense of the word. It is religion in this sense that is the subject matter of *Religions of the World.* (When the word *religion* is used in this book, which sense is meant should be clear from the context.)

Are the answers of any religion provable? Not if you are looking for scientific proof that can be mathematically formulated and verified by sense observation. There is no physical or chemical data on God or the Divine, on life after death, on heaven or eternity, just as there is no mathematical or chemical proof or neatly measurable data on honesty or loyalty or parental love. Religion deals with a dimension beyond scientific grasp. Science can tell us about the data of life that are measurable, but it leaves unanswered such questions as why life exists and what its destiny is.

religion

The response a person gives to the mystery of life; a response to the mystery of life that is organized, ritualized, and agreed upon by a group of people.

ritual

The ordered words and actions of a religious ceremony.

Science and mathematics unravel the *problems* of the universe; religion responds to the *mystery* of the universe. When a problem is unravelled, the mind is satisfied, but since mystery can never be unravelled, the mind is never satisfied but always restless. The more people solve the physical, chemical, and biological problems of the universe, the more they can apply nature to their own purposes. But no one is able to unravel the mystery of another person's freedom or the mystery of why one individual and not somebody else exists. People cannot bend mystery to their purposes—they can only give themselves to the purposes of that mystery, which is greater than themselves.

Responses are based on faith

Whether people root the mystery of life in one God, the Divine, many gods, or no God, and whether they formulate their destiny as an afterlife, an endless cycle of repeated lives, or a meaningful life that ends with the grave—their "certainty" in these answers is not scientific but is based on an act of *trust*.

Through their various beliefs, those who give a God answer to the mystery of life say, in effect, "The mystery can be trusted. It has thrust me into life and will one day call me out of life. I do not know why, but I trust there is a reason. I am an intelligent being; intelligence needs a purpose. Without a purpose, life would be unintelligible—but an unintelligible life for an intelligent being would be a cruel contradiction of my own nature. I trust that life is not ultimately so cruel. I believe, therefore, that life (and death, too, as a part of life) makes sense."

The faith of people whose answer is no-God centered (or universe-centered, or reality-centered) might be expressed this way: "People are not all there is. They are sharers of existence with All That Is. In one way or another, a person confronts the *Not-me*—that which is not himself or herself—and says, in effect, 'I can trust the *Not-me*. Reality is my friend.' Reality is not rooted in some kind of God. It is rooted in a Trustable Something, which makes it possible to say: 'Life makes sense. It is not to be wasted. It is to be responsibly lived. Death does not cancel out the meaning of a responsibly lived life.'"

But, one may ask, what about those who say there is no answer to the mystery of life? Is their response also based on faith? Of course it is, for faith is the ultimate ingredient of an inquiring mind. It must search for an answer to mystery, and it is not satisfied until it finds an answer—whatever it may be. The faith of people whose answer to the mystery of life is no answer might be expressed in this way, "I believe there is no answer to the mystery of life. That is my answer."

The influence of religion on society today

Even though religion has been a major factor influencing the development of various cultures, its influence has ebbed and flowed. The reasons for this are as diverse and as complex as human nature itself. The influence of religion is related to the political, economic, and cultural philosophies of countries as professed and practiced by their leaders. In recent times, this influence has involved the orientation of the media and the charisma of religious leaders. The influence of religion also depends on the credibility of those who profess and practice it, as well as on the religious commitment of the people in a particular society.

Currently, most of the world's leaders make their political, economic, and cultural decisions without reference to the religious beliefs of the people in their societies.[2] It is true that many of them give a passing glance to what are called human rights and do remain attentive to the religious concerns of people when these are thrust on them forcefully. For the most part, however, most leaders make their political, economic, and cultural decisions for pragmatic, secular reasons. Individuals in power may be religious, it is true, but political reasons often override their religious convictions or the religious convictions of their people in the decision-making process.

2. There are occasional exceptions. In some countries with strong Islamic rulers, for example, almost all decisions are based on the Quran, the sacred writings of Islam.

This is natural considering the complexity of the world today. On the one hand, there are countries with diverse religious expressions. No single expression could be imposed on the total population. Likewise, when various nations are dealing with each other, the religious convictions of one cannot and should not be more important than those of another. Finally, some governments are antireligious and cannot be dealt with on religious grounds. They force other governments to deal with them on strictly pragmatic economic and political terms.

A second reason that religion does not play a major role in shaping world opinion today is the secular orientation of the media. Their steady downplaying of religion and religious concerns tends to create a secular society. Religion becomes a minor concern—an individual's option rather than a community's force.

areligious

Without religion.

In countries where the media are controlled by an **areligious** or antireligious political group, the media cannot give attention to religious concerns, or present them in a favorable way. In countries where the media are not controlled, the producers of programs often choose a neutral position because of the many religious philosophies of the society in which the media operate.

This secular philosophy is reflected in much of the literature, art, theater, movies, and TV presentations available to the public. While it is true that religious topics and materials with religious themes are presented occasionally, the great bulk of material is areligious, and some materials are contrary to the philosophy of many religious groups. At times, then, religion becomes the concern of small groups and of individuals in society, rather than the concern of society in general.

Another reason that religion plays a diminished role in the political, economic, and cultural expressions of society is that many religious leaders do not exert a great influence on society. When human society was made up of literally hundreds of small groups (tribes, peoples, nations, and so on), more or less isolated from each other, a strong religious leader could mold a society along religious lines. This is what happened in the past and accounts for the great influence religion had in shaping the cultures of many peoples. At the present time, human society is global. Religious leaders influence only a small part of the global society and exert little more than moral pressure on world concerns. They contribute only one part to the total of influences that shape the expressions of world culture.

Religion's influence on world culture has also lessened today because some religions adhere to various beliefs and practices that appear to be at odds with the learning and

experience of those they address. This is especially true of
some religions in more technological countries. As a result,
religion as a whole loses its credibility with some people,
not on the major issues of life, but on the lesser aspects of
religious belief and practice that, ultimately, do not affect
people's lives. When this happens, people may not look to
religion or religious leaders for guidance in the business of
living.

A fifth reason religion may play a minor role in shaping
world affairs is that many people think of religion as something private. Most people believe in some kind of God and
do express some kind of relationship with that God. They
do the best they can to live up to their religious convictions.
But often people hesitate to bring their religious convictions into the political, economic, cultural, or social sphere.

On the other hand, some "religious" people are not really
religious. They don't live according to what they say they
believe. They fail to do so either because it is not convenient or because they do not understand the depth of
meaning in the faith they say they profess. They may opt
for the line of least resistance and simply exist in a religion
instead of really living it. They are sociologically religious.
In other words, they grew up in a particular religion and
continue in it simply because they were born into it or because it is socially correct or convenient for them to do so.
Yet they are religiously indifferent. They aren't convinced
that, in the long run, whether one is religious or not makes
any difference.[3] Their religion has little influence on their
lives; hence, it does not affect the lives of those around
them.

---

3. What is said here applies equally to people who do not hold to a response to the mystery of life that is organized, ritualized, and agreed
upon by a group. Some are deeply convinced of the reasonableness of
their faith stance, some are run-of-the-mill, and some don't think that
living by what they believe really matters.

infantilism

The living of religion on the level of children.

Two other aspects of the religious commitment of individuals that mitigate the influence of religion on world culture are religious **infantilism** and religious ignorance.

Generally, people who are lukewarm in their practice of religion are content to live their religious lives with only the barest notion of what their religion is or means. They are children, religiously, reacting as children react and content as children are content with their religious knowledge and practice. Religion occupies very little of their time and attention; it exists on the fringes of their life, rarely disturbed because it is not important to them. People whose religious life is lived on an infantile level think they know enough about religion. They make no effort either to improve their knowledge or to deepen their commitment.

This religious infantilism often creates a second problem—religious ignorance. Because they do not know enough about religion (their own or that of others) but believe they do, religiously ignorant people are apt to make snap judgments about religion, religious people, or their own or another's religion. They tend to be prejudiced or contemptuous of others' religious convictions, and show little respect for others' religious beliefs and practices.[4] This ignorance and prejudice tends to separate people into religious enclaves and prevent them from cooperating with each other, thus lessening the influence of religion on the formation of global culture.

Even though religion today may not affect politics, economics, and culture to the extent it might, it does have a strong influence on the lives of individuals. Some ninety percent of people worldwide acknowledge some religious or spiritual influence in their lives, and at least half of these testify that it has a significant influence.

Conclusion

As we have said, one of the enduring phenomena of human development is the practice of religion. It has been part of the human scene since the dawn of human consciousness. In the next two chapters, we will look at the origin of religion and the development of religion in the Western world.

---

4. Religious prejudice, of course, is not confined to people who are considered religiously ignorant. Misplaced zeal on the part of the religiously committed can sometimes blind them to the validity of another's religious convictions and can cause them to attack others, misrepresent their position, or persecute them. (Those who profess no religion can, of course, be equally prejudiced, disrespectful, and ignorant.)

It is quite widely believed today that all religions are fundamentally the same, that behind their surface differences, they all bring essentially the same message. This must be more of a pious hope than anything else, for although similar teachings do occur in more than one religion, fundamental differences of belief, attitude and behavior are so marked that it is extremely hard to pin down exactly what religion is.

For example, the attitudes of the major religions to salvation and the purpose of life are quite different. In Judaism, Christianity and Islam salvation means the survival of the individual personality in a happy existence in heaven after death. In Hinduism and Buddhism, on the other hand, salvation may mean the opposite, not the survival but the obliteration of the individual personality. . . .

Fundamental differences occur not only between one religion and another, but within each religion itself. All religions contain internal contradictions and inconsistencies. All contain sects and groups and schools of thought which reflect varying psychological attitudes on the part of believers. The American philosopher William James drew a distinction between what he called the "healthy-minded" and the "morbid-minded" religious temperaments. The first enjoys life, sees it as something to be grateful for and produces a religion of cheerful thanksgiving and praise. The second is deeply conscious of the evils of life and the viciousness of human nature, and produces a religion of guilty repentance and dread. Both attitudes coexist inside every religion, and so do other psychological categories: tough-minded and tender-minded, for instance, or emotional and unemotional, or individualist and collectivist.

Cutting across psychological differences of this kind is another constant. Each religion has what might be called a high register and a low register. The high register is the level of intellectual, educated and sophisticated belief, high-minded, philosophical and concerned with correct doctrine and the spiritual life. The low register is the level of widespread popular belief, which is far more down to earth and concerned with practical matters. The main purpose of religion at this level is to obtain the good things of life, ward off life's evils—suffering, poverty, disease, deprivation, bad luck—and secure a more enjoyable physical life after death or next time round. Trouble is therefore taken to conciliate and win the favor of the supernatural powers which have the good things of life in their gift. Popular religion tends to be polytheistic, a belief in many gods, and this is why the worship of many divine powers occurs within a monotheistic system . . . or in an atheistic system, a disbelief in any gods. . . . Accounts of religion vary considerably according to which of the two registers is stressed but all religions contain both.

Religion is difficult to define, not only because different religions are different, and give house-room to widely varying beliefs, but because they are part of the entire life of a community, part of its ethics, its art, its politics, its whole organization and outlook. Religions explain why the world and the human condition are as they are, and justify society's institutions and values. They tell people what to do or not to do, and this can extend far beyond telling you that you must not murder or steal to deciding what you may eat, who you may eat with, whom you may marry, how you are or are not allowed to enjoy yourself.

What is it that separates religion from other areas of activity? The obvious answer is belief in gods or a God, but unfortunately this answer raises problems. One is that early Buddhism did not require any belief in gods or a God, and yet it is difficult not to regard the Buddha as a religious teacher. Another is that the objects of reverence in the various religions, or at different levels of the same religion, vary enormously. They may be animals or trees, or forces sensed in the wind and the rain or in the growth of crops in the spring; or dead and living human beings, like the god-men of India or the Christian and Muslim saints; or supernatural powers conceived of a larger-than-life human beings, like the gods of ancient Egypt, Greece, and Rome; or an eternal Father or Mother, powerful and loving; or a vast impersonal It, with no human characteristics whatever.

There is no simple satisfactory definition of religion, but what seems to lie at the heart of it is a sense of the sacred, a feeling that there is another dimension to life besides the material and temporal one of ordinary, everyday experience. Behind and beyond the visible and palpable objects and creatures and phenomena of the world, there is sensed a reality which is more important, more lasting, more real, and which arouses emotions of awe and reverence. This ultimate reality may be a being or beings, a force, a principle, or something indefinable, but whatever it is, it gives a meaning and purpose to life, which without it would be a tale told by an idiot, signifying nothing. . . .

—Richard Cavendish, The Great Religions (New York: Arco Publishing, Inc., 1980), 8–9. Permission given by A.P. Watt Ltd. on behalf of Richard Cavendish.

Summary

1. Religion is natural to human beings. It is a response to the mystery of life.
2. There are many responses to the mystery of life. These responses have given rise to many different religions.
3. Religion may play a lesser role in influencing the economic, political, and cultural directions in the world today than it did in the past.

For review

1. This section states that sooner or later all people face the question of the relevancy of religion in their lives. What reasons are given?
2. Your book contends that at the center of people's religious sense there lies an encounter with mystery. What does it mean by that?
3. What are some of the responses people have made to this encounter with mystery?
4. What is the broad definition of the word *religion* that the reading gives? How does this definition differ from many people's understanding of religion?
5. Why does your book contend that people who say that they do not believe in any kind of God are religious? Do you agree? Explain.
6. Why does the text say that religion appears to not exert as great an influence on culture as it once did?

For discussion

1. In an open forum, discuss the reasons given for the diminished influence of religion in the shaping of culture. Which has had the greatest effect?
2. Discuss why many people can be classified as children in their knowledge of religion. Give reasons for your viewpoint, based on experience.
3. Do you agree or disagree with the following statement: "Your understanding of [religious things]—should it not be, perhaps, elevated to a level proportionate to your scientific knowledge of law, of history, of letters, or of biology? Would there not be a grave danger for you if in the maturity of your own judgments or of your critical acumen, you should be content to remain in the things of faith like little children, in the notions that were taught you in the course of elementary or intermediate studies?"

For research

1. In an almanac, or some source dealing with such matters, find the names of four religious leaders who have influenced world opinion.
2. Prepare a brief report on Socrates.
3. Try to find evidence for or against your book's contention that some governments are either neutral or antireligious in their political policies.
4. Survey TV listings, radio programs, and magazine and newspaper articles about religious matters. Note their quantity and placement in the overall scheme of operations.

Word list

areligious	religion
infantilism	ritual
mystery	secular

2 The Origin of Religion

Defining religion as the response a person gives to the ;mystery of life, we can say that religion is natural to human beings. **Religious systems,** or religions, however, develop from an explanation for the ;mystery of life. One person, or a group of persons, formulate an answer or give an explanation that at once makes sense and gives security to others searching for an answer, who then become believers, or acceptors, of the explanation. Those who accept a particular answer or explanation usually form a group. Over time, the group expresses its response to the mystery of life by means of **formulas,** rituals, and a **moral or ethical code.** The group acquires a name that, however loosely, identifies them as a particular group of believers who express their beliefs in a particular way.

Contrary to the thinking of scholars a century ago, many scholars today believe that early humans were as religiously aware as people today, and possibly more so. They probably had a greater sense of the ;mystery of life than many do today in our technological age. Exactly how religion began (in the sense of a group's response to the ;mystery of life), however, cannot be definitely stated. There are many theories but no certainties. Evidence suggests, however, that it began very early, in prehistoric times among our first ancestors.

Evidence from prehistory

Prehistory is generally considered to be the time prior to written records—that is, for example, in Mesopotamia,[1] it was the time prior to 3400 B.C.E.[2]; but in England it was the time before 55 B.C.E. Prehistory includes the archeological findings (bits and pieces of human tools, weapons, dwellings) and the careful speculation of **archaeologists, anthropologists, linguists,** and historians as to what these mean.

No one can assert with absolute certainty what actually did happen in prehistoric times—for no one has any *internal* record of the hopes and fears, needs and desires, or inner feelings of a prehistoric person or community. The kind of certainty reached in descriptions of prehistoric

---

1. An ancient country in Asia located between the Tigris and Euphrates rivers. Modern Iraq includes much of this area.

2. "B.C.E." (before the Common Era) and "C.E." (the Common Era) are often used today in place of "B.C." (before Christ) and "A.D." (*anno Domini,* meaning "in the year of our Lord") respectively.

religious system

A response to the ;mystery of life adhered to by a group, and expressed by means of formulas, rituals, and a moral or ethical code.

formula

A set form of words for use in a ceremony or ritual.

moral or ethical code

A system of rules or principles or laws regarding right conduct.

prehistory

The time before written records.

archaeologist

A scientist who studies the material remains of past human life and activities.

anthropologist

One who studies the science of human beings, especially their origin, nature, and destiny.

linguist

One who studies languages.

times is a *probable* certainty based on *external* information. Like detectives reconstructing an event from circumstantial evidence, present-day scientists piece together information from many sources, reconstructing a probable situation or condition and hypothesizing about what was, or could have been, done within the situation.

Experts on prehistoric religion have pieced together the elements of rather systematic religious practices among early people. Using information gained from archaeologists (ruins of ancient temples, bones arranged in special patterns in caves, **artifacts** that could have some significance only beyond use in everyday activities) and combining it with known facts about contemporary isolated preliterate tribes, experts on religion have been able to reconstruct what may have been the religious situation among our prehistoric ancestors.

The contemporary tribal societies that experts look to for insight are found in such places as Africa, Australia, South America, and New Guinea. What preliterate societies in these places have in common with prehistoric societies are that they live chiefly by hunting and gathering. "There still exist in the world today groups of people who live at a pre-Neolithic level as non-agrarian food-gatherers. . . . We can speculate that their life-patterns must be something like the life led by early man during the major part of human prehistory."[3]

What evidence is there for the existence of religious practices among early humans? What have experts on religion concluded about the religious situation among our prehistoric ancestors? To these two questions we now turn.

artifacts

Usually handmade objects representing a particular culture or stage of technological development.

A dolmen (prehistoric tomb) in the Basque region of Alava, Spain.

3. Ninian Smart, *The Religious Experience of Mankind,* 3rd ed. (New York: Charles Scribner's Sons, 1984), 28.

We know that those who lived in what is now called Europe were driven south and east by successive ice ages between 1 million and 100 thousand years ago.

Evidence of religious practices

Currently, scientists believe that humans developed from a subhuman species that appeared in Africa about 4 million years ago called *Australopithecus*. Scientists further conjecture that about 2 million years ago—again in Africa—the first type of human being appeared, called *Homo habilis*. From this species, modern people would have evolved.[4] It is known that the Peking Man (who lived in Northern China) lived 700,000 years ago, and that the Swanscombe Man (who lived in England) existed at least 300,000 years ago, and that modern people appeared 50,000 years ago.

We do not have much evidence of the development and civilizing process of human beings in the Far East and in Africa. What evidence we do have comes from Europe and the Middle East. It is from this that we **postulate** our theories about the origin of religion and formulate our definition. What is said about the origin of religion, based on current European evidence, can probably be said about its origin in other parts of the world.

We know that those who lived in what is now called Europe were driven south and east by successive ice ages between 1 million and 100 thousand years ago. The early inhabitants of Northern Europe struggled for survival through various glacial periods, which finally ended about 50,000 years ago. Evidence of this struggle is found in the caves of southern France, Spain, Austria, Germany, Bosnia, southern Russia, Palestine, and the Tigris-Euphrates Fertile Crescent. These early people were about five feet in height, stocky, and resourceful. They made tools and weapons out of stone and hunted game over a wide range. It is from these people of 180,000 to 50,000 years ago that we have our first evidence of the emergence of religious practices. The arrangement of bones in high mountain caves or deep in gorges in the earth indicates a rather advanced ceremonial or ritual for death.

Also in these caves are found skulls of bears or other "ceremonial" animals, arranged so neatly and exactly that hardly any other conclusion can be drawn than that such arrangements were purposeful and had some religious significance. In the art and sculpture of these caves and others, evidence is found of even more advanced religious practices and symbol systems.

postulate

Propose; put forward a plan or intention.

---

4. Continued research and discoveries lead scientists to revise their theories about the origin of human beings and to update their estimates of years, places of origin, and classifications.

Between 50,000 years ago and 10,000 years ago, ice caps that covered all the northern parts of the world (much like those in Greenland today) receded, and warmer climates developed. People sought out caves that, while unsuitable for living, were admirably suited to ceremonial gatherings for early forms of worship and **magic.** In these caves, they painted graphic images of deer, bison, and mammoth in such profusion and in such form as to suggest something more than a mere artistic urge or a simple pastime.

In these special caves (for early people sought shelter in other, more suitable caves or constructed rude shelters in which to live) are found not only very careful representations of the animals people depended on for food, but representations of antlered sorcerers, skin-draped dancers, mutilated hands or limbs of humans (indicating some puberty ceremony), and small statues apparently related to religious rites.

Evidence for a further development in religious symbols and practices is found in the carved figures of women (about ten inches in height) found so profusely in the caves mentioned above. These statues, dating from the late Paleolithic period (50,000–10,000 B.C.E.), seem to be directed toward another concern of early people: survival of the tribe, the clan, or the group.

During this age there seems to have arisen an urge to venerate the feminine "divine principle of survival." That these figures were religious objects can hardly be denied, for they do not fit into the practical side of early people's lives, which are characterized by crude knives, fire circles, protective walls, and animal-skin clothing. These female figures are too closely allied to the later Babylonian myth and ritual associated with the goddess Ishtar to be dismissed as anything but religious.

Further evidence of the existence of early religion is the burial ceremony that antedates the animal shrines or statuettes of women. Death in people was not indifferently observed. Animal bones were thrown carelessly away; human remains, except where there were natural disasters, were usually buried carefully and with much ritual. As in later times, for example, the time of the pyramids in Egypt, the dead were buried with the tools of life: with food, with ornaments "necessary" for the journey through death (suggesting the idea of immortality), and with companions for the journey.

magic

The use of devices, such as spells and charms, believed to have supernatural powers.

Large female figurine, Museum of Cycladic and Ancient Greek Art, Athens, Greece.

The evolution of religion

Although earlier evolutionary theories [of religion] are flawed, evidence supports the contention that ancient religious practices are different from modern ones. In an essay that avoids the pitfalls of earlier theories, sociologist of religion Robert Bellah has argued convincingly that religion has evolved from the relatively simple systems of nonliterate traditions and primitive societies to the more complex systems of literate traditions and highly developed societies.* In Bellah's view, the evolution of religious beliefs and practices is closely related to changes in patterns of economic subsistence, types of political organizations, forms of group association, and modes of communication. Major changes in religious belief systems and practices are paralleled by shifts from one type of socioeconomic system to another. For example, the development of religious organizations dominated by a priestly class emerged when a shift from simple to intensive agriculture permitted increased concentrations of population in urban centers accompanied by centralized political structures. Recognition that religion has evolved does not entail, as Bellah noted, assent to the proposition that the ultimate or holy has.

Bellah makes the point that the evolution of religion is not progressive in the sense of **better**. Change is not always progress. Modern religious conceptions and patterns of spirituality are not invariably higher or superior to earlier ones. A modern prophet like Martin Luther King, Jr., is not more or less religious than Amos of Tekoa, a Hebrew prophet of the eighth century B.C., merely because he speaks God's word at a latter point in time, just as the paintings of a modern genius like Pablo Picasso are not superior or inferior to those of Rembrandt. Similarly, the religious life of primitive people is neither more or less religious than that of moderns. It is, however, quite different, because very real differences exist between primitive and modern societies. Bellah believes that religion has developed primarily in the direction of increased role differentiation and complexity of organization rather than toward greater spirituality. Buddhism, Islam, Christianity differ from primitive religion in size, level of complexity, elaborateness of structures, and differentiation of functions as well as in their conceptions of ultimacy.**

Material achievement and complex social structures are not appropriate criteria of the truth or value of religious conceptions, but the absence of such features has sometimes made it difficult for moderns to see that tribal peoples are religious. The Apache leader Geronimo, sensitive to his people's lack of religious institutions, protested in his autobiography that the Apaches also had a religious life: "We had no churches, no religious organization, no sabbath day, no holidays, and yet we worshipped. Sometimes the whole tribe would assemble to sing and pray, sometimes a smaller number, perhaps only two or three."***

—Roger Schmidt, Exploring Religion, 2nd. ed. (Belmont, CA: Wadsworth Publishing Company, 1988), 43–44.

---

* Robert Bellah, Beyond Belief (New York: Harper & Row, 1970), 22–50.

** Ibid.
***Geronimo: His Own Story, ed. by S.M. Barrett (New York: Ballentine Books, 1971), 77.

Religion at the end of the prehistoric period

The final stage in the development of prehistoric people—from about 10,000 to 5,000 B.C.E.—indicates a rapidly developing cultural, economic, social, and religious system. During this age, there were objects and structures that indicate cults devoted to the worship and the **propitiation** of powers, forces, or deities that operate in the sky, fertilize the earth (and people), and roam the spirit world "under" the earth.

Dating from this period, scientists have found, especially in France and Spain and later in England, arrangements of stones that could suggest places of worship as well as, or mixed with, means of calculating the movements of heavenly bodies. Flat stones, table stones, circular arrangements of stones, and carefully arranged standing stones brought to the place at great labor may indicate a rather advanced, elaborately ritualized form of worship, probably of the sun, the moon, the stars, and other heavenly bodies. In the case of the famous Stonehenge ruins in England, evidence suggests that people could make extremely accurate predictions of eclipses and other heavenly phenomena by observing the heavenly bodies from certain positions within the stone circles.

Stonehenge, located in South England, was constructed by prehistoric peoples.

These evidences of early systems of nature worship among prehistoric people must not be confused with later religious systems. Religions of later periods, especially in the West after the great Greek philosophers, became more systematic and presented coherent rationales for their religious beliefs and practices. Early people did not do so—though there is evidence of a gradual development. What they were doing was working out a scheme for survival, a scheme that included not only fashioning weapons or artifacts for overcoming the forces they knew they could overcome, but also finding ways of coping with the forces they could not see but could feel—the forces, dimly conceived at first, that they "knew" they had to overcome or bargain with if they were to survive.

These early religious manifestations are forerunners of later religious systematization and worship. Just as people had moved up the evolutionary ladder only after centuries of effort, so did they move up the religious ladder.[5]

Religion among our prehistoric ancestors

Some of those who examine the evidence of religion among early people speculate that the earliest people emerged from animal awareness to human self-awareness and experienced phenomena in their world that cried out for explanation. They sought answers to the mysteries of the world in which they lived. Their answers, simplistic by our standards, were their attempt to find reasons for the phenomena they experienced.

One theory about how early people arrived at their answers goes like this. The first people were apparently most concerned about survival. Three things threatened this survival: the forces of nature, such as earthquakes, floods, forest fires, thunder and lightning; the scarcity of food; and the experience of death. Experiencing these things as they did, early people concluded that invisible powers or spirits controlled these phenomena or that the phenomena of nature were themselves forces, powers, or spirits. To cope with these forces, powers, or spirits, early people tried to develop ways to overcome the spirits, offset their power, or **placate** the power or spirit that threatened their survival. These ways seem to be the beginnings of religion.

It is further conjectured that believing firmly in the spirit world, early people explained the mysteries of their world in terms of the spirits who controlled the phenomena they experienced. The things they benefitted from—such as the sun or the plants and animals that provided food—were controlled by friendly spirits, powers, or gods. The things that threatened them were controlled by hostile spirits, powers, or gods. Early people, therefore, estab-

placate

To appease or soothe someone or some power.

---

5. As mentioned in the article on the evolution of religion in this chapter, we must be careful not to apply too strictly the notion of evolution. As noted, early people were not necessarily less adept in relating to and contemplating the ;mystery of life. With less complexities in life to distract them, they may have been better at this deeper sort of religious awareness than we are. What does seem to have undergone development is the ability to express religious faith and to separate it from other processes, such as early science or magic.

lished rituals, practices, ceremonies, prayers, songs, and chants to keep the friendly spirits friendly and to ward off the hostile spirits. As time went on (and this took many centuries or millenniums), ceremonies became more elaborate and were scrupulously followed to curry the favor of friendly spirits or to circumvent the hostility of unfriendly spirits.

Characteristics common to prehistoric religions

From what we now know about prehistoric human societies, religion played a very important role in every early society. It affected a society's structure and way of life, and how a society's members related with one another.

The following is a list of characteristics that scientists speculate were common to prehistoric religions. The list is based on the little archaeological evidence that exists from prehistoric societies and the knowledge we have of the religious practices of contemporary **preliterate** tribes. Keep in mind, however, that "though today's technologically **primitive** cultures are reminiscent of prehistoric man technologically, we must remember that the modern primitive has a culture that has undoubtedly changed during the immense span of time since Neanderthal men lived."[6]

preliterate
Before the use of writing.

primitive
Early ancestral type.

1. Belief in spirit-forces or invisible powers

Prehistoric people believed that everything was controlled by unseen nonmaterial or spiritual forces or powers. Those powers were arranged in hierarchies of power and divided into friendly or hostile powers. Those powers were both impersonal and personal. There were spirits controlling every conceivable aspect and experience of life: they made trees grow, clouds move, fires burn, the earth quake, the thunder clap, the lightning flash, the waters move, people sicken, the crops grow or fail, the hunt succeed or not, the tribe prosper or fail, and so forth. The good or evil individuals or the tribe experienced was the direct result of the work of these invisible forces or powers, which acted not only on earth but in the sky and under the earth as well.

2. Close ties to a particular area or locality

Prehistoric religions were not universal. They did not try to be **transcultural.** They were closely tied to the territory in which the people lived, to the values perceived as necessary for survival, and to the **mores** of the close-knit society that practiced them.

transcultural
Spanning more than one culture or social group; passing from one culture to another.

mores
Customs of a group that are morally binding.

---

6. *The Religious Experience of Mankind*, 28.

The world of prehistoric people was circumscribed by where the people lived. They had no notion of a much larger world where things existed that were different from what they knew. Their world was governed by mystical forces that were **capricious** and unpredictable. They did not conceive of a world governed by predictable, natural forces.

4. Concern with survival

Prehistoric religions primarily focused on ensuring the success of those practical matters that affected the survival of the tribe. Their rituals centered on the hunt, the growth of crops, success against enemies, and the birth of healthy children.

5. Manipulation, coercion, and supplication of the world of the spirits

Actions directly associated with religion became a part of early human societies. These "acts of worship," or **liturgies,** were directed to particular gods or spirits of unknown and uncertain power who affected people's lives and their life situations. The actions were designed to ward off evil spirits and to call on friendly spirits for assistance.

These actions were designed to gain the favor of the gods or spirits or to force them to act in accordance with the wishes or desires of individuals or tribes. They were performed, for the most part, by some individual in the tribe who seemed to possess special powers or influence over the spirit or force, or one who had a special relationship with the spirits or forces. They were participated in by individuals or members of the tribe who performed particular rituals or actions, sang particular **incantations,** or recited particular words at the direction of the leader or **shaman.** Such ritualistic actions are called magic.

capricious

Impulsive.

liturgy

An action associated with religious worship and practice.

incantation

A spell or verbal charm used as part of a ritual of magic.

shaman

A religious or magic practitioner who, on behalf of a group, with the aid of guardian spirits, enters into a trance-like state to make contact with the powers of the spirit world.

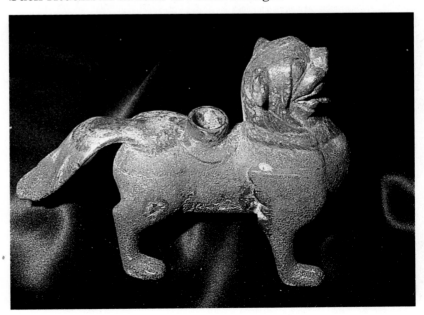

Bronze mythical animal unearthed in China in 1990. The name of this mythical creature, Bi-xie, literally means "to ward off evil."

6. Concern about death

Prehistoric people believed that human spirits lived in another world after death. They developed elaborate burial ceremonies designed to make a dead person's passage to and existence in that world happy and prosperous. Many early tribes developed magical actions or burial ceremonies to prevent the spirits of the dead from returning to disturb the tribe, or rituals designed to confuse the spirit of the dead person so that it could not find its way back to the tribe. Other rituals were designed to honor the dead and preserve the memory of heroes, kings, or leaders. In almost all cases, these acts were special religious acts—ways of dealing with the mystery of death.

7. Moral systems

Prehistoric societies had rules governing their way of life according to the particular needs of the tribe and their religious beliefs. Their moral codes included laws to protect the life of the tribe, such as laws prohibiting murder, adultery, stealing, and lying, and **taboos** and required actions based on religious beliefs.

taboo

A positively forbidden action.

Taboos, or positively forbidden actions, were the most powerful of the determining factors affecting a person's or a tribe's way of acting. They were always associated with the mysterious, or sacred, or spiritual, or **totem** forces affecting the life of the individual or tribe. Taboo actions were forbidden because they were thought to automatically produce evil. A person who performed such a taboo action was required to undergo tribal purification, a system designed to ward off the evil effects of the action. Taboos and ritual purification were serious business; they were not merely superstitions as such. They were deeply associated with the religious beliefs of the tribe, as well as its social and political structure, and were revered and observed as sacred obligations to ensure the survival of the tribe.[7]

totem

A spiritual force in an object (usually animal or plant) affecting the life of an individual or a group.

The term *totem* is applied to a natural object, a bird, an animal, a plant, or a natural phenomenon with which a primitive family or tribe considered itself closely related. The image of the totem often became the emblem or symbol of the tribe or family. Thus, the totem poles of some Native American tribes were not random collections of animal images, but symbolic representations of the sacred guardian spirits of the group.

---

7. The term *taboo* comes from the Polynesian word for negative force, *tabu;* Noa was the Polynesian name for positive force. Both were manifestations of "power"—called *mana*—in the presence of which people lived. If they experienced tabu, they had to resort to some practice—sacrifice, priestly action, magic—to offset the power of this "negative" mana.

Totem animals (loosely based on Athabascan totem pole figures, Sitka, Alaska).

8. Theology

Early societies developed a system of explanations for their religious beliefs and practices. These explanations were archaic according to our understanding of the world around us, but they were explanations that made sense to those who accepted them. These explanations laid the foundation for certain later theological systems.

9. Scripture

Some early religions in their later stages did have a body of sacred writing that was generally accepted as the sacred word or, at least, the will of the gods. Such writing originated in the word-of-mouth stories and poetry that preceded them and included the myths, explanations, words, songs, incantations, rituals, moral codes, and general theology of the tribe. The word-of-mouth stories and poetry were passed on from generation to generation, more or less intact, and formed the fabric of beliefs and practices of the tribe.

10. Prophecy

There was present in almost all early religious societies and certainly in all known early religions an aspect of "prophetic witness." This means there was a gifted, **charismatic** person who exerted through words and actions a profound and rather lasting effect on the religious life of the society that the person addressed. The person would have gained his or her authority by virtue of having experienced some extraordinary religious experience in him- or herself. In other words, this prophetic witness contains a mysterious "I am sent" element that seems to come from beyond the person's own human condition, or even his or her own wish or inclination. In fact, some religions distinguish the "true" prophet from the "false" precisely on the basis of whether he or she is overly eager to be a prophet or not.

charismatic

Having extraordinary or supernatural power or charm; persuasive.

11. Sacrifice

Gifts signify a relationship between the giver and the receiver. Archeological discoveries reveal that in early societies, gifts were offered to the powers, forces, spirits, or totems of the tribes. The gifts were offered in the form of food, items of tribal value, or sacrificed animals. When the sacrifice was tribal, the slain animal was divided and parts were offered to the power, force, spirit, or totem, and the rest was eaten by the tribal members to signify their participation in the offering, and their oneness with the spirit, force, power, or totem.

12. Designated places of worship

Archaeologists have discovered that the special places, areas, caves, rooms, or structures of early societies were set aside for religious ceremonies. Whether it be in the caves of Europe, the excavations in Africa, or the digs of the Middle East, the pattern is the same: people have been preoccupied with religious concerns in a very special way. They set aside certain places and things to express their beliefs and to show their relationship to the divine as they understood it.

Conclusion

We began this chapter by recalling that religion as a response to mystery is natural to human beings. That religious practices have been part of every human society from earliest times would seem to bear this out. Though religion as a response to mystery may be natural to us, however, not everyone is equally religious. Some people are intensely religious. Others are less so. Still others are hardly religious at all.

Among the most intensely religious, we find particularly sensitive people whose acuteness and direction of thought stand out over and above even the very best of their companions. Among these are such recognized leaders as Siddhartha Gautama (c. 563–483 B.C.E.), Confucius (551–479 B.C.E.), Abraham (c. 1950 B.C.E.), Moses (c. 1280 B.C.E.), Jesus (4 B.C.E.–29 C.E.), and Mohammed (570–632 C.E.). All of these religious leaders have contributed in one way or another to people's knowledge of and relationship with God. What their contributions have been, we shall discover as we discuss the major religions of the world.

Summary

1. Prehistory gives evidence of practices that cannot be interpreted as other than religious.
2. Religion may have begun as a result of early people's awareness of forces or powers outside of themselves that seemed to control their destiny.
3. Based on archaeological evidence and the study of contemporary preliterate tribal societies, scientists speculate that prehistoric religions had certain common characteristics.

For review

1. What is the difference between religion as a response to the ;mystery of life and a religious system?
2. Why is it impossible to say how religion began?
3. What is the evidence from prehistory showing that early people were religious?
4. What are some theories about the origin of religion?
5. Be able to name and explain at least five of the characteristics common to prehistoric religions.
6. Why does the text contend that religion is natural to people? Do you agree or disagree? Explain.

For discussion

1. In an open forum, discuss the ramifications of the following true episode: One time a man who billed himself as the world's leading atheist stood on a stage before hundreds of people and said: "If there is a God, I command [God] to strike me dead in ten seconds." He pulled out his watch and counted the seconds. After one minute, he announced triumphantly, "There is no God. If there were, [God] would be so mad at me [God] would have struck me dead."
2. Who do some people believe in a God or gods and others don't?
3. Discuss why some people are uncomfortable when the subject of religion is brought up. Why do you suppose that many people are reluctant to discuss religion in their public life?
4. Assume for the moment that we know nothing about the physical, chemical, or geological forces that produce nature's phenomena. How would you explain the existence or experience of various things that happen in nature? Take a particular instance (for example, an earthquake) and try to explain it without the help of modern scientific knowledge.

For research

1. Prepare a report on one of the following: totemism, common superstitions and their probable origins, the development of magic and its use in present-day societies, Native Americans' "happy hunting ground," prehistoric cave findings in Europe, findings from excavations in Africa.
2. Make an informal survey among your friends to find out if any of them believe in the influence of good or evil spirits in people's lives. Report your findings to the class. Cite examples, if possible, of the interest in this subject in movies and on TV.

3. At the direction of your teacher, read excerpts from *The Source* and *Hawaii* by James Michener, *The Curve and the Tusk* by Stuart Cloete, *The Spiral Road* by Jan de Hartog, or selected passages from the *Iliad,* the *Odyssey,* or *Bulfinch's Mythology* concerning primitive people's preoccupation with the life-force, the causes of death, and the attempts to ward off evil forces. Prepare a report on your reading.

4. From sources available to you, make a chart of evolution, concentrating on the period from the emergence of animals that walked upright to the positive identification of human beings.

5. Do a report on a contemporary preliterate tribal religion. Compare the characteristics of the religion you choose with the list of characteristics on pages 20–24 in this chapter.

Word list

anthropologist
archeologist
artifacts
capricious
charismatic
formula
incantation
linguist
liturgy
magic
moral or ethical code
mores
placate
postulate
prehistory
preliterate
primitive
propitiation
religious system
shaman
taboo
totem
transcultural

3 The Development of Religion in the Western World

Because the principle studies of prehistoric and early historic peoples have been made in what is known as the Western world, our discussions on the origin, growth, and development of early religions are centered on the early religions of the Western world.[1]

Our knowledge of the prehistoric religions of the Western world is based on artifacts as they are interpreted by archaeologists, anthropologists, and religious historians. Our knowledge of the early historic religions of the Western world is based on *written* records. These records consist of clay tablets, inscriptions on temple walls and statues, historical accounts compiled by palace scribes, and written copies of earlier orally transmitted legends and **myths.** These records give us a fairly accurate picture of the development of the living religions of the Western world, and an understanding of people's continuous search for an answer to the mystery of life.

Both of these can be demonstrated through an examination of three ancient historic religions—Babylonian, Egyptian, and Greek. Each of these religions shows not only the continuity and development of people's religious expression, but also that religion as such is not the invention of this or that person or group. Rather, religion is a response to the mystery of life as that mystery is interpreted from within a particular culture.

To understand ancient historic religions, it is important to remember that the beliefs, rituals, and cultures associated with each grew out of earlier religious expressions. They did not spring up whole and entire at some point in the history of the people who lived in Babylonia, Egypt, and Greece. They developed as the civilization of these areas developed.

myth

A story or tradition with a loose historical basis which serves to unfold part of the worldview of a group of people or explain a practice or belief or a natural event.

---

1. The Western world is that part of the world that lies, roughly, west of the easternmost shore of the Mediterranean. The Eastern world is that which lies east of the 60° meridian. The land area in between is referred to as the Middle East. What we know of prehistoric and early historic religions in the Orient, Africa, North and South America, and the islands of the Pacific Ocean leads us to believe that their origin and growth were much the same as that of the religions in Europe and the Middle East.

The process of people becoming civilized (that is, living in an ordered society in established territories) was long and arduous. The first human beings were nomadic: they went where they could find food and shelter. As time went on, they learned to herd animals and cultivate foods for future use.[2] When they began to settle in places favorable to the preservation of their herds and the cultivation of food, they staked out the territory as their own and took means to preserve it and to protect it from others. Clans, tribes, and peoples with similar tastes and backgrounds banded together. In time, they became a nation or a people with common purposes and goals, and eventually, with a common philosophy or explanation for the mystery of life as they experienced it.

Accepting the world of the gods as a reality, they explained the world they now encountered with a whole new set of gods—or spirits—who controlled the world in which they now lived. As time went on, these gods became the gods of their tribe or territory, and their former gods (still living, of course, in the places from which they had come), who no longer needed to be courted for favors, receded from memory and finally disappeared altogether from their religious belief system and practices.

As centuries passed, people learned more and more about the world in which they lived. They realized that they could actually control things in the world that they once thought they could not. As a result, they abandoned almost entirely their belief in nature gods and developed religious beliefs and practices associated with what they could not control—the "heavens." As time went on, the religious beliefs and practices of these people became a part of their civilizations and helped shape the economic, political, and cultural world in which each civilization developed.

In the following pages, we will look at ancient Babylonian, Egyptian, and Greek religion. These three religions have been chosen because they demonstrate the development of people's religious expression from prehistoric times and because they are the three ancient historic religions that most affected the development of the major living religions of the Western world. They were a major force in forming the culture and the mentality of the region in which Judaism, Christianity, and Islam began.

As centuries passed, people developed religious beliefs and practices associated with what they could not control—the "heavens."

---

2. History tells us that the people in Egypt, Babylon, and India were raising dairy cattle for family use and for trade with their neighbors before 5000 B.C.E.

The religion of Babylonia

The seeds of future religious development in the West were sown in the Fertile Crescent, which extended from the Mediterranean Sea through the valley of the Tigris and Euphrates rivers to the Persian Gulf. In this region, also called Mesopotamia, the city of Babylon played such a dominant role that the entire region is sometimes called Babylonia (just as in later times the name *Rome* came to stand for the entire Roman Empire dominated by the city of that name).

Babylonian religion flourished as far back as 3000 B.C.E. and continued even into biblical times. Abraham, the "father" of the Jewish people, came from the Babylonian city of Ur around 1850 B.C.E. Some of his Jewish descendants were forced to return to Babylon from their homeland more than a thousand years later, in 587 B.C.E.

Babylonian religion

An ancient polytheistic religion which originated in the Fertile Crescent and which reflected a dark outlook on life.

The Ancient Near East

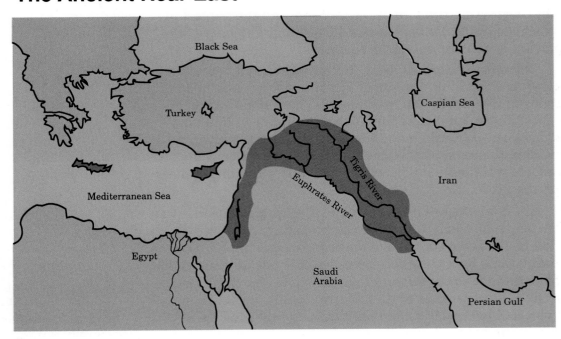

■ The Fertile Crescent

The Babylonians' lives were full of turmoil and uncertainty. They lived in a geographic area that was unsettling and unpredictable. Though the land was rich and fertile, there were frequent storms and memories of severe floods. People looked upon the world with anxiety and suspicion. For them, maintaining human life was a struggle. In addition, wars, social strife, cruelty, and slavery were part of the world they experienced.

The Babylonians' religious beliefs, their myths[3] and rituals, and their moral life reflected this uncertainty and struggle. Subject as they were to unpredictable natural phenomena, to invasion, to pestilence, to war and violent death, the Mesopotamians had a somewhat dark view of life; this was expressed in a body of myths, a set of rituals, magical practices, incantations, a priesthood, and eventually a system of **theology.**

Certain Babylonian myths explained the universe as Babylonians saw it. These myths answered basic questions about the beginning of the world, the origin of the gods, the existence of a spirit world, the role of the gods in their dealings with people, the meaning and effect of death, and the nature of the afterlife.

Like all those who went before them, the Babylonians constructed tales to put order into a universe that, to their minds, was essentially disorderly and governed by forces greater than themselves. Their chief god was Apsu, the water-god, who with the she-dragon Tiamat (who lived in and controlled the waters that frequently flooded the valley) begot Anu, the lord of the heavens and the highest of the gods; Enlil, lord of the middle air; and Ea, ruler of the moisture that irrigated the earth.

The most important deity in Babylonian religion, however, was Marduk, the son of Ea. Marduk championed the gods in the plot by the evil she-god Tiamat to destroy the gods. Marduk defeated Tiamat and split her in half, and thus formed the sky and the earth. Marduk also destroyed Kingu, the consort of Tiamat, and from Kingu's blood people were formed who will continually send up sacrifices to the gods.

These myths tell us that for the Mesopotamians, life was struggle, bloodshed, violence, and tribulation. They also tell us that life had to be made orderly by effort. In order to bring some order into society, codes of law were framed governing every aspect of life in Babylon. The most famous code of law was that of King **Hammurabi** (d. 1750 B.C.E.), who codified all the laws that had been inherited from more ancient civilizations, added necessary laws to fit his own people, and presented them as coming directly from heaven, from the sun-god, Shamash.

theology

The study of religious faith, faith in general, and religious experience.

Hammurabi

The king who codified known existing laws in the eighteenth century B.C.E.

---

3. According to the Penguin *Dictionary of Religion* (1984), a myth is a "Narrative, usually traditional, in which events are described as deeds of Gods, heroes, or other superhuman beings. . . . In the study of religion, myths, whether embodying facts or not, are seen as symbols conveying profound truths about human existence and/or superhuman reality."

The Babylonians were concerned about people's fate after death, but they took a dim view of their chances in the next life: only the gods had a good chance of living in the land of the dead. "When the gods created [humankind], for [them] they set aside death; life they retained for their own keeping," runs an old Babylonian saying. It reflects the pessimism, the doubt, the anxiety of all Babylonian life. It also gave birth to searching inquiry for answers to the mystery of life. Unlike the Egyptians, whose myths and rituals promoted the status quo, the Babylonians continually searched for answers or solutions to the negative forces that beset them on every side. Their rites and ceremonies were constructed to affect the power, to appease the god, or to achieve favor.

These rites and ceremonies (liturgies) were presided over by a priestly clan that soon had specific functions or particular **rites** that belonged to it alone. Rites took on the qualities of magic, whose purpose was to ward off evil planned by the gods.

Because Babylonians had little hope for a peaceful life after this one, this life was all that mattered. Life became a series of contests with the gods in which the Babylonians hoped to win at least some of the contests. Although there were sacrifices in the temple to the Babylonian gods, magic and **divination** became the practical religious expression of the Babylonians—divination to determine the will of the gods (or the direction of the power or divine force) and magic to coerce the gods or the forces into doing the human will.

An important development in Babylonian religion, and one directly connected with the practice of divination, was the growth of **astrology,** or the study of the stars or heavenly bodies. Elaborate charts of the heavens and the variations in placement of the stars and planets were constructed and studied to see if favorable conditions existed for undertaking an action. Because they thought the stars and planets the dwelling places of the gods, Babylonians believed that the position of the stars and their relationship with each other would tell something about the will of the gods, or at least indicate their disposition.

This form of divining the will of the gods (as well as other forms of **auguring:** casting oil on water or seeking the wisdom of a **seer,** a witch, a prophet, or a priest) was accompanied by "insurance for success" in the form of magic. Spells and incantations, mutilation and voodoo dolls (putting pins into figures of enemies), are ancient practices that carry down to the present day in many parts of the world. They are the forebearers of such practices as reading one's **horoscope,** determining one's sign, not walking under a ladder, omitting the thirteenth floor in hotels, skipping on or over cracks in the sidewalk, and knocking on wood.

rite

A prescribed form for words or actions in a ceremony.

divination

The attempt to tell the future or to discover hidden knowledge by magical means.

astrology

The study of the stars or heavenly bodies to see if favorable conditions existed for undertaking an action.

auguring

Foretelling, especially from omens.

seer

A wise person and/or one who prophecies or foretells future events.

horoscope

A chart based on the movement of the stars which is used to attempt to foretell the future.

To us, these ancient practices may seem superstitious. To the Babylonians, they were attempts to answer the perennial question about life's meaning. Had things been tranquil or the Babylonians less dissatisfied, humanity might have remained in the grip of ancient myths that now seem to provide such feeble answers. It is to the Babylonians' credit that they were *not* satisfied, that they continued to search for answers, that they scanned the heavens and the earth and the waters, that they were restless and inquiring. From them came the force that was to give birth to the cultural heritage of the entire Western world.

Sunrise at the Pyramids at Giza, Egypt.

The early Egyptian religion

The most striking features of Egypt, even in the present day, are the pyramids, the sphinxes, the desert sands, and the Nile River. Considered as curiosities or as evidence of a now dead glorious civilization, these things give us our clearest insights into **Egyptian religion.**

The pyramids are tombs of the near-divine pharaohs. These and lesser tombs, as well as burial texts and architecture, tell us the great truths of early Egyptian religion. Perhaps the most significant characteristic of this Egyptian religion was its stability. For almost 3,000 years (before Menes in 3100 B.C.E. until long after the Romans had conquered Egypt), Egyptian religion remained set in its rites, its beliefs, and its theology. This was directly due to the stability of life along the Nile River, which was as regular in its fertilization and movement as a natural force

early Egyptian religion

An ancient and serene polytheistic religion of Egypt centered around two important gods: Re and Osiris.

satellite gods

Secondary or minor gods, often in the service of a major god.

could be, to the deserts that stretched on either side of Egypt and so kept enemies at bay, and to the regularity of the heavenly bodies clearly visible over the desert sky.

In other words, the Egyptians lived a stable form of existence—they did not experience the natural or social upheavals of other early civilizations. Their lives, aside from the normal internal problems of their society, were secure.

The Egyptian gods tell nearly all we need to know about Egyptian religion. Their two chief gods were Re, the sun god, and Osiris, the god of life everlasting. There were other gods, of course, but they were **satellite gods,** whose purpose was to serve the two main gods.

Long before the Nile Valley was settled, the forebearers of the Egyptians lived in the highlands to the west of the Nile River. As these lands became arid, the people moved to the swampland around the Nile, cultivated the land, founded cities, and soon gave birth to a flowering civilization. By the year 3100 B.C.E. under the kingship of Menes, Egyptian civilization had reached a degree of sophistication unmatched in other lands. They had settled into a way of life and a religion that was to last long after the Roman invasions three thousand years later.[4]

Because the general flow of Egyptian life was stable, the emphasis in religious rites and myths was centered upon death rituals and stories. Almost all Egyptian religious ceremony centered upon elaborate burial rites designed to ensure safe passage to the land of Osiris and peace and happiness there forever.

mummification

Process of embalming and preservation of the dead practiced in ancient Egypt.

hierarchy

A ranking system based on an agreed upon classification.

The **mummification** and burial rites, which lasted seventy days for royalty, required a priesthood divided into several levels or **hierarchies** according to their various duties. Since the burial rites were thought to ensure safe passage, it was important that each action, each word, be done according to a strict rite.

Although burial rites dominated Egyptian religious practice ("salvation by rite"), the whole superstructure of Egyptian religion was based upon its elaborate myths; for if there were no gods to be appeased, what would be the sense of ritual to appease them? As obvious as this seems, it is crucial, not only to an understanding of Egyptian religion, but to an understanding of any religion.

---

4. The last known reference to Isis, goddess and sister-wife of Osiris, was in 451 C.E. Nubians were permitted to bring sacrifices to her temple on an island in the Nile. Obviously the Egyptian religion remained long after that, probably until Islam was firmly established.

Obviously, therefore, the question that comes to mind is this: Since there are gods, where did they come from? Some kind of answer is found, of course, in the elaborate myths of all early religions.

In Egypt, the creation myths eventually presented an **amalgam** of all the simple myths of pre-Egyptian society. Although Re and Osiris were preeminent in Egyptian mythology and religious systems, other gods were "created" according to the need to explain real situations faced by the Egyptians. Where did the earth and people come from? Egyptian myths give the answer: from Atum and Ptah, both creating gods who came into existence at some unspecified time in the remote past of the world of the gods.

The Egyptians "knew" that Atum (later Atum-Re) generated from his own body two other gods, Geb and Nut, the god and goddess of earth and sky, and Shu, the god of the air, who held them apart. Wondering about the origin of Atum, the "creator" of earth and heaven, the ordinary Egyptian learned that this god was the result of the thought of Ptah. People, then, were fashioned by the gods, in one account as the tears of Re, in another, on the potter's wheel of a god named Khaum.

The god Shu lifting up the goddess Nut from the god Geb.

From the vantage point of disinterested or curious study, many questions arise as to how all these gods could be consistent with each other. These questions may have arisen in ancient Egypt, too. (In fact, for a brief period around 1370 B.C.E., the pharaoh Amenhotep IV—Akhenaten—attempted unsuccessfully to do away with the **syncretism** of Egyptian myth and promote a single all-powerful deity, Aten.) In reality, the only thing that counted in Egypt was the death ritual, which provided a safe journey to the land of Osiris, so most Egyptian myth was concerned with the god Osiris.

The various manifestations of the physical universe had gods to preside over them—important gods for important duties, lesser gods for less important duties. There were city gods, village gods, temple gods, and home gods. There was a veritable storehouse of gods who kept the visible universe and the social order intact.

This seems to be the essence of Egyptian religion. It reflected an orderly view of the world (every day the sun god, Re, rode across the clear blue sky; the Nile provided regular irrigation for cultivating food; burial rituals ensured eternal safety) and people's place in that world. With few exceptions, Egyptian rites, myths, magic, and prayer continued unchanged for generation after generation. They withstood the normal developments of time and passed from the world scene only after Islam had taken over the land—about 700 C.E.

The religion of the ancient Greeks

Perhaps the greatest single influence in the development of Western civilization was the emergence of Greek culture. No other culture has had as great an influence on the development of Western society. The Greek's development of philosophy, mathematics, science, sculpture, architecture, political thought, and religion, and their influence on other civilizations of their time and subsequent civilizations marked a definite turning point in the development of human society.

As far as religion is concerned, Greek philosophical thought enabled it to move away from fear, force, power, and magic to a more rational approach. This led, eventually, to understanding religion as a relationship with whatever ultimate reality is for a particular person.

Although it is somewhat of an oversimplification, the development of religious awareness in Western civilization might be put this way:

1. Prehistoric people gave first expression to a *sense* of mystery in life.
2. Ancient Babylonian and Egyptian people *systematized* the mystery of life through myth-making.
3. Ancient Greek people *humanized* the mystery by systematically cultivating a people's-eye view of life rather than a god's-eye view of life.

The people we know today as Greeks are descended from people who probably came from all parts of prehistoric Europe and Asia Minor. There is no doubt that the last glacial period drove the inhabitants of the north into the Mediterranean coastlands, and successive invasions by the Aryan tribes from the East helped to form the ethnic group that became the Greeks of the Golden Age (fifth and fourth centuries B.C.E.).

History provides us with evidence of a civilization, called Minoan, located on the island of Crete (about 50 miles south and east of the mainland) that flourished about 1600 B.C.E. This civilization (they had five-story buildings and inside plumbing, which was not to be common again until around 1900 C.E.) was taken over by the Mycenaean civilization, which was centered in Mycenae, a city in the southeastern section of the mainland. Mycenae was the home city of Agamemnon, the famous king who led the Greeks in the battle against Troy.[5]

The major difference between the Minoan and the Mycenaean civilizations seems to have been that the Minoans were peace loving, while the Mycenaeans were inclined to war, invasion, and conquest.

Mycenae was destroyed shortly after 1200 B.C.E. for reasons still unknown to historians. Soon afterward, the northern Greek tribe called the Dorians moved into the area. Many people from Mycenae fled to Asia Minor. This brought on what is called the Dark Ages of Greece. It was not until about 750 B.C.E. that the Greece of historical influence began to arise.

---

5. Troy was a city on what is now the northwest coast of modern Turkey. The story of the battle against the city of Troy is told in the most famous epic poems of all time, the *Iliad* and the *Odyssey*, which were once thought to have been written by Homer, a Greek poet who lived in the ninth century B.C.E. Most scholars today attribute them not to a single writer but to the oral recitations of wandering bards.

It was from pre-Dorian times that the legends celebrated in Greek history and mythology came. But it was from these times and from the Dorian ages that the historical Greek religion came: ancient myths and Dorian myths intermingled in the later Greek religious myths that attempted to make sense of the everyday world and the world of the gods and spirits.

The myths of the early Greeks, like the myths of other early peoples, told of the creation of the world, the origin of the lesser gods, and the nature of the afterlife. The religious practices of the early Greeks consisted of magical acts, incantations, animal sacrifices, prayers, and ritual washings and ceremonies much like the religious practices of other early peoples.

As Greek thought developed, particularly during the Golden Age, however, **Greek religion** also developed. Greek religious thought and practice became more "humanized" by the gradual evolution of the Greek gods from natural forces into supermen and superwomen, and by the tendency to answer the question, "What is the meaning of life?" with people-oriented responses rather than with myth-oriented responses.

The usual epic mythological stories about the gods and their battles became mingled with legends about ancient Greek heroes into a kind of divine-human "gods of the round table" mythology, with the gods living on top of Mount Olympus. Zeus the Mighty, Hera, Apollo, Athena, Aphrodite, Artemis, Hermes, and Poseidon are familiar names even in our own times.[6] Magnificent temples stand today even in their ruins as mute evidence of the strength and force of Greek devotion to these gods and goddesses and what they stood for. Eventually, Greek gods, even the sky god and mother-earth goddess, were no longer mere forces, indifferent or hostile to the people. They had human characteristics (though on a more vast heroic or Olympian scale). They thought and acted in the same way that people do in the human world.

The second element of the Greek genius for "taming" the mystery of the universe to something people could cope with was their questioning instinct. They attempted to understand life piece-by-piece, step-by-step, and to build everyday explanations rather than mythical ones by accumulating a careful catalogue of what was already known. They then used known information to gain further information.

Greek religion

A humanized religion of Greece in which the gods were supermen and superwomen and which dealt with the meaning of life.

---

6. All of these gods and goddesses have Roman counterparts, whose names are equally familiar.

The development of the Greek city-states and the establishment of schools like the one at Athens set the Greeks to speculating on all areas of their lives: government, politics, society, war, mathematics, biology, religion, and so forth. Great philosophers turned their minds to explaining the reasonableness of religion. They began to draw conclusions about **deities** and religious practice in a systematic, rational way that has become standard in most Western religions.

Philosophy is not religion, but it is a useful tool for understanding the *content* of what religion responds to as the mystery of life. Philosophers such as Socrates and Plato cleared away the **accretions** of centuries and established a concern for basic principles about life. In place of many gods—undiscriminated, amorphous, of undetermined origin, purpose, or location, often animal and violent—they put a principle of good or singleness of duty. Where they found magic, witchcraft, and incantations designed to coerce the gods, they sought natural explanations for what they did not understand. When they found people subject to the fate decreed by the gods, they urged them to begin ordering their own lives to the greatest good: virtue for its own sake, social well-being, harmony, beauty, and peace. They delivered people of the Western world from a deity-fated universe (in which the whims of an animal god, an Atum or Osiris or Zeus, decided people's destiny) to a people-centered universe, where the idea of a single deity, a creative force, or an all-powerful but not vengeful God, could begin to make sense.

With the emergence of Greek thought, the search narrowed in the Western world for an answer to the mystery of life. People, prepared slowly and naturally over the course of thousands of years, were ready to accept the idea that a God—the Utterly Other, the Almighty—had created the world with people as the highest form of creation and had destined them for things greater than this earth offered.

This thought, however, was not to burst on the world. It, too, was prepared for and found its acceptance slowly. How it was prepared for and how it is expressed in Western religions are described in the next part of this book. How religion developed in the East and how it is expressed there are described in a subsequent section.

deity

A god or goddess; sometimes refers to an impersonal god.

philosophy

The pursuit of wisdom; a search for a general understanding of reality.

accretions

Additions; growth in size or extent.

Summary

1. The history of religion in the Western world reveals a trend toward more clearly understanding what is truly related to the mystery of life and what is within the realm of human understanding.

2. Archeological studies of early historic religious practices reveal people's concern about the mystery of life, survival, continuity of the tribe, death, and life after death.

3. Early myths reveal the kind of God or god(s) people believed in, their relationship with this God (or gods), and the kind of worldview held by the people of the time.

4. Early myths reflect the kind of world experienced by the people of prehistoric and early historic times.

5. The Greeks, more than any other ancient people, helped lay the foundation for a more sophisticated understanding of the world and the mystery of life. They did this through their questioning, and their searching for natural causes to the ordinary experiences of life.

For review

1. Where does the knowledge we have of prehistoric religions come from? of early historic religions?

2. Why does your book focus on the religion of the Babylonians, the Egyptians, and the Greeks?

3. Contrast the Babylonian and Egyptian views of the origin of the world, the gods, and life after death.

4. How did the practice of astrology begin?

5. What was the central concern of early Egyptian religion?

6. What role did the Greek view of religion play in the development of religious thought and practice in Western civilization? Explain.

7. How did the Greek view of the gods differ from the view of the gods of people who lived before them? Why did this development take place?

For discussion

1. Speculate why some people consult the stars or pay visits to astrologers. Is there any evidence that the stars or the planets affect people's lives?

2. Compare the relationship of the Santa Claus story or the legends about a historical figure to the myths of ancient religions.

3. Discuss why some religions seem not to have developed beyond a certain stage. Could it be because the answers to the mystery of life provided by their religious leaders satisfied them?

4. Postulate the reasons for some religions simply dying out.

For research

1. Prepare a report on the religion of ancient Rome. Include material on the cult of the emperor.

2. Prepare a report on one of the following topics: the development of ancient civilization; the pyramids and the Sphinx; Egyptian religion and culture;

the Golden Age of Greece; the influence of Rome in spreading Greek culture; the myths of Greece and Rome; the laws of Hammurabi; the Acropolis; the Trojan War; the *Iliad* and the *Odyssey;* or the theology of Amenhotep IV (Akhenaten).

3. Make a list of the major Greek gods and their role in the universe as the Greeks conceived that role. After each, put the name of the Roman god who fulfilled the same role.
4. Prepare a report on the function of myth in religion.
5. Prepare a summary of various myths of ancient religions, giving the place where the myth was used, the general content, and a probable cause for the myth's content and formulation.
6. Find out what you can about the origin of the Olympic games.

Word list

accretions

amalgam

astrology

auguring

Babylonian religion

deity

divination

early Egyptian religion

Greek religion

Hammurabi

hierarchy

horoscope

mummification

myth

philosophy

rite

satellite gods

seer

syncretism

theology

Part Two
The World's Living Religions

For the purposes of this study, the world's living religions have been divided into two major parts—the religions of the Western world and the religions of the Eastern world. The religions of the so-called Third World[1] have not been included in a separate category because, for the most part, they are either Western or Eastern, except in those areas where preliterate or tribal religions still flourish. Generally, these are in isolated pockets in Africa and on some of the islands of the Pacific and the Caribbean.

Western religions

Those religions that arose in the Middle East and are practiced in the Western world and in the Muslim countries: Judaism, Christianity, Islam.

Eastern religions

Those religions that arose and are practiced in India, China, and Japan, and are practiced in Southeast Asia and the Far East.

When we speak of the **Western religions**, we are referring to those that arose in the Middle East (Judaism, Christianity, Islam) and are practiced in the Western world and in the Muslim countries. When we speak of the **Eastern religions**, we are referring to those that arose and are practiced in India, China, and Japan, and are practiced in Southeast Asia and the Far East.

---

1. The Third World is made up of those countries that are less developed economically and educationally. Most of these countries are located in Africa, the Near East, and Latin America. Most are former colonial possessions of other nations.

One more thing needs to be said about the differences between the East and the West, and that is the mind-set or philosophical outlook of the people in each. The mind-set of the West, nurtured as it has been by the Greek philosophers, is basically earthbound, pragmatic, scientific, and deductive. The mind-set of the East is cosmic, passive, spiritual, and inductive. Each has its own way of looking at reality, a way that is peculiar to how it thinks about the world, people, things in the world, and the spiritual or nonmaterial universe. This mind-set, or way of looking at reality, has influenced not only religion itself in each area, but the beliefs and practices of the religions that flourish in each area.

Although there are many living religions by which people in the Western world live, there are three—Judaism, Christianity, and Islam—that have played a dominant role in shaping the contemporary culture of the West. These three were selected for discussion, not only because space does not allow for a discussion of each of the hundreds of religious expressions found in the Western world, but also because these three typify the development of religion in the Western world.

Many things distinguish these Western religions from the ancient religions discussed in the first part of this book. The first is that each has a known starting point, and each is dominated by a single person, or founder.

This does not mean that they have no roots that go back before their founder, even to prehistoric times. After all, every founder must have materials with which to work. It means that these religions did not just "happen" or "evolve" into being by a slow process of social accumulation. Each was formed by a definite individual.

There are differences among the three founders, of course, as we shall see. Moses founded the Israelite religion by codifying a centuries-old collection of Hebrew traditions into a unified Law of God. Jesus is remembered as having founded the Christian religion by claiming to be the sum, substance, and fulfillment of what Moses had founded. Muhammad founded the Islamic religion by passing along to humanity messages that he claimed were from the angel Gabriel, writing them down in a book called the Quran.

Since their founding, of course, each of these major living religions has developed to a greater complexity and branched into subdivisions. In our brief survey of the living religions of the Western world, we are not interested in the causes or the nature of the complexities or the subdivisions. We are only concerned with how the living religions of the Western world experience the mystery of life and respond to it.

Before beginning a study of some of the living religions of East and West, it might be useful to put the study in its proper perspective. Even though religion's influence in some parts of the world has lessened, religion is very much alive in the world. It influences the lives of most people the world over. Religion enables people to express a relationship with whatever the mystery of life is for them.

As Huston Smith, an eminent scholar who spent much of his life studying and explaining the world's religions, observed:

I write these opening lines on a day widely celebrated throughout Christendom as World-Wide Communion Sunday. The sermon in the service I attended this morning dwelt on Christianity as a world phenomenon. From mud huts in Africa to the Canadian tundra, Christians are kneeling today to receive the elements of the Holy Eucharist. It is an impressive picture.

Still, as I listened with half my mind, the other half wandered to the wider company of God-seekers. I thought of the Yemenite Jews I watched six months ago in their synagogue in Jerusalem: dark-skinned men sitting shoeless and cross-legged on the floor, wrapped in the prayer shawls their ancestors wore in the desert. They are there today, at least a quorum of ten, morning and evening, swaying backwards and forwards like camel riders as they recite their Torah, following a form they inherit unconsciously from the centuries when their fathers were forbidden to ride the desert horse and developed this pretense in compensation. Yalcin, the Muslim architect who guided me through the Blue Mosque in Istanbul, has completed his month's Ramadan fast, which was beginning while we were together; but he too is praying today, five times as he prostrates himself toward Mecca. Swami Ramakrishna, in his tiny house by the Ganges at the foot of the Himalayas, will not speak today. He will continue the devotional silence that, with the exception of three days each year, he has kept for five years. By this hour U Nu is probably facing the delegations, crises, and cabinet meetings that are the lot of a prime minister, but from four to six this morning, before the world broke over him, he too was alone with the eternal in the privacy of the Buddhist shrine that adjoins his home in Rangoon. Dai Jo and Lai San, Zen monks in Kyoto, were ahead of him by an hour. They have been up since three this morning, and until eleven tonight will spend most of the day sitting immovable in the lotus position as they seek with intense absorption to plumb the Buddha-nature that lies at the center of their being.

What a strange fellowship this is, the God-seekers in every land, lifting their voices in the most diverse ways imaginable to the God of all life. How does it sound from above? Like bedlam, or do the strains blend in strange, ethereal harmony? Does one faith carry the lead, or do the parts share in counterpoint and antiphony when not in full-throated chorus?

We cannot know. All we can do is try to listen carefully and with full attention to each voice in turn as it is raised to the divine.[2]

For review

1. When the text speaks of the "Western religions," to which religions is it referring? What are the three principal Western religions? Name the first thing that distinguishes the three principal Western religions from ancient religions.
2. In what ways does the mind-set of people in the West differ from people in the East? Explain.

Word list

Eastern religions
Western religions

---

2. Huston Smith, *The World's Religions* (New York: HarperCollins Publishers, 1991), 1–2.

View from the Mount of Olives of the Old City of Jerusalem.

"God is One."

4 Judaism

Judaism

The religion of the Jewish people characterized by belief in one God and the living out of God's law as expressed in the Jewish Scriptures.

Israeli

A native or inhabitant of the republic of Israel.

The Wailing Wall, which is the holiest place for prayer for Jews, in the Old City of Jerusalem.

Shema

The Jewish doxology which expresses the essence of that faith.

doxology

A prayer of praise to God.

The first Western religion we will study is **Judaism,** the oldest of the three principal Western religions. This religion, whose roots go back to the Fertile Crescent of the ancient Middle East, has had a profound impact on the worldview of people in the Western world. Today it is practiced in a variety of forms, not only by many **Israelis,** but by millions of Jews in the United States, Canada, and elsewhere.

The essence of Jewish faith

The heart of Jewish religious faith is best expressed in the **Shema,** a Jewish **doxology.** It is recited at morning and evening services, and often in private. The Shema expresses Judaism's strong faith in and love of God. It is taken from the Book of Deuteronomy, which is in the Jewish Bible, and goes like this:

Hear, O Israel! The LORD is our God, the LORD alone.[1] You shall love the LORD your God with all your heart and with all your soul and with all your might. Take to heart these instructions with which I charge you this day. Impress them upon your children. Recite them when you stay at home and when you are away, when you lie down and when you get up. Bind them as a sign on your hand and let them serve as a symbol on your forehead; inscribe them on the doorposts of your house and on your gates.

—Deuteronomy 6:4–9

1. In the Jewish Bible—and in this chapter—the word *Lord* when spelled with capital letters stands for the divine name, YHVH. See page 52 in this text for more about the divine name.

Chapter 4   45

Resounding through the world for over 3,000 years as the morning and evening prayers of every devout Jewish person, the cry "Hear, O Israel! The LORD is our God, the LORD alone!" proclaims the essence of Judaism. It harkens back to the desert of **Sinai,** where **Moses,** coming down from the mountain, brought to his travel-weary gathering of escaped **Hebrew** slaves the **Torah,**[2] which would make them one people bound in solemn **covenant** to the LORD. And the commands contained in the Book of Deuteronomy, chapter 6, verses 7 to 9, have been followed faithfully. Each year the works of the LORD are relived and made present to the Jewish people in the celebration of the Jewish feast days.

Today there are about eighteen million **Jews** in the world. Most live in Asia (especially in Israel), Europe, and the Americas (especially the United States). Judaism is divided into four major movements—Orthodox, Conservative, Reform, and Reconstructionist—with each having subdivisions that interpret Jewish law in a particular way.

Many Jews believe that God created the Jewish people by God's Torah. The essence of Judaism is, therefore, God, the people, and the Torah. For the Jew, however, "God" does not mean just any god, but the One and Only God, who chose a particular people—and whom a particular people chose. The Jews are not only a chosen people; they are also a choosing people.

The people are not just any motley group of individual people, but a collected, gathered, chosen family with a close-knit, mutual concern for one another that imitates the concern God has for them. The Torah is not merely a set of laws or a cultural system of teaching. It is the God-given pattern that creates the people, and it is the Jewish quest to understand God.

The Jewish religion is unique. It is about *this* God who chose *this* people to live *this* way. Other religions may express people's approach to God, but the Jewish people see their history as revealing God's approach to people. To understand its uniqueness, we must look at the Jewish religion under four headings: Jewish history, God, people, and Jewish expressions of their relationship to God.

Sinai

The peninsula extension of the continent of Asia between the Red Sea and the Mediterranean; also the name of the desert on that peninsula and a mountain from which, Jews believe, the Law was given to Moses.

Moses

Leader and prophet of the Hebrew slaves who escaped from Egypt.

Hebrew

A name for the Jewish people and their language.

Torah

The Law and teachings of the Jewish Scriptures; the first five books of those Scriptures: Genesis, Exodus, Leviticus, Numbers, and Deuteronomy.

covenant

A sacred agreement, contract, testament between two parties.

Jews

Those who belong through descent or conversion to a continuation of the ancient Jewish people.

---

2. The Hebrew word *Torah* cannot be translated simply as "Law." It includes law and teachings, summarizing a whole way of life. As it says in the Reform movement's *Gates of Prayer* (New York: CCAR, 1975): "What is Torah? It is what God has revealed to us, and what we have come to understand about God. It is the ideas and ideals, the laws and commandments, that make up our religious heritage. It is the experience of Abraham, the legislation of Moses, the vision of the prophets, the commentary of the Rabbis, the insight of the Mystics. It is the questions we ask, and the answers we receive, when we seek to understand God, the world, and ourselves. It is the way of life; the path to self-fulfillment; the design for a better world" (696).

Jewish history

Jewish Bible

Scriptures of the Jewish people.

The history of Jewish beginnings can be told in two ways: (1) through the **Jewish Bible** and the traditions surrounding it, and (2) through external historical evidence supplied by archaeologists and students of other ancient cultures. When these two versions are compared, it is apparent that the "inside story" and the story told by outside evidence are just not the same story. They do not exactly contradict each other, but neither do they entirely agree with each other; they have a completely different point of view. The Bible in Jewish tradition says, in effect, "This is the story of God's people and how God brought them together as God's people." The external evidence found by secular historians says, in effect, "This is the story of how a number of Hebrew tribes got together and came to think of themselves as God's people."

To adequately understand Jewish history, we must know both versions of the story, for each sheds light on the other. When they are put together in one composite story, the inside story is more completely understood.

The roots of Judaism go back to the Mesopotamian world of about 1900 B.C.E., where the highly complex system of nature-gods and city-gods existed in Babylonian culture. Among the many people who lived in this region were groups of wandering tribes called **Habiru.** These were not one single people but a set of loosely-related tribes of seminomads. Around 1900 B.C.E., there was a great migration of many of these clans from the area around the Persian Gulf across the Fertile Crescent.

Habiru

A name referring to a social group in the ancient Middle East who lived on the fringe of society, at times referring to roving bands, mercenaries, and foreign slaves. It may be that the Hebrews emerged from one such group.

The biblical Book of **Genesis** tells of a clan leader named **Abraham** who moved his clan away from the city of Ur because he was called by the voice of **El Shaddai** ("God Almighty") to do so. El Shaddai wanted Abraham and his wife **Sarah** to move away from a land of many pagan gods to a land where they and their descendants could worship El Shaddai as the One and Only God. This God made a mutual covenant with Abraham and Sarah (Genesis 12).

Genesis

First book of the Jewish Bible.

Abraham

Patriarch of the Hebrew people.

El Shaddai

The clan-god of Abraham and Sarah; "God Almighty."

Sarah

Wife of Abraham and matriarch of the Hebrew people.

Archeological and other secular historical discoveries have revealed some general information about the Habiru clans and their religious beliefs. Each clan had its own particular clan-god who was not stationed at any particular geographic location or city, but who accompanied the clan in its wanderings and was its faithful protector. A clan did not believe that its god was the only god in the world, but that its god was the only one who remained loyal to and protected it. This was a kind of reaction against, or adaptation of, the Mesopotamian system of nature-gods and gods stationed at particular cities.

If the biblical Abraham and Sarah's El Shaddai was typical of these clan-gods, then we do not as yet have the One and Only God of Jewish tradition. We have an intermediate understanding, a step in this direction, a step away from absolute **polytheism** (belief in many gods), but not yet the final stage of absolute **monotheism** (belief in only one God). If we could translate this clan-god concept into modern words, perhaps it would sound something like this: There may be many gods in the world, but a person (or tribe) can be faithful to only one.

Learning to believe in one God

As the story is told in the Jewish Bible, Abraham and Sarah's God was not just a clan-god but, in fact, *the* God. However, most biblical scholars realize that the Book of Genesis was written centuries after Abraham and Sarah lived (based on centuries of oral and written tradition and legend), and was edited and reedited many times before it reached its final form, around the year 500 B.C.E. (about 1,400 years after Abraham and Sarah lived). Very likely, the writers who put the story of Abraham and Sarah into its final written form read back into their lives their own more developed understanding of God.

Jewish people, who consider their Bible to be God's inspired word, recognize that God's general pattern of operation in the world is to bring about progress by slow evolution. God leads people step-by-step, not only into a growing understanding of such earthly things as agriculture, science, and mathematics, but also into a growing understanding of God. Jews understand the clan-god idea as a divinely inspired step up from absolute polytheism. They believe that God led this people through many more stages (which we shall shortly examine) to the final stage of understanding of God's absolute unity and holiness. Looking back from this vantage point, they see the early notion as the beginning of the later, more complete one. Hence, in a real sense, many Jewish people believe Abraham and Sarah were called by the One God even though they themselves may not have realized it consciously. The Book of Genesis tells their story in poetic language, revealing not exactly what Abraham and Sarah experienced but what their descendants recognized behind their experience.

polytheism

Religion based on a belief in many gods.

monotheism

Religion based on belief in only one God.

Jews celebrating Simchat Torah, the festival marking the completion and recommencing of the Torah-reading cycle.

Israelites

The Jewish people, at one time named after Israel, also known as Jacob, son of Isaac and Rebekah, grandson of Abraham and Sarah.

Exodus

The escape of the Jewish people from captivity in Egypt and their journey through the Sinai desert on the way to the Promised Land of Canaan (Israel); also the name of the second book of the Jewish Bible.

Isaac

Son of Abraham and Sarah.

Jacob

Son of Isaac and Rebekah, grandson of Abraham and Sarah.

The Jewish Bible picks up the story of the **Israelites** centuries later. After centuries of wandering, many groups settled in Egypt along the northern branches of the Nile. A series of political upheavals in the country found them at the bottom of the social ladder, reduced to slavery. Perhaps it was this unity in a common suffering that gave these groups a sense of being more than just a collection of individual isolated clans.

It was around the year 1285 B.C.E. that a powerful Hebrew leader, Moses, was able to instill in some of his lower-class comrades a sense of their own unity and their dignity as free people. Escaping from Egypt under circumstances that they celebrated as miraculous,[3] Moses' group solemnly entered into a national covenant with the LORD in the desert at Mount Sinai and expressed its newborn code of laws as the Commandments of the LORD.

The Jewish Bible, in the Book of **Exodus,** portrays the LORD as the One and Only God, the God of Abraham, **Isaac,** and **Jacob,** the God whom Abraham had called by the name El Shaddai. Again, most biblical scholars point out that the Book of Exodus probably had its beginnings in epic songs celebrating the desert escape; but additions and refinements, and newer, more complex laws were added to it over the succeeding centuries, so that the Book of Exodus as it exists today shows evidence of a "reading back into" ancient events certain insights that actually come from a later period in Jewish religious evolution.

It may very well be that Moses did not conceive of the LORD as the One and Only God in the whole world. He may have thought of the LORD only as the one national God of the newly united Israelite tribes. If that was the way he thought of the LORD, then what Moses did was to lead the Israelites to enlarge their notion of a clan-god to a national God.

Jews who take an evolutionary view of God's action upon people's understanding see in the LORD-of-Mount Sinai the second step up from Mesopotamian polytheism. For the Israelites, it made more religious sense to worship one God in common rather than for each tribe to have its own clan-god. After all, in their miraculous flight from Egypt, they had escaped as one people and sensed one power behind their escape.

---

3. On July 3, 1976, Israeli commandos staged a dramatic and very successful raid at Entebbe Airport, in Uganda, in order to free nearly a hundred Jews who had been taken hostage by terrorists while flying from Tel Aviv to Paris on an Air France flight. Even though all aspects of that operation can be explained through military plans and rational circumstances, many people describe the rescue of the hostages as nothing less than miraculous. In the same way, the biblical account of the escape of the Hebrews from Egypt looks back at the event and sees evidence of something greater than human accomplishment.

The third stage in the development of Jewish monotheism took place through the inspired preaching of the **prophets**—people of various temperaments and characters and walks of life who, over many centuries in the Promised Land, Canaan (Israel today), felt called to purify the Jewish people's understanding of what had taken place in the covenant they had entered into at Mount Sinai.

It was the prophets who made determined efforts to root out of the Jewish people the last vestiges of polytheism, the last shreds of allegiance to any nature-gods or clan-gods. It was the prophets whose inspired vision led the people to understand that the LORD must indeed be not only a national God but the God of the whole world; for the LORD had founded their nation in a miraculous escape and had many times since brought them back from capture and exile by foreign powers (chiefly the **Babylonian Exile**, from 587 to 536 B.C.E.). If the LORD was not the God of the whole world, the LORD could not have had such power over history. Therefore, the gods of other nations could not really be gods at all but were lifeless images in gold and silver and wood and bronze: lifeless images of a power that does not exist, that just plain is not—in contrast to the LORD, "Who Is."

prophet

Among the Jews, one who called the people back to the covenant and who led the people in their understanding of God.

Babylonian Exile

The capture of the Jewish leadership and exile of this group into the Babylonian empire from 587 to 536 B.C.E.

Jewish morning services in a synagogue.

The Jewish people thoroughly learned the lesson that the LORD was the One and Only God. By the time of the first century C.E., theirs was the only nation in the whole Roman Empire that did not bow to Roman gods or worship the emperor as a god, or even allow the emperor's picture to be minted on the coins they used or the Roman eagle to stand in their Temple. This was the strength of their reaction against anything that faintly resembled worship of any power but the Only One Who Is.

Zealots

A militant faction within Judaism in the first century C.E.

In 66 C.E., the **Zealots,** a faction within Judaism, led a revolt against the Romans in order to free the Jewish homeland from Roman control. The conflict, which lasted four years, ended with the Romans destroying Jerusalem and burning the Temple itself. As a result, the Jewish nation was effectively destroyed. Many Jews fled their homeland and joined their fellow Jews elsewhere throughout the Mediterranean and Middle Eastern world. Owing to a final attempt at revolt against the Romans by some Jews in 132 C.E., Jews in the Roman Empire were forbidden to practice their religion.

The Jewish religion survived the destruction of the Jewish nation and the Temple for two reasons. First, the Jews who had been in exile in Babylon had developed forms of piety not related to the Temple. Those forms of piety continued to be part of the Jewish religion after the exile even though the Jews who returned to their homeland were allowed to build another Temple. Second, the reverence the Jews had for the Torah gave them something around which to center their lives once the Temple was destroyed and their nation no longer existed.

> . . . the focus of Judaism shifted from the sacrificial rite of the Temple to the study of the Torah and its accompanying Oral Tradition in academies and **synagogues**. Thenceforth it was not the priests, who were no longer functional, but the **rabbis**(literally teachers) who held Judaism together, for their synagogues became centers not only for study but for worship and congregational life in general. Rabbinic Judaism grounded itself in the commandment to make the study of the Torah a lifelong endeavor, and Judaism acquired a distinctly intellectual dimension and character. Through the tradition of Torah-study as it developed in the **Talmud**, the mind was made integral to religious life and mental energies were introduced into piety. Study, including the kind of constant, unceasing questioning and the rigid sense of logic that pervades the Talmud, became a way of worship. In this complex, the Bible became a revealed text inviting and requiring interpretation, and interpretation was raised to the status of revelation itself.[4]

synagogue

In Judaism, a special building for worship and instruction.

rabbi

A teacher of the Jewish Torah and other written and oral traditions.

Talmud

A collection of Jewish laws and traditions; a compilation of Jewish doctrine and discipline based and built on the Torah.

---

4. Huston Smith, *The World's Religions* (HarperCollins Publishers, 1991), 310–311.

The Jewish people and the Jewish religion continued a remarkable story of survival throughout the history of the Christian Holy Roman Empire and thereafter, despite periods of dire persecution in Europe and Russia. One of the most heinous persecutions took place in the twentieth century, in Nazi Germany and throughout most of Europe. In recent times, the nation of Israel has been reestablished as a homeland for those who choose to live there and as a focal point of Jewish identity for those who live in other parts of the world.

From the highlights of Jewish religious history sketched above, we can extract some key themes in the Jewish understanding of God and people. These themes might not exist with such force in the wider world today if it were not for the presence of Judaism and its offspring, Christianity, and Islam, which sees itself as coming from the heritage of Abraham.

The God of Jewish faith

As we have said, the concept of God as Jewish people perceive God developed over many centuries. As told in the Jewish Bible, God identified God's name to Moses as "YHVH." This name is hard to translate. It may suggest God's Mysterious Beyondness if translated "I AM WHO I AM." It is also sometimes translated "I AM WHAT I AM" or "I WILL BE WHAT I WILL BE." In any case, so greatly did the Jewish people respect this name that eventually it was forbidden to pronounce it. Whenever a public Scripture reader at synagogue services came upon this name, he would pronounce simply "The Name" or, at a later period, would substitute the Hebrew word **Adonai,** which means "my Lord." This later practice continues in synagogues today.

Adonai

A Jewish name for God which means "my Lord."

But the Jewish people believe that God not only revealed God's name in the Bible, God also revealed God's nature. According to Jewish belief, God is one, personal, saving, faithful, and above all.

1. God is one.

Not much needs to be said here about this point, since it is the fundamental principle of the evolution of the Habiru tribes into "the people of God."

The closer to pure monotheism the Jewish understanding of God came, the more the Jews reacted against the beliefs of their polytheistic neighbors. They grew up in a world where natural forces were considered to have personalities: there was a sun god, a wind god, a moon god, storm gods, and so on. As belief in one God grew, the Jews had to reinterpret the symbols of the cultures surrounding them. Every one of the rival gods had to be "dethroned." The wind, instead of being a separate god, came to be thought of as "the breath of the LORD." The storms were "the anger of the LORD." The sun and moon (the chief gods in other belief systems) were really dethroned. In the creation poem of Genesis, chapter 1, the LORD doesn't create the sun and moon until the fourth day, three days after light had already been created! The various winged-lion and winged-bull gods of Babylon became mere messengers of the LORD. (From the Greek word *angelos*, meaning "messenger," we get our English word **angel**.) The ark of the covenant was covered with an empty throne in the shape of two winged bulls spreading their wings as a seat for the Unpicturable One. In these and many other ways, the Jews expressed their growing awareness that the LORD is God—not just "a god."

2. God is personal.

Jewish insight takes a definite stand that reality is ultimately personal. People are not an accident floating on a sea of blind fate; they are partners with God in a covenant, in a two-way relationship of faithfulness. This is a very key point in Jewish theology. People are not alone in life; their entire lives are spent in the presence of One Who Cares. This stands in sharp contrast to some aspects of early and ancient religion, where the power(s) over the universe could be natural forces or animal spirits, and in contrast to some Eastern religions where Ultimate Reality is an impersonal, aloof, "eternal essence."

3. God is saving.

Jewish people's conviction that God cares is based on what they experienced throughout their entire history. In their miraculous escape from Egyptian slavery, they learned that the power over the universe was on their side; theirs was a saving God. Their entire history, in fact, was experienced as a salvation history. They interpreted their temporary declines as a nation as God's punishment for their unfaithfulness to God and their unconcern for one another. They saw in their deliverance from oppression the faithfulness of God saving them, calling them to a new possibility for greatness when they would repent of their past mistakes. They learned that God takes people seriously; what they do is important to God.

4. God is faithful.

When the Jewish people found God rescuing them time after time from the punishment that infidelity had brought them to, an inspiring truth about God hit home for them: God would not divorce this people, even though they were giving God sufficient grounds to do so.[5] God keeps the covenant even when people do not. As God said to Jeremiah, one of the Jewish prophets: "You see what this people said:

angel

A messenger from God, usually considered a spiritual being.

---

5. The rather constant depiction in the Jewish Bible of the Israelites' infidelity illustrates the fidelity of God. It was not meant to show the Israelites as constantly unfaithful—they were not.

'The two families which the LORD chose have now been rejected by Him.' Thus they despise My people, and regard them as no longer a nation. Thus said the LORD: As surely as I have established My covenant with day and night—the laws of heaven and earth—so I will never reject the offspring of Jacob . . . ." (Jeremiah 33:24–26)

In Jewish eyes, it is God who calls and people who answer or refuse to respond, but God continues to call. God calls every person into being, and each person answers "Yes" or "No" to what God calls him or her to be. Those who answer "Yes" cooperate in a personal creation and become the kind of persons they are capable of becoming. If they answer "No," they choose a personal defeat and by rights deserve to become less than capability would allow. God will not force someone to become the best possible self, but God will never abandon a person: the possibility of becoming one's best self is always present, not because one deserves it, but because God has promised it.

5. God is above all.

In contrast to early and ancient religions—and to some features of superstition in any age—the Jews believe that God is not a being or spirit who can be controlled by magic, commanded by ritual, converted by prayer, or computed by human theories. It is people who must be sensitive to God's way of seeing things. God is not an extension of people, some kind of superman or superwoman. God is Absolutely Other. People can extend their control over nature, but they can have no control over God. They can pray to God for help to know and fulfill God's plan, but they dare not pretend that their plans can substitute for God's plan. They can grope after that mystery called God, but they can never wrap God up in a final formula that would protect people from the mystery of life.[6]

The Jews believe that people can pray to God for help to know and fulfill God's plan, but they dare not pretend that their plans can substitute for God's plan.

---

6. What makes the Jewish insights concerning God all the more remarkable is that they lived in the midst of more materially successful cultures whose gods apparently took care of them.

The Jewish understanding of God—so radically different from the ideas of gods among their contemporaries—led the Jews to conceive of people's place in the world and their ultimate relationship with God and other people in equally radical ways. The Jews differed from those among whom they lived in the following areas.

1. The dignity of people

Perhaps in no other way did the Jewish people differ from their neighbors so radically as in their understanding of the place of people in the world. In contrast to groups who believed that people were the slaves or playthings of the gods, or helpless in the vast scheme of things, the Jews saw people as fundamentally good because God had made them that way. (This can be seen in the creation stories in the Jewish Bible, Genesis 1:24–31 and 2:7–24.) They saw them as God's partners in making the world a suitable place to live.

In addition, because of their own experiences as slaves who were freed to become a people, the Israelites came to see in every unfortunate person a son or daughter of God. Though they were not yet enlightened enough to do away with slavery entirely,[7] the Jewish laws regulating slavery[8] were more humane than those of their pagan neighbors. Furthermore, every person was considered God's friend, not God's slave as in Babylonian and other religions; therefore, all practices such as mutilating the body in religious rites were forbidden. Forbidden also was human sacrifice, including the burning of babies, a practice in neighboring countries. The dignity of women was protected in family laws, and the rights of children were protected.

---

7. Social evolution, like all evolution, is slow. For example, the leadership of Moses in seeking the freedom of his people occurred about 1285 B.C.E., but the Emancipation Proclamation in the United States was not made until 1863 C.E.—over 3,000 years later. Even now, not all people in the United States are truly free, though they are legally free. Will people 3,000 years from now look upon people today as socially primitive?

8. In biblical times, slavery was not slavery as we understand it. It was, in fact, a form of indentured servitude in which people were able to pay debts when they were bankrupt.

2. True morality

For the Jewish people, being a good person meant a great deal more than merely conforming to a social code. It meant even more than obeying society's laws in order to be fair to others. It included these things but went much deeper. It penetrated to the ultimate motive for these things: faithfulness to God. Every Jewish person's very existence was founded upon the covenant with the LORD. The ultimate dignity of a person is that God and he or she are partners in a lifelong conversation and a lifelong friendship. God had chosen this people and they had accepted God, and both sides had sworn to be faithful.

The social code that guided Jews to be fair to other Jews was seen as God's plan for creating the people that was God's chosen family. Thus, observance of the Torah was more than a new social convention or necessity or convenience. It was the way God wanted the Israelites to live. Hence, devout Israelites observed the Torah because this was their way of being faithful to God, who was faithful to them. They observed the Torah with joy because the Torah was what God wanted for them.

The core of morality for the Jewish people was much deeper than mere external conformity to laws. The core of morality was as deep as the deepest heart of humanity—a man's or woman's capacity for personal fidelity to another person. Respect for the person of God made the Jewish people extra sensitive to the person of their neighbor, for their neighbor was also created "in God's image." Under the leadership of the prophets, the Israelites came to understand over the centuries that their original covenant to the LORD in the desert implied an obligation to be not only fair to other Jews but positively loving in their regard. The Jewish people developed a legal system designed to protect the poor, to promote justice, to extend God's benign influence from one person to another. When rulers or people fell away from these ideals, prophets rose up to warn them to change their ways lest they be destroyed; for God had intended the Jews to be God's people, a shining example of humanity for the enlightenment of the world—"the light of the nations."

3. Sin

Every religion tries to explain the mysterious sense of guilt that every person experiences. What is evil, and how did it come into the world? What makes people commit sin, and how can people overcome the evil in themselves?

a. The nature of sin. Many pagan religions showed in their myths an attempt to shrug off the problem, to put the blame for evil on something outside people. In effect they said, "Well, people are just that way—that's the way the gods made them." In the Babylonian myth of Marduk, for example, people were made from the blood of the corpse of a bad god—to imply that sin is "in people's blood"; evil was present in the very making of the universe.

The Jewish people, however, told a different story. Since they felt that the heart of humankind, the essence of humanity, lies in a capacity for personal faithfulness, they interpreted sin as personal unfaithfulness: breaking the covenant with the LORD.

In the Book of Genesis, chapters 2 and 3, a parable about the first man and woman is told. God creates a human statue out of clay and breathes the breath of life into him; from the man's rib God fashions a woman.[9] There is no evil built into them. However, faced with temptation (in the form of a serpent), the man and woman freely decide to do what God asked them not to do.

So in the Jewish view, **sin** is not a state of being into which a person is born. Rather, it is best understood as *chet,* a Jewish word that means "missing the mark." This is a term that is also used in archery, when the archer shoots the arrow and does not quite hit the bull's eye. So, too, people do "miss the mark" from time to time. The way to avoid sin, or *chet,* was to follow Torah, the Jew's guide to hitting the mark.

b. Redemption from sin. In a world where people are created evil in their nature, there can be no **redemption** from sin; the best that can be hoped is to "buy off" the gods through magic or human sacrifices.

In the world as the Jewish people saw it, where God created everything good and wants to fashion God's people as a community in God's own image and likeness, God is always trying to "buy back" (*re-deem*) God's people from their freely committed sins and the consequences of their sins. God is faithful to the covenant, even when people are not.

sin

An act or attitude which goes against the wishes or law of the God or gods; in Judaism, missing the mark or failing to follow the Torah.

redemption

A "buying back," a return to a relationship with God after individual or corporate sin.

---

9. In this feature of the parable, we see the enlightened Jewish notion of the dignity of woman—she is equal to man, not inferior to him. In a world where women were often treated with disrespect as inferior creatures, the Jewish myth portrays her as created, not from an inferior substance, but from the very substance of man.

There are actually two stories of creation in the Jewish Bible, in the Book of Genesis, the first in chapter 1 and the second in chapter 2. The rabbis brought these two stories together by saying that the first human being, who was created in the first story, was created androgynous, that is, having both male and female characteristics. The story in chapter 2 merely shows God separating that first human being into two equal parts—one man and one woman.

The prophets helped the Israelites to understand that God was always ready to rescue them from any slavery or punishment or consequences that their sins had brought upon them if they would allow God to rescue them from sin itself. Returning to the Law of God was always for them a response to the call of God to do so; the initiative was always God's; the response was the people's.

4. Destiny

The Jewish people brought a unique notion of people's destiny into the world. For them, history was forward looking. If contemporary societies (whether Jewish, Christian, Islamic, socialist, capitalist, secular, etc.) have any notion of progress in the world, if hope for a better world in the future is something we can never completely lose, it is because we have inherited this concept from the Jews. All other religions before the Jewish religion looked back to some period in the past as the "Golden Age"; the gods had created the world at that time and now everything was settled. Many of those religions (and many Eastern religions even today) conceive of history as an eternal cycle continually repeating itself. Only the Jewish God is continually creating. God is creating the people of God.

Beginning with their escape from Egypt and continuing with their conquest of the Promised Land, their constant rescue from enemy capture, and their re-creation after exile, the Jewish people came to depend upon the LORD to be continually at work re-creating the covenant people.

The prophets taught them to long for the day when sin would be conquered, when people would love each other, when God would bring their community to such great perfection that it would be the light of the world. Then all nations would "beat their swords into plowshares" (Isaiah 2:4) and live in peace and harmony. This "Golden Age" is today called the **Messianic Age**[10] because at its center would be a royal ruler who would be an ideal person to rule an ideal people.

Today's Jewish people still long for the Messianic Age, although they interpret it divergently. Orthodox and Conservative Jews believe the messiah will come to inaugurate the kingdom of God at the end of time. Reform Jews believe that no one person, but all people, will be God's anointed community at the end of time. All religious Jews believe that, in the end, all people will accept God's name. Their *Aleuu* prayer reads:

Messianic Age

A "Golden Age" with a royal ruler who would be an ideal person to rule an ideal people.

---

10. From the Hebrew word *messiah,* meaning "anointed one" (because Jewish kings were anointed with oil during the coronation ceremony). In Jewish tradition, the messiah will be a human being who comes to reinstate Jewish political sovereignty by throwing off the yoke of oppressors.

We therefore hope in You, O Lord our God, that we shall soon see the triumph of Your might, that idolatry shall be removed from the earth, and false gods shall be utterly destroyed. Then will the world be a true kingdom of God, when all mankind will invoke Your name and all the earth's wicked will return to You. Then all the inhabitants of the world will surely know that to You every knee must bend, every tongue must pledge loyalty. Before You, O Lord, let them bow in worship; let them give honor to Your glory. May they all accept the rule of Your kingdom. May You reign over them soon through all time. Sovereignty is Yours in glory, now and forever. So is it written in Your Torah: The Lord shall reign for ever and ever. Such is the assurance uttered by the prophet: "The Lord shall be King over all the earth; that day the Lord shall be One and His name One."[11]

Arising out of this belief in a future "Golden Age" is the Jewish notion of the resurrection of the dead. All early religions believed in some kind of "soul-land" where departed spirits went. But since there was for them no future "Golden Age" on earth, there was no particular reason for the dead to return. However, the Jewish insight that God is continually at work perfecting creation through God's people made them uncomfortable with the notion that the dead are forever removed from this world. If God takes this world so seriously that God is continually resurrecting this chosen community throughout history, then does God not take this world seriously enough to resurrect each individual member of the community at the end of history? Such was the principle that brought the hope for bodily resurrection into Jewish consciousness[12] during the centuries immediately preceding the Common Era.

A Jewish cemetery in New York City.

---

11. The Rabbinical Assembly of America, *Weekday Prayer Book.*

12. Today Orthodox and Conservative Jews still believe in the resurrection of the body; Reform Jews do not, but they do believe in immortality.

Jewish expressions of their relationship to God

All religions have some form of ritual called **worship,** whereby people stand before reality greater than they are and act out what it means to be human and what kind of relationship they have with that reality.

If people think reality is a group of natural forces who "have it in for them" because they are an evil creation made from the corpse of bad gods, then people try to "buy off" the forces, for example, by sacrificing human babies or the most perfectly formed young man or young woman.

On the other hand, if people think reality is the creation of a loving, personal God, who is creating a people of loving concern in his or her image and likeness, then people open themselves to the creative activity of God:

We must praise the Lord of all, the Maker of heaven and earth, who has set us apart from the other families of earth, giving us a destiny unique among the nations. We therefore bow in awe and thanksgiving before the One who is Sovereign over all, the Holy One, blessed be God.[13]

Because the Jews experienced God as a person, their primary symbol for relating to God was not a "natural" symbol, such as a bear or the sun, but a "personal" symbol—the *word.* Whereas other gods created the hard way (through winning a battle), the LORD created just by giving the *word:* "Let there be light . . . Let there be an expanse in the midst of the water, that it may separate water from water. . . ." (See the Jewish Bible, Genesis 1.)

When God created the chosen people, God did so by the word of Torah. When God wished to re-create the Jewish people after each of their fallings-away, God's word came to them through the prophets. And the fundamental relationship, the covenant, was itself a word of promise between God and the chosen people.

Thus it is that although the Jewish people had many forms of worship, the one they put most emphasis on, and the heritage that they have passed to the rest of the world, involved worship through word.

Their special worship services, when each Jewish person turned his attention directly to the LORD, were (and are now) conducted principally in their synagogues.[14] Jewish synagogue services are based on the principle that prayer is not a monologue. Rather, it is a dialogue: God talking to people and people responding. There is a rhythm, and an alternating, between reading the word of God (excerpts from the Jewish Bible) and responding to that word in

worship

Religious ritual of adoration of forces, a deity, or deities.

A Torah scroll.

13. *Gates of Prayer,* 615.

14. The Jewish people had only one Temple—in Jerusalem—where God "resided." All other Jewish worship services were held in special buildings or places where the people could gather for worship and instruction. The word *synagogue* comes from the Greek word for "gathering of people."

prayers, sacred hymns, preaching and explanation, and exhortation. For the Jewish people, worship is not a passive watching; it is an active correspondence with God.

Because worship is a dialogue for the Jewish people, God has to speak to them. They believe God does so through God's word, the Bible. The first five books of the Bible are the Bible's core. They are known as the Torah.

Beginning at the time of Moses, the people were reminded that they had been saved through the mighty acts of God. They responded with prayers and hymns of thanksgiving. After the time of Moses, these same exploits were read to the people in ritual services, and they responded with promises of fidelity to God, just as their ancestors had done. As centuries rolled on, other collections of books were added to the original. Some contained history; some contained collections of songs and hymns that came down from their forebearers. Some were created to fit special services, and some books contained a record of the preaching of the prophets.

These were not all considered one collection of equal value until the Babylonian Exile, when the Jewish population was defeated and their leaders deported to Babylon.[15] There, in the absence of Temple worship, it was only the Torah and the traditions surrounding it that kept the people together. Synagogue services had their roots in the **Sabbath** meetings of this time. At the meetings, these various writings, as well as the Torah, were read and explained to the people as God's half of the dialogue. The people responded with their sacred hymns. The books (actually in scroll form) that were most commonly used in this way became standard and were gradually considered as much God's word as the Torah was. Thus, it became possible to conceive of them as one collection, and to codify them into the Jewish Bible.

It is impossible to measure the influence of the Jewish religion upon the Western world. From its beginnings in polytheistic times to its dedicated loyalty to the One God today, it is a remarkable monument to people's ability to respond to the mystery of life and, in responding, to be transformed.

Sabbath

A day of worship and rest; in Judaism, from sundown on Friday to sundown on Saturday.

---

15. Some material was added to this collection, probably in the second century of the Common Era. Among these are Ecclesiastes and the Song of Songs.

A woman at the Wailing Wall, Jerusalem.

Jewish Scriptures as an expression of the Jewish relationship with God

The Jewish Scriptures, like the sacred writings of other religious traditions, came together over a long period of time. The stories that are found in the Jewish Bible of the origin of the world and of their ancestors were part of Jewish folklore long before they became a part of their sacred writings. At first these stories were handed down by word of mouth. Eventually they were written down and then codified. This codification took place around 550 B.C.E., when many of the Jewish leaders were in exile in Babylonia. It was also at the time of the Babylonian Exile that the Jewish sacred literature was divided into three parts: the Torah, the Prophets, and the Writings. The first part of the Jewish Scriptures to be codified was the Torah, followed by the Prophets, and then, only centuries later, closer to the first century C.E., the Writings.

The Torah, also known as the Law or the Pentateuch, consists of the five "books of Moses": Genesis, Exodus, Leviticus, Numbers, and Deuteronomy. These books are the principal, or most important, part of the Jewish Bible.

Genesis contains the stories of creation (Adam and Eve, Noah and the Flood, and so forth) and the stories of the Jewish **patriarchs and matriarchs**, the famous ancestors of the Jewish people (Abraham and Sarah; Isaac and Rebekah; Jacob, Rachel, and Leah; and others). Exodus is the story of the escape from slavery in Egypt and of the covenant made with the LORD (and contains the Ten Commandments). Leviticus is a book about Jewish worship and about their priesthood. Numbers is a book about the experiences of the Jews in the desert. It contains a listing of the people who made the escape from Egypt. Deuteronomy contains another version of the Torah proclaimed on Mt. Sinai and an explanation of it.

patriarchs and matriarchs

The famous ancestors of a people.

The Prophets, as the name indicates, contains the activities and the words of the prophets. It is divided into two parts: the Former Prophets (often referred to as the Judges and the Kings of Israel—Saul, David, and Solomon) and the Latter Prophets (the ones who passed judgment on Israel and reminded them of their promises to God, such as Isaiah, Jeremiah, Ezekiel, and so forth). The Writings contain all the other material of the Jewish Bible, like the Psalms, the Proverbs, the Chronicles, Job, and the Festival Scrolls.

In all, the Jewish Bible contains thirty-nine books, all of which were (and are) referred to as "the books of the law," "the holy books," or simply, "the books." They not only occupy a special and sacred place in Jewish history and worship, expressing the relationship of the Jewish people with their God. They also form the first part of the Christian Bible (called the Old Testament or the Hebrew Scriptures) and are considered to be among the great pieces of writing in world literature.

Most Jews believe that their Bible is inspired. That is, they believe that God inspired the writers to write what God wanted to say to the people. Most Jews consider the Bible as God's book—a book containing a message for God's people sent by God through holy writers.

If the Exodus and the Sinai covenant "made" the Jewish people a religious nation, their Bible has kept them so. It has played a major role in making the Jewish people what they are, and has been a major force in shaping the culture of Western civilization.

The Talmud

One cannot speak of the Jewish Bible and/or the Torah without speaking of the Talmud and the Mishnah, or as it is sometimes called, the Mishna-Talmud.[16]

The Talmud, also known as the oral Torah, is a collection of Jewish laws and traditions consisting of the Mishnah and the Gemara. The Mishnah is a collection of oral laws handed down by word of mouth that was collated, edited, and revised by Rabbi Judah ha-Nisi around 200 C.E. The Gemara is a collection of commentaries on the Mishnah. There are two principal editions of the Talmud. The first is the Palestine edition, put together by the rabbinical schools in Palestine about 400 C.E. The second, larger and more definitive, was put together by the rabbinical schools in Babylon about 500 C.E.

---

16. *Talmud* comes from the Aramaic word meaning "teaching." *Mishnah* is an Aramaic word meaning "oral teaching." Aramaic was once the language of the Jews.

The Talmud is generally described as an interpretation of the Pentateuch and a divinely revealed guide of morals and conduct. It developed as a collection of materials used to settle complicated problems concerning the obligations imposed on Jews by the Torah.

The Talmud, then, is a compilation of Jewish doctrine and discipline based and built on the Torah. It is considered as having equal value and authority in Jewish life with the Torah and is subject to the same discussion and interpretation. Although the Torah, strictly speaking, is the first five books of the Jewish Bible, it is, more broadly, the whole body of Jewish law contained in the Pentateuch and the Talmud.

Jewish feasts and celebrations

The nature of Jewish religious awareness and their religious philosophy and spirit are best understood through their religious services, feasts, and celebrations, which uniquely express this people's relationship with God. The general nature of Jewish synagogue services was described earlier; some of their major feasts and important religious observances are described below.

The Jewish Sabbath

For the Jewish people, observance of the Sabbath is at the foundation of their faith. The work week is brought to a focused close on the seventh day, which is kept holy. The Sabbath recalls the completion of creation and the Creator's rest on the seventh day and refreshes and strengthens the participants. Traditionally, preparations for the home, which is the center of Sabbath celebration, and for the members of the family and their guests are completed before sundown on Friday evening. The Sabbath ends at sundown on Saturday.

The mother lights two candles shortly before sunset on Friday and prays a blessing. After the readings and prayer in the synagogue (or the home), family and guests gather for the evening meal. A special hymn is sung and each of the children blessed by the parents. The wine and the day are blessed, then the two loaves of twisted white bread (called hallah). The meal follows. Songs, teachings, and prayers complete the celebration for the evening.

The Sabbath day is joyful and festive. Saturday is marked by a morning synagogue service with a reading from the Torah, study, rest, a late afternoon service, and a culminating meal with concluding prayers.

The mother in a Jewish family lights the two Sabbath candles.

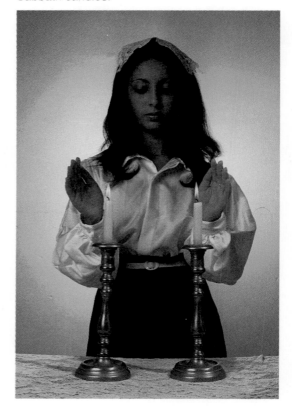

Autumn celebrations

Rosh Hashanah is a two-day festival for the new year. The blowing of the shofar, a ram's horn used in biblical times, is part of this celebration. There are communal prayers and an extended liturgy in the synagogue with readings from the Torah and the Prophets which emphasize life and hope.

Rosh Hashanah

Jewish celebration of the new year.

The blowing of the shofar.

Ten days later, the period of penitence that began with Rosh Hashanah concludes with **Yom Kippur,** the Day of Atonement. Yom Kippur is a day of penance and renewal that includes fasting and self-examination. The synagogue service that is part of this day includes confession, prayers for pardon, and a prayer asking for absolution from sins against God. In an ancient part of the service, the people pray that God will soon unite all people and do away with wickedness. Also in the service is a memorial for those who have died, with the prayer that others will follow their good examples. The service concludes with the blowing of the shofar.

Yom Kippur

The Jewish Day of Atonement.

In the same month of the Jewish calendar (Tishri, the seventh month), the harvest festival of **Sukkot** is celebrated. Popular names for this feast are the "Feast of Booths" or "Feast of Tabernacles." The festival recalls the wilderness travels under Moses; no permanent dwellings could be built, so booths or tents were used. This joyful holiday lasts for nine days, during which the family eats its meals and spends time in a little booth. The booth has an open roof of leaves or branches and is decorated with fall fruits, vegetables, flowers, and branches. In the synagogue ceremony, a palm branch with sprigs of myrtle and willow is held in one hand, and a citron (lime) is held in the other.

Sukkot

The Jewish autumn harvest celebration; Feast of Booths or Feast of Tabernacles.

The symbols are waved in every direction because God, who gives the harvest, is everywhere. The eighth day is the Solemn Assembly and the ninth Simchat Torah.

Winter celebrations

Hanukkah, the "Feast of Dedication" or the "Festival of Lights," commemorates the rededication of the Temple after it was desecrated by Antiochus Epiphanes in 168 B.C.E., when he set up pagan idols there and ordered the Jews to worship them. This event led to the Maccabean revolt and religious independence. When the Temple was finally cleansed, pure olive oil was needed for the lamp, but only enough oil for one day could be found. The feast recalls the miracle by which the oil lasted for eight days. Hanukkah is celebrated in December, and one more candle is lit on each of the eight days. The season celebrates religious freedom and loyalty. As part of the family celebration, gifts are given to children and games are played on each of the days.

A menorah being used during the celebration of Hanukkah.

Purim, the "Feast of Lots," takes place later in winter. It recalls the biblical story of Esther, who caused the defeat of an enemy of the Jewish people in Persia. Prior to Purim there is a fast which recalls Esther's three-day fast before approaching the king on behalf of her people. As with Hanukkah, Purim is not a biblical requirement. The Book of Esther is read in the synagogue, and the festival is celebrated with parties and other forms of entertainment, gift giving, and charity to those in need.

Pesah or Passover

The Jewish spring festival recalling the Exodus; includes the seder meal.

seder

The Jewish ritual meal of Passover.

Celebration of the Passover meal.

Shavu'ot

The Jewish feast celebrated on the fiftieth day after Passover; the Feast of Weeks or Pentecost.

Spring festivals

Pesah, or Passover, is celebrated with a ritual family meal and with special synagogue gatherings over eight days. It has roots in a spring farming feast, but it recalls in detail the escape from Egypt. Passover begins with the **seder** meal. Near the beginning of the service, the youngest child asks four questions, beginning with, "Why is this night different from all other nights?" The father then relates the story of the Exodus.

The meal includes lamb to recall the slaying of a lamb before the last of the plagues, the death of the firstborn, afflicted the Egyptians. The houses of the Israelites were passed over because of the blood of the lamb on the doorposts. Because the Israelites left Egypt quickly, they baked wafers of unleavened bread, or matzah, to take along. This is the only kind of bread eaten during Passover. Other foods includes unseasoned horseradish (recalling the bitterness of Egyptian slavery), chopped apples mixed with nuts, cinnamon, and wine (recalling the mortar used by the Jews to make bricks in Egypt), a roasted egg (a sign of the freewill offering that accompanied the sacrifice of the paschal lamb in the Temple), vegetables such as parsley or radish (symbolizing life, hope, and redemption), and salt water for dipping the vegetables (symbolic of tears).

Four cups of wine are served, two before the meal (halfway through the Haggadah or Exodus reading) and two after the meal. They stand for the four ways the redemption of Israel is announced in the Book of Exodus. A glass of wine is poured for Elijah, the prophet who foretold the coming of the messiah, and the door is opened for a time as a sign of welcome to him.

Shavu'ot, the "Feast of Weeks," is also known as "Pentecost," meaning the fiftieth day after Passover. Originally a spring harvest celebration, it is considered the birthday of the Jewish religion, recalling the time Moses received the Ten Commandments on Mount Sinai.

Eastern Orthodox Churches still set their date for Easter according to the date of the Jewish Passover, but the Western Christian and Jewish calendars no longer agree. Shavu'ot in Reform Judaism is the day for confirmation ceremonies.

The Jewish population of the United States since the mid-twentieth century has stood at between five and six million—two or three percent of the total population of the country. Jews came to America in three waves of successively greater size. The first wave consisted of Sephardic Jews who came in the colonial period. The second wave consisted of German Jews who came in the mid-nineteenth century. The third and greatest wave was of Eastern European Jews who came to America between 1881 and 1920. . . .

The first Jewish community in America was in the Dutch settlement of New Amsterdam (later New York). In 1654 a boatload of Spanish and Portuguese Jews came to New Amsterdam. . . . By the time of the American Revolution there were about 2,500 Jews in the thirteen colonies. . . . Jews came to those colonies which practiced religious toleration. . . .

In central Europe Jews had lived on the margins of society, making a living by filling niches that were new or that no one else cared to fill. Jews found similar niches on the frontier in America. The typical Jewish immigrant from Germany started out as a backpack peddler. An outfitter, generally an earlier immigrant, would set him up with a backpack and a supply of manufactured goods. He would walk from farm to farm, selling his goods. When he saved up enough money the peddler would buy a wagon and increase his stock. As soon as he had saved enough money and scouted out a good location, he would settle in a town and open up a shop of his own. Many of the great department stores in America, including Gimbel's and Macy's, were started by German Jews who had begun with a peddler's backpack. . . .

[T]he Jews of Eastern Europe ceased to hope for Enlightenment to solve their problems after the pogroms of 1881. That year began the flood of East European Jewish immigration to America. From 1880 to 1900 nearly a million Jews came to America. From 1900 to 1920 over a million more came. Altogether, perhaps half the Jews of Eastern Europe transferred to the United States in those years. . . .

The kind of economic opportunities that had existed in the mid-nineteenth century for German Jews were no longer available. The immigrants crowded into terrible slums in the major East Coast cities, especially New York. . . . Despite the poverty, very few Jews returned to Europe. . . .

This mass of poor immigrants worked their way up the economic scale and into American society more rapidly than any other immigrant group in American history. The immigrant generation sacrificed themselves and their own lives so that their children could have a better life. Their primary weapon in the struggle was education. . . . The first and second generation Jews worked their way out of the factories to become successful small businessmen, but their children usually declined to enter the business. More often, they went off to college and became professionals.

—Reprinted from *Settings of Silver: An Introduction to Judaism* by Stephen M. Wylen. Copyright © 1989 by Rabbi Stephen M. Wylen. Used by permission of Paulist Press.

The LORD said to Abram, "Go forth from your native land and from your father's house to the land that I will show you.

I will make of you a great nation,

And I will bless you;

I will make your name great,

And you shall be a blessing.

I will bless those who bless you

And curse him that curses you;

And all the families of the earth

Shall bless themselves by you."

Abram went forth as the LORD had commanded him. . . . Abram took his wife Sarai and his brother's son Lot, and all the wealth they had amassed . . . and they set out for the land of Canaan. When they had arrived in the land of Canaan, . . . the LORD appeared to Abram and said, "I will assign this land to your offspring." And he built an altar there to the LORD who had appeared to him.

—*Genesis 12:1–7.*

View from Mt. Sinai.

And the LORD continued, "I have marked well the plight of My people in Egypt and have heeded their outcry because of their taskmasters; yes, I am mindful of their sufferings. I have come down to rescue them from the Egyptians and to bring them out of that land to a good and spacious land, a land flowing with milk and honey. . . ."

—*Exodus 3:7–8.*

In the days to come,

The Mount of the LORD's House

Shall stand firm above the mountains

And tower above the hills;

And all the nations

Shall gaze on it with joy.

And the many peoples shall go and say:

"Come,

Let us go up to the Mount of the LORD,

To the House of the God of Jacob;

That He may instruct us in His ways,

And that we may walk in His paths."

For instruction shall come forth from Zion,

The word of the LORD from Jerusalem.

Thus He will judge among the nations

And arbitrate for the many peoples,

And they shall beat their swords into plowshares

And their spears into pruning hooks:

Nations shall not take up

Sword against nation;

They shall never again know war.

—*Isaiah 2:2–4.*

A psalm of David, when he was in the Wilderness of Judah.

God, You are my God;

  I search for You,

  my soul thirsts for You,

  my body yearns for You,

  as a parched and thirsty land that has no water.

I shall behold You in the sanctuary,

  and see Your might and glory,

Truly Your faithfulness is better than life;

  my lips declare Your praise.

I bless You all my life;

  I lift up my hands, invoking Your name. . . .

—*Psalm 63:1–5.*

A season is set for everything, a time for every experience under heaven:

A time for being born and a time for dying,

A time for planting and a time for uprooting the planted;

A time for slaying and a time for healing,

A time for tearing down and a time for building up;

A time for weeping and a time for laughing,

A time for wailing and a time for dancing;

A time for throwing stones and a time for gathering stones,

A time for embracing and a time for shunning embraces;

A time for seeking and a time for losing,

A time for keeping and a time for discarding;

A time for ripping and a time for sewing,

A time for silence and a time for speaking;

A time for loving and a time for hating;

A time for war and a time for peace.

—*Ecclesiastes 3:1–8.*

There are seven kinds of Pharisees: a "shoulder" Pharisee, a "wait-a-bit" Pharisee, a "calculating" Pharisee, an "economizing" Pharisee, a "show me my fault" Pharisee, a Pharisee out of fear, and a Pharisee out of love. The "shoulder" Pharisee carries his good deeds on his shoulder (an exhibitionist); the "wait-a-bit" Pharisee says: Wait for me while I perform a virtuous act [he is ostentatious]; the "calculating" Pharisee balances a wrong act with a virtuous act, crossing off one with the other; the "economizing" Pharisee speculates as to how he can economize and do a good deed with his savings; the "show me my fault" Pharisee asks to be shown any act of wrongdoing on his part that he may redress it by a virtuous act. The Pharisee of fear [of God] is like Job; the Pharisee of love [of God] is like Abraham. No one is as beloved as the Pharisee of love, like father Abraham. Father Abraham transmuted his evil impulse into good, as it is written, "You found his heart faithful to You" (Neh 9:8).

—*The Talmud, The Tractate Berakhot, Yerushalmi 9:5 (14b).*

Summary

1. Jewish faith is based on a covenant relationship with the God of the Jewish people.
2. The Jewish belief in one God is the cornerstone of succeeding religious faiths of Western civilization.
3. Jewish religious faith is expressed in Jewish life, whose heart and soul is the Torah, which is explored in depth in the Talmud.
4. Jews recall their history and their faith in the celebration of their religious feasts.

For review

1. What is at the heart of Judaism?
2. Can you describe in general terms the differences between the Jewish religious understanding and the religious understanding of the people among whom they lived? To what do you attribute these differences?
3. How does the history of Jewish beginnings as told in the Jewish Bible differ from what we know of Jewish beginnings from other sources?
4. How did the Jewish understanding of God arise because of their history? To whom did the Jewish people ascribe their successful escape from Egypt? How does this differ from the history of other peoples of the time?
5. If the acts of God were revealed in Jewish history, what function does the Jewish Bible play in revelation?
6. Describe how the understanding of God's nature developed as Judaism evolved.
7. How have the Jewish people influenced the thinking of others concerning the future?

For discussion

1. Discuss the significance of the Jewish religious experience on people's understanding of God. Has it helped you better understand who God can be for you? In an open forum, exchange ideas about God with your classmates.
2. Relate how the Jewish Bible can be seen as God's word to people.
3. Review what you find most appealing about the Jewish religion now that you have had a brief introduction to it.

For research

1. Prepare a chronological chart of the early development of the Jewish religion.
2. Prepare a report on the geography, agriculture, and climate of the modern state of Israel.
3. Present a report on the Star of David and the Menorah.
4. Prepare a report on some aspect of the Holocaust.
5. Research the Hasidic Jews, or the Hasidic Jews residing in the United States.
6. Investigate the stereotypes alleged against the Jews in their long history as a people.

Word list

Abraham	patriarchs and matriarchs
Adonai	Pesah
angel	polytheism
Babylonian Exile	prophet
covenant	Purim
doxology	rabbi
El Shaddai	redemption
Exodus	Rosh Hashanah
Genesis	Sabbath
Habiru	Sarah
Hanukkah	seder
Hebrew	Shavu'ot
Isaac	Shema
Israeli	sin
Israelites	Sinai
Jacob	Sukkot
Jewish Bible	synagogue
Jews	Talmud
Judaism	Torah
Messianic Age	worship
monotheism	Yom Kippur
Moses	Zealot
Passover	

5 Christianity

Judaism was conceived in the events associated with the lives of the patriarchs, matriarchs, and Moses and the experience of the people in Egypt and the desert. It was born in the covenant made with God on Mt. Sinai. **Christianity** was conceived in the appearance of **Jesus** and was born when certain followers of his said they experienced the divine presence at **Pentecost,** fifty days after they said they experienced him alive following his death by crucifixion.

Christianity can be understood only in terms of that Pentecost experience—as this experience is told by those involved in it. This extraordinary experience was reported by Luke, a physician and chronicler of the first days of the followers of Jesus. In his **Acts of the Apostles** in the **Christian Scriptures** (the New Testament in the Christian Bible) he wrote:

> When the day of Pentecost had come, [the close followers of Jesus] were all together in one place. And suddenly from heaven there came a sound like the rush of a violent wind, and it filled the entire house where they were sitting. Divided tongues, as of fire, appeared among them, and a tongue rested on each of them. All of them were filled with the **Holy Spirit**. . . .
>
> Now there were devout Jews from every nation under heaven living in Jerusalem. And at this sound the crowd gathered and was bewildered, because each one heard them speaking in the native language of each. Amazed and astonished, they asked, "Are not all those who are speaking Galileans? And how is it that we hear, each of us, in our own native language?" . . . All were amazed and perplexed,

Christianity

Religions based on a belief in Jesus and his teachings.

Jesus

The person on whom Christians base their faith; considered human and divine by most Christians; the second person of the Trinity, in Christian understanding.

Pentecost

The Jewish festival of Shavu'ot, commemorating the giving of the Ten Commandments by God to Moses; the Christian feast celebrated fifty days after Easter, which celebrates the gift of the Holy Spirit to the first Christians.

The Holy Spirit descending upon the first Christians at Pentecost.

Acts of the Apostles

A book in the Christian Scriptures which tells the story of the early Christians.

Christian Scriptures

The New Testament of the Christian Bible.

Holy Spirit

The third person of the Trinity, God's Spirit, as understood by Christians.

saying to one another, "What does this mean?" But others sneered and said, "They are filled with new wine."

But Peter, standing with the eleven, raised his voice, and addressed them, "Men of Judea and all who live in Jerusalem, let this be known to you, and listen to what I say. Indeed, these are not drunk, as you suppose, for it is only nine in the morning. No, this is what was spoken through the prophet Joel:

'In the last days it will be, God declares,
    that I will pour out my Spirit upon all flesh,
        and your sons and daughters shall prophesy,
    and your young men shall see visions,
        and your old men shall dream dreams.
    Even upon my slaves, both men and women,
        in those days I will pour out my Spirit. . . . '

"You that are Israelites, listen to what I have to say: Jesus of Nazareth, a man attested to you by God with deeds of power, wonders, and signs that God did through him among you, as you yourselves know—this man, handed over to you according to the definite plan and foreknowledge of God, you crucified and killed by the hands of those outside the law. But God raised him up, having freed him from death, because it was impossible for him to be held in its power. . . .

"This Jesus God raised up, and of that all of us are witnesses. Being therefore exalted at the right hand of God, and having received from the **Father** the promise of the Holy Spirit, he has poured out this that you both see and hear. . . .

"Therefore let the entire house of Israel know with certainty that God has made him both Lord and Messiah, this Jesus whom you crucified."

Now when they heard this, they were cut to the heart and said to Peter and to the other **apostles,** "Brothers, what should we do?" Peter said to them, "Repent, and be baptized every one of you in the name of Jesus Christ so that your sins may be forgiven; and you will receive the gift of the Holy Spirit. For the promise is for you, for your children, and for all who are far away, everyone whom the Lord our God calls to him."

—Acts of the Apostles 2:1–8, 12–18, 22–25, 32–33, 36–39.

God the Father

The first person of the Trinity, as understood by Christians.

apostles

Twelve men who followed Jesus and (with the exception of Judas, who was replaced) became leaders of groups of early Christians.

This account reveals four things about the origins of Christianity and tells what a Christian is:

1. The followers of Jesus experienced him alive after he had been put to death. This they described as his **resurrection.** (This experience is explored in the Christian Bible, the **Gospel** according to Matthew, chapter 28; the Gospel according to Mark, chapter 16; the Gospel according to Luke, chapter 24; and the Gospel according to John, chapter 21.)

2. The experience of Pentecost began to make clear to the followers of Jesus who he really was. This they spoke about and explained. The record is contained in the New Testament.

3. A Christian is a person who believes what the apostles said about Jesus, is baptized in his name, and follows the way of life prescribed by Jesus. There are many kinds of Christians—**Protestant, Catholic, Orthodox,** for example—who interpret the way of life Jesus prescribed in different ways, ways they think help best live the life they believe Jesus commanded.[1]

4. Christianity did not begin as a religion separate from Judaism. It began as a plea to the Jewish people among whom Jesus had lived to accept him as the promised Jewish **messiah.**[2]

Today, there are over 1,833,000,000 Christians living in every quarter of the world.[3] About 239 million live in North America; 436 million in Latin America; and 414 million in Europe. There are 285 million in Asia; 327 million in Africa; and 23 million in Oceania (Australia, New Zealand, and the islands of the South Pacific).

resurrection

A rising from the dead; belief in the resurrection of Jesus is common among Christians.

Gospel

One of four books in the Christian Scriptures which deal with the life and teachings of Jesus; literally, the word means "good news."

Protestant

The term encompasses a large number of Christian Churches which formed at the time of the Reformers (sixteenth century) and thereafter; used to describe most Christian denominations which are not Catholic or Orthodox.

Catholic

The word *catholic* means "universal"; *Catholic* (as in Church) refers to the Christian Church centered in Rome under the authority of a pope.

Orthodox

The word *orthodox* literally means "right worship"; *Orthodox* refers to the Christian Church of the East which separated from the Roman Church in 1054 C.E.

messiah

Someone sent by God to lead the Jewish people to their days of glory.

---

1. In the United States, estimates of the number of Protestant denominations or Church bodies, depending on how one defines those terms, vary from 250 to over 2,000.

2. The circumstances which caused the separation of Judaism and Christianity are too complex to be discussed in this survey.

3. According to David Barrett, author of *World Christian Encyclopedia,* Christianity is the first truly universal religion. It is found in every country and among all people, including many nearly inaccessible tribes.

Who is Jesus for Christians?

If the Jewish breakthrough in people's religious aware-ness was so remarkable, so, too, was the emergence of Christianity. Briefly, this is the story of its founder and the beginnings of the religion:

Details of Jesus' birth and early life are few. Some sto-ries have been included in the Christian Scriptures in the Gospels according to Matthew and Luke. Other stories have come from other oral and written sources. According to Christian tradition (scriptural and non-scriptural), Jesus was born in Bethlehem, a small town southwest of Jerusa-lem, about 5 B.C.E. His parents took him to Egypt for a short period to escape a threat to his life posed by Herod, the Rome-appointed king. After returning from Egypt, Jesus and his parents settled in Nazareth, a town in Gali-lee, a Jewish province in the northern part of Palestine.

Stained-glass rendering of Jesus.

Jesus grew up in Nazareth and worked as a carpenter until he was about thirty years old. At that time, he moved from Nazareth to Capernaum, a town on the northern shore of the Sea of Galilee.

At this point, the story is picked up in all four Gospels, although not every event is recorded in each Gospel. One day, this Jewish man from Galilee appeared at the Jordan River where a Jewish prophet known as John the Baptizer was preaching a baptism of repentance for the forgiveness of sins.

After being baptized, Jesus began his own mission of preaching that the reign of God was at hand and that people ought to repent and believe in the "good news." For nearly three years, throughout Palestine, he preached the good news. He preached about God's love for people and about how people should live together in loving concern for each other. According to the Gospels, Jesus attracted many followers by his words and good works.

Jesus' career as a preacher was marked by an unusual ability as a speaker and by many signs (healings and other miraculous events) that led a great number of people to accept him as a messenger of God.

During his years of preaching, Jesus came into conflict with some of the more powerful religious authorities. He was arrested and tried in the Jewish court as one who sub-verted the people. He was then tried in the Roman court as an enemy of Caesar.

Sentenced to death by the Romans—the military, eco-nomic, and political rulers of Palestine at the time—Jesus was first scourged and crowned with thorns. He was then forced to carry a cross to a hill of execution outside the walls of the city of Jerusalem. His **crucifixion** involved being nailed to a cross until death. After a Roman guard ran a spear through his heart to insure his death, he was taken down from the cross by his friends, anointed with burial oils and herbs, and buried in someone else's tomb. He was, perhaps, thirty-three years old.

As later events showed, Jesus was an extraordinary person with great influence on the lives of large numbers of people, the course of history in much of the world, the development of many civilizations, and many people's awareness of the nature of God and the relationship that all of creation has with God.

As unique as the person and career of Jesus was, the event which told his followers who he was and how unique he really was, was his resurrection from the dead. His followers said they saw him alive, talked with him, ate with him, and met with him on several occasions after he had been buried. When they became convinced of who they believed him to be, they preached about him, not simply as the messiah, but as the Son of God—God Himself, expressing Himself as a human person.

In general, this is what Christian faith is about: Most Christians believe that Jesus is the Son of God who became a man, lived in a particular place during a particular historical time, was put to death, rose from the grave to a new life, and lives now as the Lord of the universe and the Lord of history.

As Christians see it, God's self-revelation was gradual, and God's self-revelation in Jesus is the logical climax to people's search for an answer to the mystery of life.

For those Christians who accept Jesus as the risen Lord and the Son of God, four main questions about life are answered: (1) What is the nature of God? (2) What is the meaning of human existence? (3) What is the meaning of death? and (4) How does a person live a meaningful life? The Christian answer for each of these gives a security, a faith, and a hope that is distinctly Christian.

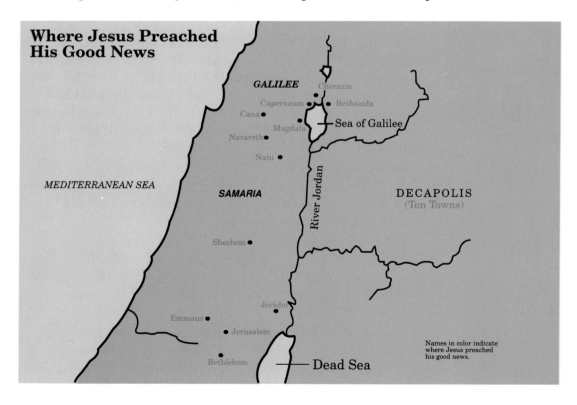

Where Jesus Preached His Good News

GALILEE — Chorazin
Capernaum — Bethsaida
Cana
Magdala — Sea of Galilee
Nazareth
Nain

MEDITERRANEAN SEA

SAMARIA

River Jordan

DECAPOLIS
(Ten Towns)

Shechem

Jericho
Emmaus
Jerusalem

Names in color indicate where Jesus preached his good news.

Bethlehem — Dead Sea

Trinitarian

Characterized by belief in one God in three persons; in general, the Christian understanding of God.

The roots of Christian faith are firmly planted in the soil of the Jewish heritage from which it sprang. (Jesus was a Jew; his trusted apostles were Jews; his first followers were Jews.) God is identified as not just any god, but as the Almighty Creator of the universe—in other words, the God of the Jewish people. And yet, although the Christian belief is thoroughly Jewish in it roots, it is organized along principles that came directly from the early Christians' experience of Jesus and from their community life after his resurrection.

The basic structure of the Christian belief in God is **Trinitarian.** The only way the early Christians could explain what they experienced in Jesus and heard from him was to say that *The One God is so personal that this God is really three persons.* They did not say this because it "made sense"; they said this because they believed that was the way Jesus' disciples remembered experiencing and learning of God when they were with Jesus.

The external events of Jesus' life do not by themselves adequately convey the impact this extraordinary man made upon his followers. People saw him as a prophet, but there had been many prophets, including John the Baptizer, and none of them had started a new religion. He was a martyr, but many reformers had been killed, and none of them had galvanized a following that claimed to experience his living presence among them after his death. Such was his power that after his death his disciples enthusiastically told everyone they met about his life, death, resurrection, and teachings, despite threats to their own lives.

The apostles and the other early followers of Jesus believed that the same God they had known since childhood had raised Jesus from the dead, made him Lord of the universe, and sent his own breath of life (Spirit) into them. This is what they preached. From that time on, it was impossible for those who believed in Jesus to think of God in terms other than what the apostles had preached. For them, Jesus and the Spirit of God were part of their awareness of God.

But why did early Christians think of God as three persons? And why, if they accepted the idea of three persons, did they not think there were three gods? The reason lies in their Jewish heritage about God and in the people's experience of Jesus while he lived among them.

The Jewish people did not picture God as having to "do" anything to achieve God's goals. God did not have to fight wars, trade with other gods, or perform acts of magic. The Jewish God was not an enemy of the people, a benevolent despot, or an indifferent spirit living in a world all God's own. God was almighty, personal, loving, and faithful.

For the Jews, God created by giving a command, gave life by breathing the breath of life into living things, and sustained all things in existence by God's act of will. They pictured God as acting in the universe through the divine spirit and through the divine word.

After the resurrection and Pentecost experiences, the apostles and other early Christians recalled that Jesus used these two ideas to refer to himself and his work: he claimed to have the spirit of God, and he spoke with authority about how people should live.

Stained-glass window showing Jesus entering Jerusalem.

As Jesus went around doing good and preaching the good news (as his followers called it), many people sensed in him a uniqueness and authority that was more than that of a prophet. He seemed to have the spirit of God and to speak of God in a new way. In reflecting back on the life and teachings of Jesus, the writer of the Gospel according to John spoke of him saying, " 'The works that I do in my Father's name testify to me. . . . My sheep hear my voice. I know them, and they follow me. I give them eternal life, and they will never perish. No one will snatch them out of my hand. What my Father has given me is greater than all else, and no one can snatch it out of the Father's hand. The Father and I are one' " (John 10:27–30), and " 'If I am not doing the works of my Father, then do not believe me. But if I do them, even though you do not believe me, believe the works, so that you may know and understand that the Father is in me and I am in the Father' " (John 10:37–38).

Jesus' followers remembered him speaking in God's name on his own authority (for example, in the Gospel according to Matthew, chapters 5–7, Jesus used phrases like: "You have heard . . . What I say to you . . . "; or expressions like, "Do this," "Do not do . . . ," "Ask," "Seek," and so on.) According to the Gospels, when he performed some miracle, it was always done by him in his Father's name.

So, reflecting upon this uniquely authoritative person, who treated God's Spirit and God's word as his own (and whose life of good works backed him up), early Christians came to this conclusion: *Jesus was the Word of God!* They believed that just as God had spoken in creation and in their Scriptures, so did God speak to them in the person of Jesus. For them, Jesus as the Word of God was actually God.

But, if the Word of God (Jesus) was really a divine person, Jesus' first followers naturally asked themselves about God's Spirit. Remembering what Jesus had said, the first Christians recalled that Jesus not only possessed God's Spirit, as they understood it, *he also had God's Spirit to give!* Before his resurrection Jesus is quoted as saying, " 'I will ask the Father, and he will give you another Advocate, to be with you forever. This is the Spirit of truth, . . . The Advocate, the Holy Spirit, whom the Father will send in my name, will teach you everything' " (John 14:16–17a, 26).

The first followers of Jesus experienced the fulfillment of this promise at Pentecost. They came to believe that Jesus and the Father were one, but that Jesus was distinct enough from the Father that Jesus could ask the Father to send the Spirit—he and the Father were one and the same God but two separate persons. And since Jesus promised them Another One like himself, Another whom they experienced as God's Spirit, they came to believe that God's Spirit, like God's Word, was one and the same God but a *third* person of God.

This belief in the Trinity (Tri-unity) of God has never been adequately explained by Christians, for they believe it is beyond anyone's power to explain completely. They believe that the early Christians discovered it, not by understanding, but from what they saw and heard when with Jesus. They believed that they met God's Word personally in Jesus, and they felt God's Spirit personally at Pentecost as Jesus promised.

The Christian view of human existence

Steeped as they were in their Jewish heritage that people are created in God's image, the first Christians came to believe that they are destined to share God's life through Jesus. In other words, Christians believe that it is through Jesus that they are saved from an existence outside of God.

Christians believe that all people were born to share in God's life. They believe that people possess a unique dignity and ought to be regarded with the respect that belongs to things that are sacred—that are God's. They believe that people are created for more than simply an existence in this world; they are destined to live with God forever. This view brought a special meaning to human existence for Christians.

For Christians, people belong to God, and they have been created by God, claimed for God by God's Son, Jesus, and formed into God's people by the action of the Holy Spirit. For Christians, people are not foolish mistakes of a blind force, playthings of the gods, or even servants of the Utterly Other. They are, through Jesus, the **Christ,** God's children.

This view of the meaning of human nature and of human existence greatly influenced the pattern for living among Christians. For the first Christians, who, as we said, were Jews, the pattern for living was, in addition to the Torah, a person—the man Jesus who had come to live among them. They accepted and put into practice his emphasis on the command from Judaism to love others for the love of God. This, too, gave meaning to their lives.

Christ

A Greek term roughly equivalent to "messiah"; used by Christians to refer to Jesus.

Christians working at a food bank.

A statement of belief which is prayed by many Christian Churches

*We believe in one God,
the Father, the Almighty,
maker of heaven and earth,
of all that is seen and unseen.
We believe in one Lord, Jesus Christ,
the only Son of God,
eternally begotten of the Father,
God from God, Light from Light,
true God from true God,
begotten, not made, one in Being with the Father.
Through him all things were made.
For us and for our salvation
he came down from heaven:
by the power of the Holy Spirit
he was born of the Virgin Mary, and became man.
For our sake he was crucified under Pontius Pilate;
he suffered, died, and was buried.
On the third day he rose again
in fulfillment of the Scriptures;
he ascended into heaven
and is seated at the right hand of the Father.
He will come again in glory to judge the living and the dead,
and his kingdom will have no end.
We believe in the Holy Spirit, the Lord, the giver of life,
who proceeds from the Father and the Son.
With the Father and the Son he is worshiped and glorified.
He has spoken through the prophets.
We believe in one holy catholic and apostolic Church.
We acknowledge one baptism for the forgiveness of sins.
We look for the resurrection of the dead,
and the life of the world to come. Amen.*

The meaning of death for Christians

For all people, death is a great mystery. Since the time of Jesus, Christians believe they have the answer to that mystery. For Christians, life after death is more than a hope; it is assured.

As Christians understand the accounts of Jesus' resurrection in the Gospels, the early Christians' experience of Jesus alive after death means three things: (1) Death is not the end of existence. (2) The whole person lives on through death and experiences a new dimension of existence called the risen life. (3) This new person lives with God and experiences the life of God unencumbered by the limitations of earthly existence—the limitations of time and space, the limitations of sin, and the limitations of the necessities required to sustain life here on earth.

Christians believe that because of Jesus, they can face death with courage and joy. For them, death is the moment of the total person's passing into that eternal dimension of life for which he or she was created. Death is not the end. It is the means by which a person enters into full participation in the life of God.

What is a meaningful life for Christians?

The Christian response to the question about how one leads a meaningful life has a two-fold answer given to Christians by Jesus as reported in the Gospels. His answer was not new; it was an important part of the Jewish Law. The interesting thing is the way the two commandments are linked to each other in the following passage.

> *One of the scribes . . . asked him, "Which commandment is the first of all?" Jesus answered, "The first, 'Hear, O Israel: the Lord our God, the Lord is one; you shall love the Lord your God with all your heart, and with all your soul, and with all your mind, and with all your strength' [Deuteronomy 6:4–5]. The second is this, 'You shall love your neighbor as yourself' [Leviticus 19:18]. There is no other commandment greater than these."*
>
> —Mark 12:28–31.

For Christians, this response of Jesus (made in different words on different occasions) summarizes the philosophy by which a person should live. It encompasses two things: (1) the person's relationship with God, and (2) the person's relationship with people.

baptism

Initiation into the Christian community by water (immersion, pouring over the head, or sprinkling) and the words, "I baptize you in the name of the Father and of the Son and of the Holy Spirit."

Lord's Supper

Celebration (in some Christian Churches, remembrance) of the last meal Jesus had with his friends in which he blessed and shared bread and wine and asked them to do this in memory of him.

sacrament

A sign or symbol which expresses the Holy as understood by members of a particular religion; for Christians, a sacrament is a visible sign of the action of Jesus in their lives.

Like all other religious people, Christians express their belief in action. Believing in the divine dignity of people, Christians are expected to express their relationship to God by making it possible, through various acts of love, for people with few material advantages to experience a condition of existence that goes beyond the constant search for food, shelter, and clothing. Through their acts of charity, Christians believe that they worship God in every person by doing for people what God has intended: making life worth living.

Believing also in the divine worth of life, Christians celebrate life in their acts of worship of God. Believing that they are united with Christ through **baptism,** Christians come together to celebrate the **Lord's Supper** in imitation of Jesus at the Last Supper, when he asked his followers to celebrate his presence among them. There are differences between Christian Churches in their understanding of the Lord's Supper. Some Churches consider the celebration to be a remembrance only, while others believe that there is a "communion" between persons and God in the person of Jesus which takes place in the sharing of the bread and wine.

Various Christian groups celebrate other life situations (marriage, coming to maturity, ministry, death, and so on) in their own ways. Most Christian groups call some of these celebrations (especially baptism and the Lord's Supper, or Eucharist) **sacraments,** because they believe their lives are made more holy and their relationship with God is strengthened through them.

Some Christians come together to celebrate the Lord's Supper in imitation of Jesus at the Last Supper.

One of the best attended of all church services, of whatever denomination, is the Harvest Festival, responding as it does, even in a secular and industrial age, to an innate feeling that thanks should be rendered "for all good gifts around us." Urban congregations who have never handled agricultural machinery, sing, in churches decorated with fruit and flowers, "We plough the fields and scatter the good seed on the land," a German hymn composed by Matthias Claudius (1740–1815). In compensation, "the fruits of the earth" is in some places given a broad interpretation and mechanical products are displayed.

In England 1 August . . . was known as Lammas (Old English hlafmaese: "loaf festival"), when bread from the first corn to ripen was brought to church to be blessed. No provision was made for this service in the **Book of Common Prayer** . . . . "Harvest homes," feasting after the sheaves were brought in, nevertheless remained a folk festival and in 1843 R.S. Hawker, Vicar of Morwenstow, Cornwall, tried to restore a religious meaning by using bread made from the ripe corn during a special Sunday Eucharist. Its popularity spread and Harvest Thanksgiving figures in most modern service books. In the United states it coincides with Thanksgiving Day . . . , recalling the gratitude of the first settlers in Virginia and Massachusetts for their survival from the threat of starvation.

—J.C.J. Metford, The Christian Year (New York: Crossroad, 1991), 122.

Relationships with people

Taking their cue from Jesus with regard to their relationships with people, Christians summarize Jesus' message by recalling his words: "This is my commandment, that you love one another as I have loved you" (John 15:12). Christians consider this saying to be a summary of Jesus' way to live because no other counsel given by him occupies so important a position in his teachings. For him, it was to be the distinguishing mark of a Christian's life: "By this everyone will know that you are my disciples, if you have love for one another" (John 13:35).

This teaching was so important that Paul, an early Christian, writing to Roman Christians from Corinth, Greece, about 57 C.E., did not hesitate to say: "The commandments, 'You shall not commit adultery; You shall not murder; You shall not steal; You shall not covet'; and any other commandment, are summed up in this word, 'Love your neighbor as yourself.' Love does no wrong to a neighbor; therefore, love is the fulfilling of the law" (Romans 13:9–10). For Christians, love of neighbor is the starting point of all ethical considerations.

For Christians, love is the key to a meaningful life—love of God and love of neighbor. It opens a person's heart, they believe, to the spiritual and social realities of human existence.

The priesthood and ministry in Christianity

All Christian groups have persons who are designated, often ordained, to be **priests** or **ministers** of religion. These persons are specially trained to minister to the religious needs of their people. They preach the gospel, teach, lead the religious celebrations of their groups, and administer the affairs of their group.

Priest of the Greek Orthodox Church at a traditional festival.

Major branches of Christianity

For the first millennium after Jesus, there was more or less one Christian Church. Although it was not an officially recognized religion until 380 C.E. and was often not well organized (due to problems of distance and communication), the Christian Church held together until 1054. Tensions between the Church in the East and the Church in the West culminated in the **Great Schism,** which split the Christian Church into the Roman Catholic Church in the West and the Orthodox Church in the East.

In the sixteenth century, the Church in the West was again faced with division. The Protestant Reformation began with Martin Luther's separation from the Roman Church and continued with further divisions under John Calvin, Henry VIII of England, and others.

Some Christian Churches do not consider themselves to be part of any of the three major branches. This is particularly true if they originated after the Protestant Reformation and did not split off from an existing group.

Roman Catholicism

The Roman Catholic Church is centrally organized under the pope in Rome. The structure of the Church is hierarchical, that is, the pope, who is bishop of Rome, has authority over all other bishops. Most bishops are in charge of a diocese, a geographic area with up to several hundred parishes. Each parish is administered by a priest, deacon, or lay administrator and serves a few to several thousand households. Pope, bishops, and priests are **celibate.** The pope and bishops have teaching authority in the Church.

The primary liturgy of the Roman Catholic Church is the Eucharist, sometimes referred to as the Mass. Seven sacraments are celebrated in the Catholic Church: baptism, Eucharist, confirmation, marriage, holy orders, reconciliation, and anointing of the sick.

A number of somewhat national Churches are in communion with the Church in Rome but celebrate their liturgical services in a more culturally adapted way. While the major **Rite** is the Roman (or Latin or Western) Rite, others include the Byzantine Catholic Rite, the Maronite Rite, and the Coptic Rite. In some of these Rites, liturgies and sacraments have different names, for example, chrismation instead of confirmation.

Great Schism

The division of the Christian Church into the Roman Catholic Church and the Eastern Orthodox Church.

celibate

Unmarried; abstains from sexual intimacy.

Rite

A division of a Christian Church using a particular liturgy.

The Eastern Orthodox Church

In general, Eastern Orthodox Churches are self-governing on a national level, the Church of Russia, for example. They do, however, consider themselves to be in communion with each other. The titular or honorary head of the Eastern Church is the Patriarch of Constantinople, who is first among equals with the patriarchs of the other Churches.

Teaching authority in the Eastern Orthodox Churches is shared with the laypeople, but the number of beliefs considered to be dogma are fewer than in the Roman Church. Bishops are selected from among the monastic clergy. Parish priests may be married, although they must marry before being ordained a deacon (the step before priesthood).

The seven sacraments are referred to as mysteries, and many liturgies are rich and elaborate celebrations. The veneration of **icons** is an important part of Orthodox prayer life. Icons are religious images that are painted in a particular way. They are highly symbolic and are displayed extensively in churches and homes.

Protestant Churches

Protestantism is much harder to summarize than were the previously discussed branches of Christianity. There is very little uniformity among the many Protestant Churches, due primarily to the large number of groups with varying beliefs and structures. However, 85 percent of Protestants belong to twelve denominations; most of these denominations are part of or are derived from the four major early Protestant branches: Lutheran, Calvinist, Anglican, and Anabaptist.

Early Protestant Churches had several common characteristics, such as belief in the Bible as the one source of revealed truth, an understanding that the person is justified (made right with God) by faith alone, and an emphasis on the priesthood of all the faithful. Today, there is much diversity in dogmas and teachings among the Churches. Interpretation of the Bible varies: literal, private, accommodated to the Scripture scholarship of the last century. Most Protestant Churches celebrate the two sacraments of baptism and the Lord's Supper.

While some Protestant Churches are organized in ways similar to the Roman Catholic Church or the Eastern Orthodox Church, others have a very loose connection between congregations, and still others are single-congregation independent Churches. Local congregations number from a few families to thousands of people. Most Protestant Churches have ordained ministers, both men and women, and all allow marriage for their ministers.

icon

A religious image common to Eastern Christianity which is painted to a conventional model and has high symbolic significance.

Fresco of Mary and Jesus, Rongovos Monastery, Tsepelevo, Greece.

Christian pluralism

Probably the most pervasive issue facing modern Christians is the fact of religious pluralism, within and outside the boundaries of Christianity itself. This is not new—diversity within Christianity is as old as the religion itself, and Christianity grew up in an environment of many religions. What is new—essentially since the late eighteenth century—is the acceptance and tolerance of diversity within the ranks. Whereas Christians in earlier times fought desperately to assert the superiority of their version of the faith, to prove that theirs was the one true way, modern Christians have accepted the existence of a variety of Christianities. The outward framework for this has been the **ecumenical movement**, the association of churches to share ideas and cooperate on work where they can agree. Shortly after the turn of the [twentieth] century, a number of American denominations formed the federal Council of Churches; later they reorganized as the National Council of Churches and gradually joined with churches in other lands to form the World Council of Churches. Not all denominations belong; indeed, some conservative groups who thought the council was too liberal have formed alternative organizations. Still, however, the ecumenical spirit is present, and the joint work has enabled the churches to accomplish social work and missionary efforts that would have been beyond the capacity of individual churches.

Nevertheless, the ecumenical movement skirts the issue that lies at the root of the problem of pluralism: the issue of truth. Is there one theology or way of thinking about Christianity? Is there one path to God that is better than the others? Are there a few basics, at least, that we can say Christians must agree on in order to consider themselves truly Christian? Particularly in a religion that traditionally has emphasized doctrine or belief, this would seem an important issue. Yet at present, neither theological faculties in seminaries nor bishops in council nor lay believers, with their involvement in daily practice, are moving toward any new agreement. Except in Fundamentalist churches, there has been a move away from relying on doctrine, so new developments may not come through great theological syntheses. Additionally, Christians have renewed their interest in ritual, especially since the **Second Vatican Council** (1962–1965); possibly the ancient sacraments may provide a new basis for unity. But nothing is certain; it is not even clear that most Christians feel any strong need for greater unification in the faith.

—Sandra Sizer Frankiel, "Christianity," Religious Traditions of the World, edited by H. Byron Earhart (HarperSanFrancisco, 1993), 588–589.

ecumenical movement

The promotion of a worldwide Christian unity or cooperation.

Second Vatican Council

The official gathering of Catholic bishops (1962–1965), at which representatives of many other religions were present as observers.

The Christian Scriptures

Bible

The book of sacred writings for Christians, which includes the Hebrew Scriptures (Old Testament) and the Christian Scriptures (New Testament); the Bible is a collection of many smaller books.

The Christian Scriptures, the codified and standardized sacred writings of the Christian people, are commonly known as the **Bible.** The Christian Bible has two parts: the Old Testament (Hebrew Scriptures), which contains the materials of the Hebrew Bible, and the New Testament (Christian Scriptures), which is an authorized collection of some of the writings of early Christianity.

The Christian Scriptures have four parts: the Gospels, the Letters, the Acts of the Apostles, and the Book of Revelation. The Gospels contain the traditions about Jesus. The Letters were addressed to individuals and Christian communities and dealt with how to live Jesus' way of life. The Acts of the Apostles gives the history of the early Christian community. The Book of Revelation is the Christian book of prophecy. The Gospels are the most important part of the Christian Scriptures because they contain what Christians believe are the teachings and actions of Jesus. They are the norm by which Christians explain and profess their faith.

There are four Gospels, the Gospel according to Matthew, the Gospel according the Mark, the Gospel according to Luke, and the Gospel according to John. These are four versions, or traditions, of the meaning of Jesus. There are twenty-one Letters, thirteen attributed to Paul and eight written by other apostles or close associates of the apostles. The Acts of the Apostles and the Book of Revelation are single books.

revelation

That which God has disclosed to people about God, human beings, the meaning of life and death, and the world as a whole.

Christians believe that their Scriptures are inspired by God, and are, for them, **revelation.** These books tell Christians what God wants known about God, the origin of the world, God's plans for people, and how to live.

Christian feast days

Christian feast days

Days of Christian celebration to recall God's saving actions in Jesus.

liturgy

Public acts of worship.

Christian feast days, or days of Christian celebration, are recollections of God's saving actions in Jesus in the past, and celebrations of God's saving actions in Christ in the present. The celebrations in church of these feast days, or **liturgies,** as they are called in many Christian Churches, are examples of the Churches' official, public worship of God in Christ.

Although various Christian groups celebrate these actions in various ways, and each group has its own special feast days (such as Worldwide Communion Sunday among many Protestant groups or Ascension Thursday among Catholic and Orthodox groups), all Christian groups celebrate three major feasts: Easter Sunday, Pentecost Sunday, and Christmas Day.

Easter Sunday, the most important feast day for Christians, recalls and celebrates what most Christian groups believe was Jesus' resurrection from the dead. These Christians believe that Jesus rose from the dead on the Sunday after his death by crucifixion. They believe that he rose to a new dimension of existence called the risen dimension. It is, however, more than a celebration of a past event. It is also a celebration of a present reality for Christians: Jesus' presence in his Church and the resurrection of all people to a new life in God.

Pentecost Sunday recalls and celebrates what Christians believe took place some fifty days after Jesus' crucifixion. They believe that on that day the Holy Spirit came to the apostles and other early Christians to enlighten them about Jesus. This feast is not, however, simply a celebration of a past event. It is also the celebration of a present reality for Christians: the action of the Spirit in the continuing creation of the world, and the Spirit's action in the life of each Christian.

Christmas Day, December twenty-fifth, celebrates the birth of Jesus. Although it recalls and celebrates a specific event in history, it also celebrates what is for Christians a reality: the presence of God in the world and the presence of Christ in his community of believers.

In addition to these yearly feasts, Christian groups come together for worship each Sunday (or Saturday, in some cases). For them, Sunday is "the Lord's day." It is a day set aside each week specifically for worshiping God as a community. They do this through special liturgies, rest, and recreation. For the early Christians, Sunday eventually replaced the Jewish Sabbath for two reasons: (1) because Christians believe that Jesus rose from the dead on Sunday and (2) to remind Christians that they are called to a new life in Christ through their baptism.

Easter Sunday

The Christian celebration of the resurrection of Jesus.

Christmas Day

The Christian celebration of the birth of Jesus.

Wooden figurines of Joseph, Mary, and the Child Jesus.

rld

Selections from the Christian Scriptures

When [Jesus] came to Nazareth, where he had been brought up, he went to the synagogue on the sabbath day, as was his custom. He stood up to read, and the scroll of the prophet Isaiah was given to him. He unrolled the scroll and found the place where it was written:

"The Spirit of the Lord is upon me,

because he has anointed me to bring good news to the poor.

He has sent me to proclaim release of the captives

and recovery of sight to the blind,

to let the oppressed go free,

to proclaim the year of the Lord's favor."

And he rolled up the scroll, gave it back to the attendant, and sat down. The eyes of all in the synagogue were fixed on him. Then he began to say to them, "Today this scripture has been fulfilled in your hearing."

—Luke 4:16–21.

In the beginning was the Word, and the Word was with God, and the Word was God. He was in the beginning with God. All things came into being through him, and without him not one thing came into being. . . . And the Word became flesh and lived among us, and we have seen his glory; the glory as of a father's only son, full of grace and truth. . . . No one has ever seen God. It is God the only Son, who is close to the Father's heart, who has made him known.

—John 1:1–3, 14, 18.

When Jesus saw the crowds, he went up the mountain; and after he sat down, his disciples came to him. Then he began to speak, and taught them, saying:

"Blessed are the poor in spirit, for theirs is the kingdom of heaven.

"Blessed are those who mourn, for they will be comforted.

"Blessed are the meek, for they will inherit the earth.

"Blessed are those who hunger and thirst for righteousness, for they will be filled.

"Blessed are the merciful, for they will receive mercy.

"Blessed are the pure in heart, for they will see God.

"Blessed are the peacemakers, for they will be called children of God.

"Blessed are those who are persecuted for righteousness' sake, for theirs is the kingdom of heaven.

"Blessed are you when people revile you and persecute you and utter all kinds of evil against you falsely on my account. Rejoice and be glad, for your reward is great in heaven, for in the same way they persecuted the prophets who were before you."

—Matthew 5:1–12.

"Do not let your hearts be troubled. Believe in God, believe also in me. In my Father's house there are many dwelling places. If it were not so, would I have told you that I go to prepare a place for you? And if I go and prepare a place for you, I will come again and will take you to myself, so that where I am, there you may be also. And you know the way to the place where I am going." Thomas said to him, "Lord, we do not know where you are going. How can we know the way?"

Jesus said to him, "I am the way, and the truth, and the life. No one comes to the Father except through me. If you know me, you will know my Father also. From now on you do know him and have seen him."

Philip said to him, "Lord, show us the Father, and we will be satisfied." Jesus said to him, "Have I been with you all this time, Philip, and you still do not know me? Whoever has seen me has seen the Father. How can you say, 'Show me the Father'? Do you not believe that I am in the Father and the Father is in me? The words that I say to you I do not speak on my own; but the Father who dwells in me does his works. Believe that I am in the Father and the Father is in me; but if you do not, then believe me because of the works themselves. Very truly, I tell you, the one who believes in me will also do the works that I do and, in fact, will do greater works then these, because I am going to the Father. I will do whatever you ask in my name, so that the Father may be glorified in the Son. If in my name you ask me for anything, I will do it.

"If you love me, you will keep my commandments. And I will ask the Father, and he will give you another Advocate, to be with you forever. This is the Spirit of truth, whom the world cannot receive, because it neither sees him nor knows him. You know him, because he abides with you, and he is in you.

"I will not leave you orphaned; I am coming to you. In a little while the world will no longer see me, but you will see me; because I live, you also will live. On that day you will know that I am in my Father, and you in me, and I in you. . . ."

—John 14:1–20.

When the hour came, [Jesus] took his place at the table, and the apostles with him. He said to them, "I have eagerly desired to eat this Passover with you before I suffer; for I tell you, I will not eat it until it is fulfilled in the kingdom of God." Then he took a cup, and after giving thanks he said, "Take this and divide it among yourselves; for I tell you that from now on I will not drink of the fruit of the vine until the kingdom of God comes." Then he took a loaf of bread, and when he had given thanks, he broke it and gave it to them, saying, "This is my body which is given for you. Do this in remembrance of me." And he did the same thing with the cup after supper, saying, "This cup that is poured out for you is the new covenant in my blood."

—Luke 22:14–20.

Love is patient; love is kind; love is not envious or boastful or arrogant or rude. It does not insist on its own way; it is not irritable or resentful; it does not rejoice in wrongdoing, but rejoices in the truth. It bears all things, believes all things, endures all things.

Love never ends. . . . And now faith, hope, and love abide, these three; and the greatest of these is love.

—Paul's First Letter to the Corinthians 13:4–8a, 13.

For all who are led by the Spirit of God are children of God. For you did not receive a spirit of slavery to fall back into fear, but you have received a spirit of adoption. When we cry, "Abba! Father!" it is that very Spirit bearing witness with our spirit that we are children of God, and if children, then heirs, heirs of God and joint heirs with Christ. . . .

—Paul's Letter to the Romans 8:14–17a.

Summary

1. Christians are those who believe that Jesus is the Son of God who became a human being.
2. Christians believe that Jesus is the final step in God's self-revelation to people.
3. Most Christians believe that God's self-revelation shows us that God is Triune, a Trinity of three persons in one God.
4. Christians believe that all people are called to share God's life forever in a risen dimension of existence.
5. Christians believe that God's law can be summed up in two commandments which come from the Hebrew Scriptures: "Love God with all your heart. . ." and "Love your neighbor as you love yourself."

For review

1. What is the central belief of Christians?
2. Why is the Pentecost experience important in Christianity?
3. What is the chief source for the world's understanding of Jesus? Explain.
4. In what way is the Christian concept of God different from other ideas of God? What motivated Christians to express their understanding of God in this manner?
5. When Christians say the roots of Christianity are found in Judaism, what do they mean?
6. According to Christian belief, what is the key to meaningful relationships with people? How is this similar to or different from other religions you have studied?
7. What does a belief in the resurrection of Jesus mean for Christians in regard to their own destiny?
8. What does Christian worship essentially celebrate?
9. What are the principle feast days of Christians? What do they celebrate?

For discussion

1. Chart the essential differences between Catholic, Protestant, and Orthodox Christians.
2. Compare rituals and practices of Judaism with those of some Christian Churches. What are the similarities? differences?
3. Speculate what might happen if a person like Jesus began to preach and teach today.

For research

1. Organize a report on the art and architecture of early and medieval Christianity. If possible, illustrate your report.
2. Prepare a report on the priesthood and the ministry in various Christian religious groups.
3. Read Matthew 5–7 in the Christian Scriptures and prepare a synopsis of its contents.

4. Read the First Letter to the Thessalonians in the New Testament. Be prepared to say why it is a letter and what its various parts are about. Where was Thessalonia?

5. Read chapters 27 and 28 of the Acts of the Apostles in the New Testament. Be prepared to capsulize their focus in a news report.

6. Research the role of monasteries in the history of Europe. Prepare a report on their contributions, both positive and negative.

7. Find out which Christian denominations have congregations in your city or town or nearby urban area.

Word list

Acts of the Apostles	Holy Spirit
apostles	icon
baptism	Jesus
Bible	liturgy
Catholic	Lord's Supper
celibate	messiah
Christ	minister
Christian feast days	Orthodox
Christian Scriptures	Pentecost
Christianity	priest
Christmas Day	Protestant
crucifixion	resurrection
Easter Sunday	revelation
ecumenical movement	Rite
God the Father	sacrament
Gospel	Second Vatican Council
Great Schism	Trinitarian

6 Islam

Muslim

An adherent or believer in Islam.

minaret

Muslim tower with balconies used for the announcement of prayers.

Allah

The God, in Islam.

Islam

The religion of Muslims.

There are Muslims among every race, except perhaps Native Americans. They live in every part of the world, on the steppes of Asia, in the thick jungles of Indonesia and the Philippines, across India and Pakistan, throughout the Middle East and North Africa, even in the cities of Europe and North America. Only 20 percent of Muslims live in the Arabic countries, including those in Northern Africa. At least twenty-five million live in Europe and up to five million in the United States. So powerful a force is Islam that nearly 100 percent of the people in Arabic countries and North Africa profess Islam.

Muslims chant a sacred prayer five times a day. Called from the **minarets,** they pray: "There is no God by **Allah,** and Muhammad is His Prophet!" At the times of prayer Muslims everywhere prostrate themselves in submission (**Islam**) to Allah.

Muslims at prayer, Jersey City, New Jersey.

Islam is the proper name of this religion of 1.2 billion people, a religion which some misname "Mohammedanism." Muslims resent having their religion called Mohammedanism because they consider God, not Muhammad, as central to their faith. The word *Islam* comes from the Arabic word *Salam,* meaning "peace," or "surrender." Hence, "the perfect peace that comes from total surrender to Allah" is Islam.

People who profess Islam are called Moslems, or, most commonly today, Muslims, a term derived from the word *Islam*. *Muslim* means "an adherent of," or "believer in," Islam. Muslims are "those who submit" to God under the name of Allah, and honor **Muhammad** as Allah's messenger and prophet.

Allah means *"the* God." It combines the Arabic article *al*, meaning "the" with the Arabic word *Illah,* meaning "God." Allah ("Blessed be His Name," Muslims add) is the same God Jews and Christians worship. Muhammad, Muslims believe, is the last prophet; the list of these messengers of God include Adam, Abraham, Noah, Isaac, Job, and Isaiah, David, John the Baptizer, and Jesus.

Today there are two major sects in Islam. The "Sunnis," found principally in the Middle East, Africa, and Indonesia, trace their origins to the elders associated with Muhammad. The "Shi'a," found mostly in Iran, Iraq, Pakistan, and India, trace their origins to Ali, Muhammad's son-in-law.

Muhammad

The last of God's prophets or messengers, according to Islam.

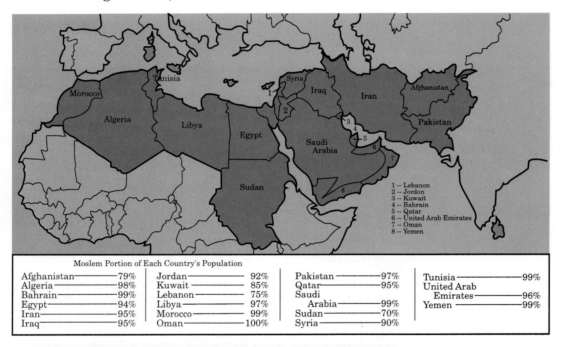

Moslem Portion of Each Country's Population

Afghanistan	79%	Jordan	92%	Pakistan	97%	Tunisia	99%
Algeria	98%	Kuwait	85%	Qatar	95%	United Arab
Bahrain	99%	Lebanon	75%	Saudi		Emirates	96%
Egypt	94%	Libya	97%	Arabia	99%	Yemen	99%
Iran	95%	Morocco	99%	Sudan	70%		
Iraq	95%	Oman	100%	Syria	90%		

What is Islam?

Islam is faith in Allah and in his prophet Muhammad, "the last and the greatest of prophets," and observance of the five obligations, or rituals, sometimes referred to as "The Pillars." For Muslims, the phrase "There is no God but Allah and Muhammad is his prophet" is not simply a slogan or a pious phrase. It is an act of faith.

Brought to life as it was in the hot, barren desert of the Arabian peninsula (known now as Saudi Arabia) in 622 C.E., Islam was a boon to a people whose ancient religion was dying out and whose lives and fortunes were subject to

jinn

Sprites or spirits (sometimes described as similar to elves or fairies) capable of taking on human forms and of influencing human beings for good or evil; spiritual beings between humans and angels.

Quran

The holy writings of Islam; alternative spelling: *Qur'an. Koran* is the previously used English form of the Arabic word meaning "book," or "reading."

Ishmael

Son of Abraham by the servant woman Hagar.

Makkah

The holy city of Islam, located in Saudi Arabia; in the West, often spelled *Mecca.*

the fates of the desert **jinn,** or spirits, the marauding of desert Bedouins, the whims of the ruling class, and the exploitation of the merchants.

Centuries of contact with Judaism and the Christians of the Near East, Egypt, and North Africa had readied the people of Arabia for at least a notion of one God. What was unique about Muhammad's preaching was not monotheism, but *the idea of a single God who spoke to His people through His prophet, calling them to a new way of life and a new concept of religion.*

Even though some claim that Islam is a curious mixture of Judaism and Christianity, it is incorrect to think of Islam as an amalgam of Judaism and Christianity suited to a desert people. Many things in Judaism and Christianity do converge in Islam—and not by accident—but Islam is as different from Judaism and Christianity as Christianity is different from Judaism.

Muslims believe, as do Jews and Christians, in *the* God. They believe that God spoke to Abraham, that Moses was God's prophet, that Jesus was a great prophet (here departing from the Jewish concept of Jesus), but that he was, like Abraham and Moses, *not* God (here departing from Christians). They believe that Muhammad is the last and the greatest of prophets and that he brought them enlightenment from God's messenger, the angel Gabriel, in the form of sayings or revelations which have been written into the **Quran** (Koran). They believe that there is a direct line from Abraham to Muhammad through **Ishmael,** the half brother of Isaac, the son of Abraham, who settled in Palestine and fathered the Jewish people. According to the Jewish Bible, the mother of Ishmael was Hagar, the maidservant of Sarah.[1]

They believe that the "great nation" promised to Hagar and her son is the Arabian nation brought to its promise by the efforts of Muhammad. And they believe that Jerusalem is a holy city because it was a holy city for their revered prophets. It was the city where Solomon's Temple was built, where Jesus taught and worshiped, and it was the city from which Muhammad ascended to heaven in the company of the angel Gabriel. A sacred Muslim shrine, the Dome of the Rock, was built on the spot where this took place. The shrine was built in the seventh century of the Common Era and remains one of the world's most famous sights. It was toward Jerusalem that Muhammad turned to pray. Later, he directed his prayers toward **Makkah,** which is now the holy city of Islam.

But Islam is not part Judaism and part Christianity. It is a religion with its own beliefs, rituals, and practices.

---

1. See Genesis 16:1–16 and 21:1–21.

The origin of Islam

Muhammad, "The Seal of the Prophets," was born about 571 C.E. in Makkah, an Arab town in western Saudi Arabia, about 800 miles east of Cairo, Egypt. His parents were members of the Quraish, a leading tribe in the city. Because his father died before Muhammad was born and his mother died when he was six years old, Muhammad was taken care of by his grandfather.

When Muhammad was nine years old, his grandfather died. One of his uncles took him in, and Muhammad worked as a shepherd and then in his uncle's caravan business. Since his people in Makkah used to travel to Syria and Yemen in business caravans, perhaps Muhammad also made some trips to those lands. Eventually he learned the principles of the Christian and Jewish religions that were to influence his later thinking about God.

Muslim with Islamic literature, Malaysia.

Tradition tells us that in spite of the chaotic and immoral situations he faced, Muhammad was honest, upright, trustworthy, and faithful to his duties. The names later applied to Muhammad—"The Upright," "The Trustworthy One," "The True"—were earned, it is said, during this period of his life.[2]

When he was twenty-five, he was hired by a wealthy widow, Khadija, to manage her business. His uprightness and honesty impressed her, and eventually they were married. Khadija played an important role in his life, for she was the first to believe his visions of what should be done for the people of Makkah. When the people of Makkah opposed Muhammad and persecuted him and his followers, she remained his steadfast companion. She encouraged him, supported him, and was always at his side. If there had been no Khadija, there may have been no Islam.

---

2. The name *Muhammad* means, in Arabic, "highly praised." It has been borne, after him, by more males than any other name.

The messenger of Allah

Muhammad was a compassionate, sensitive man. He was troubled by the inhumanity he saw every day, by the barbarism, drunkenness, murder, stealing, and general lawlessness and immorality which destroyed any claim the common man and woman had for security and peace. He often went off by himself to pray and meditate, seeking a solution to the problems he saw which were destroying his people and his city. For several years, he went, whenever possible, to his "place of solitude":

A mountain on the outskirts of Mecca, known as Mount Hira, contained a cave, and Muhammad, needing solitude, began to frequent it. Peering into the mysteries of good and evil, unable to accept the crudeness, superstition, and fratricide that were accepted as normal, "this great fiery heart, seething, simmering like a great furnace of thought," was reaching out for God.

The desert jinn *were irrelevant to this quest, but one deity was not. Named Allah, he was worshiped by the Meccans, not as the only God, but as an impressive one nonetheless. Creator, supreme provider, and determiner of human destiny, he was capable of inspiring authentic religious feeling and genuine devotion. Certain contemplatives of the time, called* hanifs, *worshiped Allah exclusively, and Muhammad was one of their number. Through vigils, often lasting the entire night, Allah's reality became for Muhammad increasingly evident and awesome. Fearful and wonderful, real as life, real as death, real as the universe he had ordained, Allah (Muhammad was convinced) was far greater than his countrymen supposed. This God, whose majesty overflowed a desert cave to fill all heaven and earth, was surely not a god or even the greatest of gods. He was what his name literally claimed: He was the God, One and only, One without rival. Soon from this mountain cave was to sound the greatest phrase of the Arabic language; the deep, electrifying cry which was to rally a people and explode their power to the limits of the known world.[3] La ilaha illa 'llah! There is no god but God![4]*

---

3. Within 100 years of Muhammad's death the Muslims had penetrated from India to Spain across the whole northern section of Africa.

4. Huston Smith, *The World's Religions* (New York: HarperCollins Publishers, 1991), 224–225.

Muhammad became so convinced of this truth that he felt a compulsion to preach it in order to free his fellow Makkans from the superstition, idolatry, suffering, and degradation to which they were subject. One night as he was in deep meditation, he felt such an utter compulsion, tradition tells us, that he heard a voice say three times, "Proclaim." "What shall I proclaim?" asked Muhammad, in complete terror.

Proclaim in the name of your Lord Who creates,

creates man from a clot!

Proclaim, for your Lord is most Generous;

Who teaches

by means of the pen,

teaches man what he does not know.

—Adapted from The Quran, 96:1–5.

He rushed home, and suffering from the physical manifestation of the vision—trembling, sweating—he related his experience to his wife, Khadija, who comforted him and told him that God would take good care of him because he was kind and cared for the poor and needy.

The rest of Muhammad's life was spent in uncompromising and unrelenting effort to bring the message of Allah to the people. Muhammad was a kind, gentle person, but he could be hard as nails in his devotion to his mission. He bore no illusions about himself ("God has not sent me to work wonders; he has sent me to preach to you." "I never said that Allah's treasures are in my hand, that I knew the hidden things, or that I was an angel. . . . I am only a preacher of God's words"), and he suffered the fate of all prophets: persecution, ridicule, humiliation.

The causes for the opposition are not hard to find. It often happens that leaders of established religions, fearing any sort of deviation from the standard line, at first hold prophets in contempt, then try to silence them. Failing this, they use the righteousness of religion to instigate persecution. In Muhammad's case, they feared, first, that his monotheism would cut into the revenues paid at the shrines in their temples.[5] Second, they resented his vision of humanity, which insisted that all people are equal (this threatened the rigid social structures which enabled the upper class to exploit the poor). Third, his moral code, which was stricter than theirs, threatened to upset the licentiousness, murder, illegal traffic, and degradation of women which was an entrenched way of life for some among the upper classes in Makkah.

---

5. In one temple in Makkah there were over 360 shrines—one for every day in the year.

Hegira

Muhammad's flight from Makkah to
Yathrib (Medina).

For his pains, Muhammad and his few followers were literally run out of town. They fled to Yathrib, later called Medina, the "City of the Prophet of God," about 270 miles north of Makkah. This flight, tragic as it was for those concerned, turned out to be an important event in the history of Islam, for the date of this **Hegira** (flight)—622 C.E.—is the Islamic cutoff point in reckoning dates. It also marks the end of Muhammad's period of vision and preaching alone and the beginning of the activity to establish his "religion." It was not thought of either as "his" or a "religion"—it was simply his total effort to bring the message of God to the people by whatever means were available.

The results of his preaching were meager at first. After three years he had less than forty followers, but in ten years he had made such an impression by his zeal, courage, and honesty that he had more than 5,000 followers. Assuming the leadership of the town to which he had fled, Muhammad proved to be a skillful leader, consummate politician, and fierce warrior—all in the name of Allah, whose humble servant Muhammad continued to be. For ten years, Muhammad struggled to establish his message and his way of life. He succeeded, for upon his death in 632 C.E., he had virtually all of Arabia under his control. One hundred years later (when Muslim expansion was halted by their defeat in a decisive battle at Tours, France, by Charles Martel), Muslims controlled virtually all of the civilized world around the Mediterranean and into India.[6]

The Spread of Islam in the Eighth and Ninth Centuries

▨ Represents Islamic controlled areas in the 8th and 9th centuries

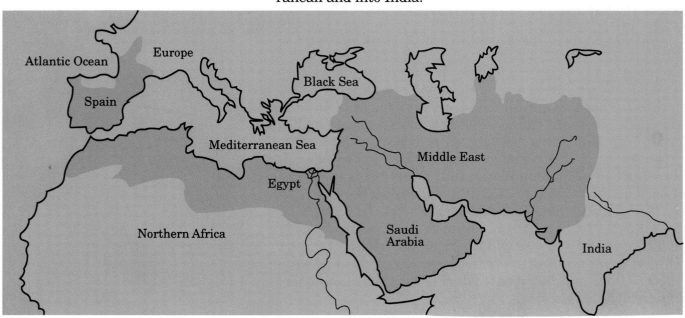

---

6. It must be clearly understood that although Islam originated in Arabia and is often thought of as "Arabian," it is *not* a racial or ethnic term. There are Berber Muslims, Persian Muslims, Philippine Muslims, Indian Muslims, and North American Muslims, just as their are German Catholics, Mexican Catholics, Chinese Catholics, or American Jews, Australian Jews, and English Jews.

The Muslim way of life

What was it that made Islam so successful? Aside from the fact that the people were ready for political and religious reform, Islam is basically simple. It has no complicated theology or theological system (Why speculate? say the Muslims. It's all God's work), no list of miraculous events, no elaborate liturgy, and no complicated moral code. It is based on five principles, or Pillars, as they are called in Western circles, which are basic to Islamic life.

The five principles, or obligations, imposed by the Quran, Islam's Scripture, give Islam an uncomplicated, universal faith and practice which has endured, virtually unchanged, for over 1,300 years. The five obligations are:

1. A profession of faith (*shahada*)

All Muslims publicly profess acceptance of Allah as the One God and Muhammad as the messenger of God. This is the Creed of Islam, the **shahada.** Other beliefs are secondary to it. They believe that angels are spiritual beings who carry out the will of Allah, and that the Quran is Allah's infallible and eternal word. They believe that prophets are the messengers of God, and that there will be a day of judgment and resurrection, at which time those faithful to the Quran will be rewarded and those who fail to observe its obligations will be punished.

2. The obligation to pray (*salat*)

The Muslim duty to pray, **salat,** which binds men only, is fulfilled in two ways: private prayer, which can take place any time in any place, and public, or formal prayer, which is obligatory five times during the day. On arising, at noon, in the afternoon, at sunset, and before retiring, the faithful Muslim answers the call to prayer by, first, a ritual purification with pure water. (In case water is not available or cannot be used, clean earth or sand can be a temporary substitute.) The Muslim then stands erect, facing the principle house of worship in Makkah, and recites the first chapter of the Quran. Then the person bends forward, rises, kneels, touching the forehead to the floor in adoration of Allah, sits up and leans back on the heels, all the while reciting words of prayer and concentrating on Allah. These actions may be repeated during the time allotted for this formal prayer.

shahada

Islamic public profession of acceptance of Allah as the One God and Muhammad as the messenger of God.

salat

The duty of Muslim men to pray, including the obligatory five times daily.

mosque

The Muslim house of prayer and worship.

Imam

The leader of prayer in a mosque.

If at all possible, a Muslim man tries to go to a **mosque,** the Muslim house of prayer and worship, upon hearing the call to prayer. There he joins other Muslims, first removing his shoes, then aligning behind a leader who calls the group to prayer. Muslims make a special effort to go to the mosque at noon on Friday, the Muslim Sabbath, at which time the leader, called an **Imam,** preaches a sermon.

Sultan Hassan and Rafi mosques, Cairo, Egypt.

In towns that are predominantly Muslim and ruled by the Sharia, or Quranic law, the call to prayer is made from the minaret, a tower attached or close to the mosque, by the muezzin (moo-ez-in), the Islamic prayer announcer. The minaret and the sound of the call to prayer are characteristic of Muslim towns.

3. The giving of alms (*zakat*)

zakat

The Muslim obligation to give alms for the care of the poor and needy.

Every Muslim has the obligation of giving at least 2 $\frac{1}{2}$ percent of his earnings per year to charity. This giving of alms is called **zakat.** The money is given for the care of the poor and needy. Muslims believe that only by giving to the poor, either directly or indirectly, can a person's wealth be "purified," or be pleasing to God.

4. The obligation to fast (Ramadan)

Ramadan

The Muslim obligation to fast during the ninth lunar month in the Arabian calendar.

The fourth major obligation required of every adult Muslim is **Ramadan,** or fasting during the ninth lunar month,[7] called Ramadan. Unless excused due to sickness, old age, or journey, adult Muslims abstain from food, drink, and

7. Ramadan does not come at a fixed time in the solar calendar. Muslims count their religious months by the lunar cycle, which is about ten days shorter than the solar-year cycle. Thus, this ninth month of the Islamic calendar rotates within thirty-five years in all seasons.

sexual activity from just before dawn until after sunset every day during the month. When the fast is broken after sunset, special prayers are recited and special passages from the Quran are read.

At the end of the month, Muslims celebrate the "Post-fast Festival," the most important Muslim holiday. The second most important Muslim festival is the "Festival of Sacrifice" celebrated on the tenth day of the twelfth lunar month. This festival marks the end of the pilgrimage season and is kept in honor of Abraham, whose son Ishmael went to Makkah, according to Muslim tradition, and became the "father" of all Arabic peoples.

5. The pilgrimage to Makkah (*hajj*)

Every adult Muslim has an obligation to visit Makkah and to pray at the **Ka'ba,**[8] the rectangular sacred shrine of Islam located in the courtyard of the Great Mosque, built, Muslims believe, by Abraham and Ishmael. The shrine contains the sacred Black Stone of Muslim veneration. Those who are able make the pilgrimage, the **hajj,** more than once, but the obligation is fulfilled by visiting Makkah once during a person's life. Not all Muslims, of course, can make the pilgrimage, but hundreds of thousands do. They come on foot, by donkey, horse, camel, cart, bus, car, ship, airplane, or jet. The pilgrimage is considered the highlight of a Muslim's life—"more important than birth or death."

The pilgrimage, or *hajj*, has several complementary elements. Upon entering Makkah, pilgrims perform the ablutions, or cleansings, and dress in white robes. The pilgrims then circle the shrine seven times and kiss the sacred Black Stone. After that, they make a barefooted ceremonial run between two set points in memory of the search for water made by Hagar, the mother of Ishmael.

Having completed these "preliminaries," on the eighth day, pilgrims begin the pilgrimage proper. First they listen to a long discourse in the Great Mosque. Then they set out for Mina and Arafat, two cities five and thirteen miles from Makkah. At Arafat, pilgrims stay from noon to sundown listening to sermons by Imams. The night is spent in the open. The next day the pilgrims throw seven stones on a large stone heap, symbolizing their rejection of Satan. Following this, the pilgrims sacrifice a sheep or a goat, have their heads shaved or trimmed (women pilgrims clip a very small part of their hair), and prepare to leave this consecrated state. The pilgrims return to Makkah, visit the Great Mosque again, and drink the water of Zamzam, which comes from a very ancient

Ka'ba

The rectangular sacred shrine of Islam located in the courtyard of the Great Mosque in Makkah.

hajj

The Muslim obligation to make a pilgrimage to the Ka'ba in Makkah.

---

8. *Ka'ba* (Kah ba) is an Arabic term meaning "cube."

well. Muslims consider this water very blessed because they believe it comes from a well that sprang miraculously by the power of God for Abraham's son Ishmael.

The pilgrims then relax for a day or two and prepare to return home. There they share the trip and their experiences with family and friends. The pilgrim receives a new title, "Hajji," a term of respect and pious envy. It means, "One who has made the hajj."

A religion of centers

There are other things of great importance to the faithful Muslim, like the prohibition against alcohol, pork, and gambling, the things Muhammad believed caused the downfall of the people of Makkah.

Many Muslims celebrate various religious feasts and holidays, such as Maulid, which marks both the birth and death of Muhammad. All Muslims put great store in complete submission to Allah and heartfelt gratitude to Allah for all things He provides. Central to every Muslim's life is unquestioning faith in Allah, the acceptance of Muhammad as the last and the greatest of the prophets, reverence for the Quran, and the observance of its laws. One source put the things that are important to Muslims this way:

Islam may be described as a religion of centers. God is the center of realities. The Ka'ba is the center of worship. The mosque is the center for the community. And the Prophet Mohammed, who called for recognition of all the preceding missions and who cautioned against his being considered more than human, is the central model and ideal example of righteous conduct.

The divine teachings, laid down by God, are eternal and unchangeable. They are compatible with the needs of all times and all situations. Whether stated specifically or categorically, or in general terms such as the lawfulness of all that is useful and the prohibition of harmful things, they are not subject to human whims. Islam today is the same Islam as when it was born fourteen centuries ago. There is no modern or ancient Islam, no Oriental or Western Islam. Reform movements aim at the return of the faith to its original purity and the removal of the ramifications of cultural traditions misunderstood in some areas to be part of the religion.

Islam is a religion of moderation, catering to spiritual and material needs. Neither should outweigh the other. While it is virtuous and righteous to be generous and charitable, arrogance and extravagance are condemned. A good Muslim observes the law of Islam, including the obligatory and supererogatory rituals, but a Muslim also endeavors to earn a living and to enjoy the lawful pleasures of life.[9]

Muslims at prayer, Jersey City, New Jersey.

9. From Miami-Dade Community College, *Student's Guide to the Long Search.* Copyright © 1978 by Kendall/Hunt Publishing Company. Used with permission.

Marriage and social relationships in Islam

Islamic marriage is a time for great rejoicing and celebration. In traditional settings, which are dominant still in most Muslim regions, the parents serve as matchmakers. Young women are not allowed to go out looking for a husband, although they may express their preferences and they have the right to refuse someone selected for them. A man may initiate the matchmaking, but he normally does not approach a prospective bride directly. Propriety and custom require indirect negotiations with the woman's father or other male guardian. The betrothed pair are not permitted to be alone together before marriage, although they may sometimes enjoy each other's company in the presence of other responsible adults such as parents.

Islamic law has strict regulations concerning relations between the sexes. The concept of mahram *refers to the permitted degrees of close blood relationship within which males and females may not marry and thus may associate socially with each other. . . . There are no prohibitions regarding socialization between females with each other or males with other males. This leads to a two-sided, but not divided, society among Muslims. . . . Proper Muslim men do not normally inquire about female members of a non-kinsman's family, although it is expected that a general inquiry about the well-being of the family as a whole be offered. . . .*

The Qur'an permits Muslim men to marry up to four wives concurrently, provided all are treated equally. Since this is a practical difficulty—many would say impossibility—there is a wide consensus that marriages should be monogamous except in special circumstances. . . . Women are permitted only one spouse at a time. Divorce is allowed for both partners, but it is generally easier for the man to dissolve the marriage. . . .

The marriage ceremony is a simple affair of writing up and signing a contract between the partners. There is no specific ritual connected with the ceremony, at least as a requirement, although it is customary for someone to recite a passage of the Qur'an and to deliver a brief inspirational speech. . . . It is after the legal ceremony of signing that the real marriage festivities begin. These celebrations vary widely according to region, but all Muslims consider it important to launch the marriage with a happy time for relatives and other guests to the extent that means and circumstances permit. This typically includes special and abundant food, new clothes, Qur'an recitation by a hired professional, music, dancing (folk types prevail, with each sex dancing together), bright lights and decoration, dramatic performances (e.g., shadow puppetry in Java), and other activities. . . .

—Frederick M. Denny, "Islam," Religious Traditions of the World, *edited by H. Byron Earhart (HarperSanFrancisco, 1993), 683–684.*

Kurds at an Islamic wedding, Dogubayazit, Turkey.

The achievements of Muhammad

The assessment of the lives and works of great men and women must always be made in the light of the times in which they lived, what they were trying to do, the realities of the real situations they faced, and the capacity of the people to absorb and to implement their programs. This is especially true of Muhammad. He was trying to shape and form a society. Measured by their results, his efforts rank with the greatest achievements of civilization. Among the more important achievements of Muhammad, the following stand out:

1. Muhammad formed a people formerly divided into classes and ridden with superstition and polytheism into a proud, fierce, monotheistic people among whom all persons, theoretically, are equal.

2. He impregnated his society with an overwhelming awareness of the majesty, power, and transcendence of God.

3. Muhammad gave them a list of sayings as direct revelations from God, later codified and standardized to form the Quran, or Islamic Scriptures. The book has greatly affected the lives and thinking of vast numbers of people.

4. Muhammad improved the status of women from property or chattel to respected members of society. He forbade the killing of baby girls, insisted that women have a right to inheritance, discouraged divorce, forbade licentiousness, encouraged education for women, and limited the practice of **polygamy** within bounds which were more humane than was the custom in harems of his time. By present-day standards in Europe and North America, Muhammad's reforms concerning the status of women may not seem so earthshaking, but in the world in which he lived, his reforms were monumental.

5. He insisted on absolute racial equality. In his view and in his preaching, Muhammad saw every person as a creature of God—hence, there is no such thing as the superiority of one race over another.

6. Muhammad successfully challenged the economic inequalities of the Arabian world of his time and based his economic statutes on charity and brotherly love. In a world full of human misery and exploitation of the poor, he injected the principle that each person is everyone's concern and that social welfare called for serious effort by all.

7. Muhammad insisted on religious toleration. Christians, Jews, and Hindus lived in relative peace and harmony under Muslim rule, although they were not given the same degree of rights as members of the official Muslim religion.

polygamy

Religious practice that allows a man to take more than one wife.

The charge that Muslims lived by the sword is only partly true; their record is no better and certainly no worse than any other nation professing to bring "the faith" to "pagans, infidels, and unbelievers." That **jihad**, or "holy wars," were carried on by corrupt caliphs is unquestionable, but these were wars of conquest, using religion as a means to stir the emotions and bolster the courage of the fighting men.

Viewed as a whole, however, Islam unrolls before us one of the most remarkable panoramas in all history. . . . [It contains] the development of a fabulous culture, the rise of literature, science, medicine, art, and architecture; the glory of Damascus, Baghdad, and Egypt, and the splendor of Spain under the Moors. . . . [And] the story of how, during Europe's Dark Ages, Muslim philosophers and scientists kept the lamp of learning bright, ready to spark the Western mind when it roused from its long sleep.[10]

jihad

Islamic holy war to spread Muslim rule.

Ceramic tiles and Arab script decorate the Dome of the Rock, the Muslim shrine on what had been at one time the site of the Temple in Jerusalem.

10. Huston Smith, *The World's Religions* (New York: HarperCollins Publishers, 1991), 267.

Jihad: holy wars

The purpose of jihad is not, as Westerners often assume, to spread Islam, but to spread Muslim rule. It is involved with missionary activity only insofar as out-and-out pagans (all those who are not "possessors of scripture"), once their territory has been conquered, can only choose between death and conversion. By contrast, Christians and Jews—the Zoroastrians were soon made "People of the Book" as well, out of political necessity—need but pay tribute. When all such arrangements were properly organized, this tribute was collected in the form of a head tax, something the Arabs were long familiar with from the Sassanid dynasty. It was justified, all the way into the late-Ottoman period, by the fact that non-Muslims were exempt from military service.

In this sense, the jihad was considered the permanent duty of Muslims so long as any part of the earth was still not subject to Muslim sovereignty. A formal peace with non-Muslim states was therefore fundamentally impossible, although an Islamic government might always see its way to a temporary armistice. At any rate, not all Muslims were obliged to serve under arms; there simply had to be a sufficient number in the field.

All Muslims have to take up arms only when Islamic territory is attacked by a non-Muslim power. . . . many prescriptions of Islamic martial law, especially those not directly based on the Qur'an, have been repealed by Islamic governments themselves. Some jurists go so far as to give jihad an interpretation altogether different from its basic meaning, because the word means only "to strive, to labor," with the usual addition of "on God's way." But this must not be connected with the business of war; early on, in fact, it was applied to the struggle with oneself, to asceticism. Nowadays this sense of jihad is often given prominence in order to stress Islam's readiness for peace.

—Josef van Ess, "Islamic Perspective" in Christianity and the World Religions by Hans Küng (Garden City, NY: Doubleday, 1986), 102–103.

Islam's Scripture: the Quran

Islam cannot rightly be understood apart from the Quran, the sacred writings of Islam. Its 78,000 words are divided into 114 chapters, which, Muslims believe, were dictated to Muhammad by the angel Gabriel during twenty-two years of specific ecstatic, prophetic moments. As with Judaism and Christianity, it was the message, not the messenger, that was important. Muhammad was only the inspired prophet who passed on the word of God, which he received from the angel.

The Quran is a collection of Muhammad's recitations made during his moments of ecstasy which were written down by his faithful followers. These sayings, or recitations, were codified and standardized about 650 C.E., around twenty years after Muhammad's death.

Muslims believe that the Quran completes and corrects all previous Scriptures (the Torah of the Jews and the Gospels of the Christians) and is the final revelation of God. They believe that all the words in the Quran are the words of God spoken to Muhammad through the angel Gabriel; hence, they cannot be changed in any way whatsoever. For Muslims, the words of the Quran are absolute, complete, and infallible. Because they are, they regulate every phase of Islamic law, religion, culture, and politics. They are the sole guide of the true believer's life.

In addition to the Quran, Muslims preserve a body of sacred tradition called **Hadith,** a collection of Muhammad's words, sayings, explanations, and examples designed to help the true believer follow the Quran exactly.

Thus, the Muslim learned from the Qur'an that he must pray. But he learned from the Hadith the particular form of prayer appropriate for a Muslim as commended by the practice of Mohammed. From the Qur'an, the Muslim learned that he must give alms. But he learned particular procedures for giving alms from the Hadith as it cited custom and advice of the Prophet in this respect. In each case, the Muslim traced the Hadith tradition back to prescriptions and prohibitions laid down by the Prophet, and the practices he followed from former times or initiated himself to be the way of Islam.[12]

Hadith

A collection of Muhammad's words, sayings, explanations, and examples to help the believer follow the Quran.

---

12. John R. Whitney and Susan W. Howe, *Religious Literature of the West,* copyright © 1968, 1971, Augsburg Publishing House, 252.

Muhammad did not want these "ways, judgments, and actions" written down, lest they be confused with the revelations of the Quran. However, after his death, his close followers collected those oral traditions of what Muhammad had said and done concerning the revelations and formed them into a collection of things that would guide the true believer in his observance of the prescriptions in the Quran. A typical story in the Hadith, for example, tells how Muhammad was taken by a mysterious animal to Jerusalem and carried into heaven, where he met Abraham, Moses, and Jesus. This incident is believed to have taken place at "the rock" in Jerusalem, a spot not too far from where the Jewish Temple had stood. The place is enclosed under the famous Dome of the Rock, a sacred Muslim shrine.

Among the basic doctrines of the Quran are four major themes: (1) Allah is the all-powerful One who created the world. (2) Allah, who created people for Himself, will do with them as He wishes. (3) People, therefore, must perform the tasks Allah has assigned to them. (4) The day of judgment will find people deserving of reward in heaven or punishment in hell.

Interpretations of various sayings in the Quran are made from time to time, but the sayings of Muhammad which reveal the eternal truths (and, of course, reflect the culture, climate, and topography of Arabia) are, according to Muslims, sufficient guidance for any person. "What need have we of a savior?" Muslims say. "We have a book that tells us how to live." Muslim life, from the Hegira in 622 C.E. to the present time, is a reflection of the sayings of the Quran and the five Pillars of Islamic life.

Some Muslims have difficulty adjusting to modern life and interpreting their tradition in light of modern science, psychology, and anthropology. Coming out of a tradition with a somewhat static concept of people and the universe, Islam presented a worldview much different from that of the present day. Muhammad believed, however, that religion needs to speak to people in their own terms and not in terms of a past culture. For that reason, Muslims today are faced with the task of interpreting their religion in light of today's insights.

Devout Muslims, like devout Christians, Hindus, or Jews, are called on to balance their loyalties to the revered past with the imperatives of the present and future. They, like so many others, are forced into the painful task of distinguishing between the essentials of their religion, which should always remain, and the minor details, which are conditioned by time and place and therefore need to be changed to enable them to live in the world as they experience it. They express their pieties—observing those things which can be reasonably observed—in a world no longer bound by the desert or the necessities of eking out an existence in a hostile world.

Rally outside Al-Salam Mosque, Jersey City, New Jersey.

This is the Book which contains no doubt; it means guidance for those who fear Allah;

who believe in the Unseen, are steadfast in prayer, and spend out of whatever We have provided them;

who believe in the Revelation that has been sent down to you as well as what was sent down before you,

While they are convinced about the Hereafter;

such people hold on to guidance from their Lord; those will be successful.

—*The Quran 2:2–5.*

You who believe, act steadfast towards Allah, as witnesses for fairplay, and do not let ill-will toward any folk incriminate you so that you swerve from dealing justly. Be just: that is nearest to heedfulness; and heed Allah. For Allah is well-acquainted with all you do.

—*The Quran 5:8.*

The believing man said: "My folk, follow me; I'll guide you along the path of common sense. My folk, this worldly life is to be enjoyed only [briefly]; the Hereafter is the Home to settle down in. Anyone who commits some evil deed will merely be rewarded with something else like it, while someone who acts honorable, whether it is a man or a woman, provided he is a believer will enter the Garden. He will be provided for there without measure."

—*The Quran 40:38–40.*

It is Allah Who has sent down the Book as well as the Scales for Truth. What will make you realize that perhaps the Hour may be near? The ones who do not believe in it would like to hurry it along, while the ones who do believe are apprehensive about it for they know it is the Truth. Are not those who want to discredit the Hour [acting] in extreme error? Gracious is Allah towards His servants. He sustains anyone He wishes; He is the Strong, the Powerful!

—*The Quran 42:17–19.*

By the morning bright,

and at night when all is still

your Lord has not forsaken you nor is He annoyed.

The Hereafter will be even better for you than the first [life] was.

Your Lord will soon give you something which will leave you satisfied.

Did He not find you an orphan and sheltered [you]?

He found you lost and guided [you].

He found you destitute and made you rich!

Thus the orphan must not be exploited;

and the beggar should not be brushed aside.

Still tell about your Lord's favor.

—*The Quran 93:1–11.*

And they have been commanded no more than this:

To worship Allah, offering Him sincere devotion,

as righteous seekers [after Truth]—and to keep up prayer and pay the welfare tax.

That is the Religion Right and Straight.

—*The Quran 98:5.*

Have you seen someone who rejects religion?

This is the person who pushes the orphan aside

and does not promote feeding the needy.

It will be too bad for the prayerful

who are absent-minded as they pray,

who aim to be noticed

while they hold back contributions.

—*The Quran 107:1–7.*

—By permission of the Publisher of Amana Books, Inc. The Quran, translated by T.B. Irving, 1988. P.O. Box 678, Brattleboro, VT 05302.

Summary

1. Islam is a religion whose name describes its essence: total surrender to God.
2. Muslims believe that Muhammad is the last and the greatest of a long line of prophets sent by God to reveal the Divine will to people.
3. The five major obligations of Islam are total surrender to God, daily prayer, almsgiving, fasting and self-restraint during Ramadan, and a pilgrimage to Makkah.
4. Islam's Scripture, gathered into a book called the Quran, consists of the sayings Muhammad received from the angel Gabriel, God's personal messenger to Muhammad.

For review

1. What is Islam? Where did it arise? What are some of the probable causes for its emergence?
2. What expression constitutes the Muslim act of faith?
3. Briefly summarize the major events of Muhammad's life.
4. What are some of the traits Islam has in common with Judaism and Christianity?
5. What experience sparked Muhammad's move to change the conditions of life for the people of Makkah?
6. What is the significance of "Hegira," "Medina," and "Makkah" in Islam?
7. What are the five obligations, or Pillars, of Islamic life? Briefly describe each.
8. Why are Jews, Christians, and Muslims considered as "people of the book?"
9. What is the Quran for Muslims?
10. What are the two sacred shrines of Islam? Explain the significance of each.
11. In what areas of the world is Islam the dominant religion? What were some of the causes for the rapid spread of Islam after Muhammad's death?
12. What did Muhammad accomplish for Arabic society?

For discussion

1. Discuss the tensions between Arabs and Israelis in light of what you know about Judaism and Islam. What other issues might be involved?
2. Discuss the impact of modern science on religions formed centuries ago. What effect might the advance of learning have on religious people? Explain.
3. What are the advantages and disadvantages of having a government which is highly influenced by religious laws?

For research

1. Research the origins of the medieval Crusades.
2. Prepare a report on Arab contributions to learning in Europe in the Medieval period.
3. Prepare a report on the influence of Islam on the history, art, and architecture of Spain.

4. See if you can find out why Muslims are forbidden alcohol, pork, and gambling.

5. Prepare a report on Zoroastrianism.

Word list

Allah

Hadith

hajj

Hegira

Imam

Ishmael

Islam

jihad

jinn

Ka'ba

Makkah

minaret

mosque

Muhammad

Muslim

polygamy

Quran

Ramadan

salat

shahada

zakat

Section Two
The Living Religions of the Eastern World

Celebrants with joss sticks at the Nine-Emperor God festival in Singapore. A "joss" is a Chinese idol or cult image. A "joss stick" is a stick of incense that is burned in the presence of a joss.

When students of religion in the West turn their attention to Eastern civilization, they are entering a world largely unfamiliar to them. As pointed out earlier, the mind-set of people raised in the cultures of the East is vastly different from the mind-set of people influenced by Western culture.

People of the East have their own ways of looking at reality, and their own ways of responding to that reality. Among Eastern peoples, generally, contemplation is valued more highly than in the West, and actions are done not so much "to get things done" as to be the right kind of person. For Eastern peoples, style is more important than ostentatious display, and manners more important than results. Politeness, civility, respect, and passivity are hallmarks of Eastern peoples because their ways of looking at the world and at people develop in them a timelessness and a sense of proportion that is foreign to those raised in Western societies.

It is impossible to include all the religious systems of such a vast part of the world, but we will survey two countries and two major religions of each. From the land of India, we will survey Hinduism and the reaction against it, Buddhism. And from the land of China, we will survey Confucianism and the reaction against it, Taoism.

The religious systems examined here are not limited to the lands with which they are originally associated. Buddhism, for example, has spread beyond India and is adhered to by millions of people in China. On its way through China, one branch of Buddhism was filtered through Taoism and reached Japan in the form of Zen Buddhism, which is now one of the major religions in Japan.

7 Hinduism

Half a world away from the metropolitan centers and capitals of the Western world live over 886 million people, of many racial mixtures and divided into thousands of **castes** speaking sixteen languages and over 800 dialects. These are the people of India, the largest nation in the Indian subcontinent. In spite of this tremendous diversity, the people of India have corporately had a spiritual impact on the world that would not have been possible without a unity and identity that is hard to define but is unmistakably present.

Musician at a Hindu evening prayer service.

India is the country that produced the powerful concept of nonviolence. It has developed the practice of meditation more fully than almost any other culture. It has produced a remarkable atmosphere of toleration for differences of opinion. At the same time, India for centuries suffered from the poverty common to colonized and underdeveloped countries. While the standard of living increased dramatically for the middle-class sector in the latter decades of the twentieth century, inadequate shelter, nutrition, and education still plague many people. What makes India what it is—with both its strengths and its weaknesses—is Hinduism.

What is Hinduism?

Hinduism, the basic religion of India, is marked by a fundamental openness of mind: openness, above all, to the depth of things and to the infinite. Hinduism instinctively refuses to stop at a particular idea or truth and to think that that is the limit of knowledge or experience. Hinduism constantly, restlessly searches beyond the limits of what is already known.

Hence, for Hindus, ultimate reality is unknowable by the rational mind. It is knowable, however, through intuition—direct "insight" into the divine through contemplation. No one, they believe—much less any one religion—can claim for itself absolute and final truth. Hindus believe that all religions are partially true insofar as they are attempts to be open to the Ultimate, which may or may not be a Person, a Father, a Creator, a Ruler, a Savior, a Spirit, a Power, or a Force. For them, Ultimate Reality, or **Brahman,** is the ground of being, the source and essence of the universe.

Hinduism is not like many religions, with boundaries and groups within it. It is, in some sense, a gathering of many religions. Each Hindu interprets the religion in his or her own way. As a result, it is difficult to compare Hinduism with other religions.

Hinduism is an insight (or rather, several diverse, or many times even contradictory insights) into the nature of reality, and the entrance of the entire person into reality by means of insight. Hinduism brings together many mythologies, yoga disciplines, beliefs, and speculations. It constantly adapts to new situations with new forms.

There are almost 733 million Hindus in the world today. Most Hindus live in India, but they can be found also in all the other countries of South Asia, in many of the cosmopolitan urban centers of Southeast Asia, in eastern and southern Africa, in the Persian Gulf States, on the northeast coast of South America, and in many large cities in Europe and North America. In the United States, Hinduism and its offshoot, Buddhism, enjoyed a singular popularity in the latter part of the twentieth century among some people, mostly young adults. They found that the Eastern experience of religion provided practical spiritual techniques or methods (meditation, mantras, chanting) which enabled them to experience the sacred or the mystery of life.

Hinduism

The basic religion of India, marked by contemplation and self-denial for religious reasons.

Brahman

For Hindus, the transpersonal ultimate divine reality (or the Absolute, or the Godhead), primal source of the universe and ultimate goal of all beings.

The origin and growth of Hinduism

Unlike Judaism, Christianity, and Islam, Hinduism does not have a founder. Rather, it is the crystallization of the religious instincts of the people of India through the ages. Its beginnings are shrouded in mystery.

Prehistoric Indian people worshiped nature gods, forces of power, and spirit gods, and had religious rituals and ways of coping with the particular forces of nature they experienced. All of these are reflected in Hinduism as we know it today. The land and the climate of India shaped and molded the Indian concept of the gods, and the geography of India played as important a role in the gradual development of what was eventually to become modern Hinduism as any other factor.

India[1] is framed on the north by the majestic Himalaya Mountains, which prevented invasions from that direction (and consequently, the religion-shaping forces of China and the Far East), and on the west by the lands that are today Pakistan, Afghanistan, Iran, and Iraq (the Persian territories of 2500 B.C.E.). Its western boundaries were open to successive invasions, the most significant of which—as far as religious development is concerned—was the Aryan. This is the same wave of northwestern European tribes that swept over Greece, Syria, and Mesopotamia, bringing their nature gods, and their gods of war and fire and destruction, of power and force, of fertility and generation. Other invasions, from the Greeks under Alexander, in 327 B.C.E., to the European conquest after Vasco de Gama's arrival, in 1498 C.E., influenced Indian religion but did not basically change it.

Perhaps the chief characteristic of the Hindu religion is its comprehensiveness. Hinduism has long absorbed (enfolded or included) in its religious concepts the religious philosophies, theology, ritual, and ceremony of many other religions. Hinduism is flexible and has an ability to "see" in other religions an expression of its own beliefs and practices.

---

1. The name *India* and the word *Hindu* come from the Sanskrit word *Indus,* the Persian name for the river flowing from Tibet through Kashmir and Pakistan to the Arabian Sea. Sanskrit is an Indo-European language that has been used as the literary and religious language of India since 1200 B.C.E.

Believing that they have only a partial vision of Brahman, of sacredness itself, Hindus see in other religions a manifestation of the limitless expressions of Brahman. They see the Hebrew God, the Muslim God, and the Trinity of Christianity as various manifestations of their own Ultimate Reality, which can manifest Itself as **Brahma,** the Creator; **Vishnu,** the Preserver; **Shiva,** the Destroyer; or as any other particular god. Thus, the Hindus see the various major religions as alternative and comparatively equal roads to the same Reality, the prime source of all things and ultimate ground of all being. Reality, for the Hindus, can have many faces and many names—still it is One Reality.

If flexibility and adaptability are characteristic of Hinduism, what, then, *is* Hinduism, if it is not some shapeless grabbag of various religions? Arising as it did from people's basic encounter with their universe and shaped as it was by centuries of speculation, Hinduism presents a complex symphony of magic, faith in a universal power, a kind of nature worship, a polytheism, a **panentheism,** and a system of theological-philosophical reflection on the deities that rival the complex theologies of the West. Some Hindus are monotheists who devote themselves to one of the gods, and some are atheists.

Perhaps the simplest way to describe Hinduism (or rather, the religion of India, since there are many expressions of Hinduism) is to describe its concept of Ultimate Reality, its understanding of self, and a person's path to Ultimate Reality (Brahman).

Brahma
The Hindu god who is the Creator.

Vishnu
The Hindu god who is the Preserver.

Shiva
The Hindu god who is the Destroyer.

panentheism
Belief that the whole of reality is in God.

The images on the outside of this Hindu temple in Malaysia are some of the many gods of Hindu mythology.

The Hindu concept of Ultimate Reality

Brahman (the universal Spirit), the Hindus contend, cannot be defined, described, or properly conceived by the human mind because the mind evolved to cope with the problem of survival in this universe. It deals with, or conceives of, only finite objects. Because The Great One is not finite, because It is the Power Beyond, the Unsearchable, the Unknowable, Brahman can be comprehended intuitively, but never rationally. Perhaps the best description of the Hindu idea of the Absolute comes in the prayer of Shankara, a great Hindu philosopher: "O Thou before whom all words recoil."

The Hindu concept of Ultimate Reality is dealt with most clearly in their Scriptures, especially in that segment known as the **Upanishads,** which claims, "He assumed all forms to reveal himself in all forms. He, the Lord, is revealed in all forms. . . ." The Hindu Supreme Reality is not, however, a mass of nothing. That the Absolute cannot be described does not make a thing of it. Thus, the Hindus, feeling incapable of defining (and thus limiting) Brahman, encourage believers to conceive of Brahman in the way that is best for the individual. For all, the Absolute is Brahman. For one type of believer, the Absolute is Saguna Brahman, the Father—provident, almighty, all-wise, concerned about each present moment. For another type of believer, the Absolute is Nirguna Brahman, the goal, an infinite and transpersonal being, infinite consciousness, infinite bliss. For both, Brahman is the Supreme Reality or Being—the one from whom all things have come and toward which all ultimately return. The following three points might be made about the concept of the Absolute from a Hindu point of view:

1. The one God is **not masculine or feminine;** *he is* **not a person** *the way a human being is. The all-encompassing and all-penetrating One is not an object, "about" which a man might make statements from a superior distance. . . .*

2. . . . God is **not neuter,** *either. . . .* **neither** *can God be* **impersonal** *or, still less,* **subpersonal.** *. . . In the Hindu view the primordial One, or Brahman, is at the same time, universal consciousness, to which real powers are ascribed: an unlimited capacity to know (omniscience), to will (absolute freedom), and to act (omnipotence).*

3. God as the primal reality, therefore, **comprises** *the masculine, feminine, and neuter, the personal and the impersonal. In him* **all the contradictions** *of the created human world are . . . affirmed (conserved), denied (relativized), and overcome (transcended).*

—*Heinrich von Stietencron, "Hindu Perspectives," in* Christianity and the World Religions, *by Hans Küng (Garden City, NY: Doubleday, 1986), 208, 209.*

Upanishads

A collection of philosophical and mystical texts dealing with Atman and Brahman; they are appended to the Vedas and are a major part of the Hindu Scriptures considered to have divine origin.

If Ultimate Reality is so conceived, for example, either personally or impersonally, it follows that a person in relation to that reality will be affected by an individual particular belief. That is why the Hindus have many degrees of relationship to the Supreme Reality and many paths to it.

Hinduism contains a heritage of many gods[2] without seeing in this a contradiction, for it recognizes these many gods as attempts on the part of people to understand a particular aspect of Brahman. One explanation it offers is that the various gods are "faces" of Brahman. Realizing that all explanations are inadequate to Reality, it allows people to approach the One Reality in whatever way or in as many ways as are useful. If a person finds it congenial to come to Brahman through relating to many gods, this is as acceptable as if a person were to admire white light by admiring its rainbow colors refracted through a prism.

Many contemporary Hindus, even unsophisticated ones, regard all the gods (or the names of the many gods) as one. Some Hindus are even monists, transcending a dualism which separates the individual from Brahman. Contemporary Hindus, polytheistic or not, worship one supreme and genderless deity with three modes of being: creating, preserving, and destroying.

---

2. It is said that the Hindu "god list" contains 330 million gods. Over and above all, and penetrating all existence, of course, is Brahman. The three most important manifestations of Brahman are Brahma, the Creator; Vishnu, the Preserver; and Shiva, the Destroyer.

Counting the gods

An old Hindu story tells of a holy man who tried to count the gods. Although he was the son of a brahmin priest and could have enjoyed a life of wealth and ease, he decided at the age of 20 to travel across India for a year or two to ask people which god and goddesses they worshiped. In great cities and humble villages he wrote down the name of every god in a large book. When he filled one book, he started another. From the furthest Himalayas to the burning plains of the south he saw magnificent temples filled with beautiful statues, as well as crude stone idols. He discovered thousands upon thousands of dif-ferent deities and finally, at the age of 93, he began adding up all the names he had written. The task alone took another seven years, and finally, on his deathbed the holy man wrote on the last page of the last book the grand total of all the gods in India. He wrote: "One."

—Leonard J. Biallas, World Religions: A Story Approach *(Mystic, CT: Twenty-Third Publications, 1991), 158.*

The Hindu concept of self

Atman

The true self or soul of each individual, the soul being divine and eternal and beyond the ego or personality.

nirvana

In Hinduism, a state in which a person is united with his or her deepest self, Brahman.

reincarnation

Rebirth into a higher or lower form of life according to how well or how poorly a previous life was lived.

moksha

Release from the endless cycle of rebirth

According to Hinduism, at the core of each person's existence is a reservoir of being that never dies called **Atman.** This Atman is beyond the ego or personality. For all Hindus, Atman is the true self or soul and is divine and eternal. Some Hindus see Atman as being identical with Brahman. It is the Brahman within every person and everything, the universal soul. For these Hindus, Brahman-Atman is the source of the many living beings but is one with those beings. Most Hindus believe, however, that there are many Atman, all of which are distinct but not separate from Brahman. For them, each Atman is rooted in or grounded in Brahman eternally and is a distinct form of the divine.

Unfortunately, according to Hinduism, people are not aware of the hidden greatness within. Instead of identifying themselves with the Total Being that is their innermost soul, they identify themselves with their surface self and the happenings of daily life. They do this out of ignorance, or illusion, or selfishness, and the result is suffering. It is possible to come to an awareness of what one is in essence, to identify with that hidden self, and, thus, to achieve union with the Eternal within (**nirvana**), but only with great difficulty. For most people, getting through the illusion to the core of the self takes several lifetimes. Hence, people die and are reborn again and again—they are **reincarnated.**

Hindus believe that the true self can be found only in a profound search for Atman, that inner being, or power, of each person, which is the extension of Brahman and/or is identical with Brahman. Union with Brahman is the only way to freedom from an endless cycle of reincarnation. Once a person attains union with Brahman, he or she is no longer bound up with suffering, hatred, emotions, and passions. Having attained **moksha,** or release from the endless cycle of rebirth, such a one is utterly free of the unreal self and enters the state of eternal union, or true self.

In order to achieve this unity, each person must be reborn until the "sheaths" have been shed that prevent one from either attaining mystical union with Brahman (what most Hindus believe) or realizing that his or her unchanging essence is identical with Brahman (what some believe). To shed the "sheaths" a person must lead a life of constant striving to get rid of whatever interferes with self-perfection. For this reason a true moral life—a life in which a person rejects selfishness, curbs his or her desires, and does "the good"—insures a better condition in the next incarnation. On the other hand, a person who does not lead a true moral life is "sheathing" the self, or regressing, and hence may go back to a previous or worse state, perhaps as an insect or snake or rodent or even a magnificent stallion.

Like all beliefs that have their foundations in the past, the Hindu doctrine of reincarnation has evolved. It may have arisen from the belief that the Atman must go somewhere, because it does not simply die but has a destiny beyond this tangible life. Unlike the Jewish, Christian, and Muslim belief that a person has but one chance—this life—Hindus propose that a person has several lives, that everyone is reborn into a higher or lower form of life according to how well or how poorly a previous life was lived. Belief in reincarnation is not simply belief in being born again as an animal, an insect, or a reptile. It involves a more complicated procedure than fate. It is determined by each person's life and how closely each one approaches the knowledge and final awareness of his or her true self. Hence, for Hindus, salvation does not mean being reborn (in the Christian sense); it means being freed from the endless cycle of reincarnations—achieving nirvana.

Hindus, then, believe that they have lived before and will live again until they reach nirvana. Their life cycles will perhaps be endless, monotonous rounds of experiences until by self-discipline (hence, the need for yoga, or devotions to lesser deities) they, at some future time, enter complete union with Brahman or realize their identity with Brahman, the Eternal within.

Street scene, Jodhpur, India. Hindus consider cows sacred because they are the most giving of all animals.

Some Hindus may opt for a passive resignation or disengagement in the face of the endless cycle of rebirths (why fight it?). But the more active and positive Hindu response to life is to work with the **law of karma** as the law of spiritual freedom. Thus, a person engages in good thoughts and actions in order to build up karma (merits) for a more favorable rebirth and performs duties and rituals faithfully in order to realize liberation or salvation. Mahatma Gandhi is an example of a Hindu who stressed action in this world, thus popularizing the movement for Indian nationalism and independence from Great Britain.

law of karma

The moral law of cause and effect; the Hindu connection between how one acts and the consequences for those actions.

Hindu ways to union with Ultimate Reality

yoga

A system of physical and mental discipline designed to achieve a spiritual purpose.

A truly religious person, according to Hinduism, is one who seeks to transform his or her nature, to become a truly complete human being. But because there are basically four kinds of persons (reflective, emotional, active, experimental—with an infinite variety within the four kinds), there are four ways to reach this goal. These four ways are the four kinds of **yoga**—specific directions or means to achieve the goal, the union of a person's self with Brahman. Yoga involves physical and mental exercise designed to bring about this integration or union, to realize moksha.

Yoga is not primarily a scheme for physical training or exercise; it is designed to achieve a spiritual purpose. The purpose of yoga is to correct the false identification of self with what is apparent and to seek that which lies underneath the layers of illusion—one's true self. The true practitioner of religious yoga is one who is seeking the true self: the "I" who possesses body and mind, but which cannot be equated with either of them.

Depending on the type of person one is, upon his or her particular bent, he or she can achieve this union with the Supreme Reality through knowledge, love, work, or psychological experience.

1. Through knowledge (Jnana Yoga)

The union of one's Atman with Brahman through knowledge is for the person inclined to thinking, for the reflective person. The kind of knowledge someone following this path seeks, however, is not factual knowledge but intuitive. A person arrives at that intuitive knowledge through a three-step process.

The first step is to be introduced to the insight that what one is in essence is Being itself. Having come to that theoretical understanding, a person then undertakes to come to a felt sense of that truth. That is step two and it is accomplished through a reflective process. In step three, then, a person begins to think of his transient self in the third person and begins to identify with his essential self, which is Being itself. The sense of identity with the Eternal Spirit is so great that a person no longer "feels" the finite, the sensible—he becomes insensitive to pleasure and pain alike. He develops complete control over his body because he "withdraws" from it. For this **yogi**, Brahman is an impersonal goal, a depth, a reality to be sought, the ultimate in being. The way to Brahman through knowledge is difficult—it is reserved for the very few.

yogi

Practitioner of yoga.

2. Through love (Bhakti Yoga)

A far easier way to the Supreme Reality is through love. The practitioners of this form of yoga have a personalist view of Brahman, and therefore direct toward Brahman that strongest of human emotions—love. The practitioner of knowledge yoga conceives of Brahman as an impersonal sea of being. The devotee of love yoga sees Brahman as one to whom love is directed in adoration. For the Hindu Bhakta, this love is expressed to one of the personal deities, one of the manifestations of Brahman. The Bhakta seeks to love Brahman in word and action, and for no other motive than simply Brahman's own self.

The Bhakta distinguishes four kinds of love, hence four ways of looking at Brahman. The first is love of Brahman as protector, provider, and benevolent master. The second regards Brahman as friend or intimate companion. The third regards Brahman as a loving father, and the fourth regards Brahman as one's beloved, one's intimate, one's divine spouse. The ultimate is reached when all things are love because Brahman is loved.

3. Through work (Karma Yoga)

A third way to Brahman—for those inclined to be active—is the way through work. Hindus realize that everyone must in one way or another be active. But often, people do their work merely for the sake of ego-inflating success. For the Karma yogi, however, work (caste duties) is performed as an act of devotion—as a service to Brahman, who gives the energy for working and thus is working "through" the person. Considering work a part of the eternal purpose, the Karmi does each act as if it were the only thing and the last thing he or she has to do. Distracting desires are discarded and a calm is achieved that stems from concern with the eternal as opposed to the turmoil that stems from personal anxieties. Actions are performed in a spirit of non-attachment to results. This produces good karma (merits), which is necessary for salvation. Thus, work is a liberating thing, freeing the person from the sense of frustration and limitation that others experience in work.

4. Through psychological experience (Raja Yoga)

The fourth path to Brahman is the Raja or royal Yoga. The practitioner aims to reintegrate self into the deity by way of psychological experiment or examination. Such an experiment or examination, however, does not refer to a doctor-patient relationship. It refers to a self-examination and perfection that uses life's personal experiences to delve into one's deeper self to discover the inner Being that can only be reached when the external layers of concern are stripped away. Within each person's being, Hindus believe, is this inner Being, or Being itself, which is hidden because of the distractions and necessities of the world.

Hindus view a person as a "layered" being. What we see and feel affects our outer layer, but by successive yoga practices, a person can "peel away" the layers and thereby enter completely into self, where nothing distracts and nothing draws one from the Utter Reality. A person in this stage has reached the Ultimate; he or she is "back" into the Being from which all things come. This person has become the master/king/raja and is not dependent on anything outside of himself or herself.

In Raja Yoga, yoga is practiced to its most intense degree to discipline the body and the mind so that one is not distracted by anything—not joy or sorrow, pleasure or pain, happiness or irritation. The Raji work long hours to secure such control (the classic yoga position, for example, is legs crossed, foot resting on thigh, spinal cord absolutely erect, hands palm up on the lap, one atop the other, eyes half-opened) that he or she can virtually stop breathing. The Raji seeks such absolute control over the body and mind that concentration will lead to complete absorption in Brahman, a perfect union of the "real" self with the Eternal Essence.

In these four methods of yoga, Hindus encourage each individual to conceptualize Brahman and to worship as his or her idea dictates. They believe that because no *one* thing can represent Brahman, neither can many things. Hindus are not exclusivists, insisting on one form rather than another. Neither are they indifferent to forms. They respect every person's right to conceive of the Inconceivable in his or her own way.

The stages of life according to Hindu belief

guru

A spiritual director, teacher, or guide, in the Hindu tradition.

In Hindu belief, a normal, harmonious life consists of four stages. The first is that of a learner. Under the direction of a **guru,** or spiritual director, a true Hindu opens himself or herself to life in such a way that no matter what his or her status or caste, he or she seeks to learn to live that life to its utmost. Interestingly, everything in Hinduism is predicated on one's being a male. Being a woman is a punishment in the sense that a person in "his" former life did evil deeds of such a nature as to bring about rebirth as a female—causing "him" to start over, as it were. Thus, Hindu women live exemplary lives in order to be born again as a male.

The second stage is that of marriage or the prime of life, where one should engage himself totally in his family, his vocation, and his community life. Most Hindus are content to remain in stage two. But the responsibilities of family and work, like the joys of youth, are meant to be left behind eventually in the pursuit of nirvana. If life has been lived fully and properly, the third stage will not involve a cessation of activity. It will be devoted to achieving a mature self-understanding.

The fourth and most exclusive of the Hindu's stages is the last, the state of *sannyasin*. It is the stage—arrived at after the prolonged spiritual examination of stage three—in which a person neither loves nor hates, seeks or desires, goes forth or resists. He simply is at rest in the Holy Power with all his faculties. In this stage, he prepares himself for his passage to the unknown—that which lies beyond this earthly life.

A Hindu holy man.

What lies ahead depends on one's karma. According to the law of karma, one's thoughts and actions in past lives and in the present life produce consequences or effects (karma, good and bad) that determine a person's status and fortune in this and future lives. One who has lived rightly, who has faithfully fulfilled his or her social role, will be rewarded in the next incarnation. Being born to a low caste or into another animal form is understood as a kind of punishment for acts committed in previous lives. On the other hand, an animal may advance to a human caste and then proceed upward to higher castes in a series of lifetimes.

Morality in Hinduism relates to making good decisions that will advance the person in his or her next incarnation. This aspect of Hindu belief explains some of the things that characterize India in the minds of Western visitors—images of sacred cows, holy men, starving people, and the caste system. Among these, none is so hard to understand or accept as the caste system. It can be explained, perhaps, by saying that the same view of people that permits such diversity in religious thought and expression also permits the caste system to continue, even without official recognition or permission. It can also be explained in part by the fact that, for Hindus, there are different paths to the Universal One, different life patterns appropriate to various stages in a person's life, and different positions or stations in life in the social order because of the way a person lived in his or her former life.

The formal caste system began around 300 B.C.E., probably resulting from a combination of invasion, ethnic and religious differences, health and fertility requirements, and religious taboo. No one knows for sure. But, in India, the normal differences in any society—of intellectual and spiritual leaders, of administrators and politicians, of manufacturers (producers), and of laborers—became fixed and rigid in four classes, which are then divided into many castes (today there are over 2,300). In the course of time, a group of untouchables emerged. These social outcasts became the dregs of Indian society.

So rigid did the caste system become in India that marriage outside of one's particular caste or level was forbidden, and rising from one level to another very difficult. In addition, privileges of caste created severe burdens for those of the lower castes.

A proliferation of castes within castes led to a society that included undeserved privilege, exclusiveness, rigidity, and heartless cruelty to lower castes. The lowest castes—the untouchables—are not slaves in the strictest sense, but they are subject to quite harsh treatment.

One of the reasons the caste system can remain in Indian society today is the Hindu concept of people's nature and destiny. To the Hindu, the important thing is not the external; it is internal union with Brahman. If a person makes progress in the present life in the search for union with Brahman, he or she will be reincarnated into a higher caste in the next life. This upward progress will continue from one life to the next until he or she completely identifies with his or her Atman, thereby achieving union with Brahman. If one does not make progress in the present life toward that goal, he or she deserves his or her own fate.

Ethnic Indian woman at a Hindu prayer service.

Hinduism is a religion which can, perhaps, be best described as the search for human awareness, the search for the real self, whether this be by practices of ancient worship, the devotions of later insights, or the sophistication of the ultimate yogi. Accepting the idea of the eternal cycle, the Hindu by one way or another seeks incorporation into the unknowable Brahman.

This is the heart of Hinduism. There may be a multitude of lesser gods, but there is one ultimate Brahman; all others are but "faces" of the true. They may be true in their own right, but they are, nonetheless, distinct from and inferior to the Alone. Hence, the Hindu can tolerate all kinds of temples and gods and devotions and practices. Whether his devotion or sacrifice is directed to **Krishna** or Shiva, or **Kali** or Parvati or Surya (the sun god, symbolized by the rays of the sun in Hindu devotional images) or the multi-armed images in Hindu temples, the true Hindu hopes for peace and encompassment in the Brahman cradle—or final rest.

Hindu Scriptures

The Hindu Scriptures, or body of sacred writing, are a collection of sacred hymns, stories, legends, commentaries, ritual directives, myths, philosophy, and theological speculation.

The Hindu Scriptures, like the Scriptures of other religions, had their origin in oral tradition dating back many centuries. That oral tradition was codified and standardized in written form sometime between 1500 and 800 B.C.E. Unlike the Scriptures of the religions of the West, however, the Hindu Scriptures are not selective. They are, literally, collections of the religious wisdom of the Hindus over the centuries.

The Hindu Scriptures fall into two categories, *shruti* ("that which is heard") and *smirti* ("that which is remembered"). Writings considered *shruti* contain knowledge believed to have come from the insights of *rishis* (holy persons or seers). As a result, such writings are treated with utmost reverence. Writings considered *smirti* had their origins in the remembered sayings, teachings, stories, epics, and commentaries of the respected gurus of Hinduism. They are not held in as high esteem as *shruti* writings, but they are an important and respected part of the Hindu sacred writings because they are "infallible guides to right conduct."

The *shruti* writings are divided into three parts: the **Vedas,** the **Brahmanas**, and the Upanishads.

The Vedas are four collections of religious material containing prayers, ritual, liturgy, hymns, and spells and charms of a popular nature. They are, basically, Hindu prayer books. The Brahmanas are a collection of writings for priests containing directions for sacrifice. The Upanishads are a collection of

Krishna

A popular and important incarnation of Vishnu in Hinduism.

Kali

The Hindu goddess who destroys evil.

Vedas

Four collections of religious material containing prayers, ritual, liturgy, hymns, and spells and charms of a popular nature.

Brahmanas

A collection of writings for priests containing directions for sacrifice.

philosophical commentaries dealing mostly with Indian deities. While the Vedas deal with nature worship and polytheism, the Upanishads contain speculations on the ultimate order of things.

The writings considered *smirti* are more extensive than the *shruti* writings. Among the literature in this category are the *Mahabharata* and the *Ramayana,* two religious epics containing sacred history for the Hindus. The first is the story of the earliest inhabitants of the Indian subcontinent, the Mahabharata, while the second is the story of Rama, one of the manifestations of Vishnu. Another piece of literature in this collections of writings is the **Bhagavad Gita,** which is the story of Lord Krishna, who is the source of the manifestations (avatars, incarnations) of Vishnu. The *Bhagavad Gita* is probably the most popular book of Hindu Scripture, for in it is found the message that there are many ways to salvation, all of which are valid.

Bhagavad Gita

A book of Hindu Scripture containing the story of Lord Krishna, who is the source of the manifestations of Vishnu.

Worshipers bathing in the Ganges River at Varanasi (Benares), India's holiest city.

Hindu worship

Hindu worship is basically individual, though at times groups of Hindus seem to be praying together because they are in the same place at the same time.

The Hindu's day begins with washing or bathing. If possible, the Hindu bathes in a river, reciting certain prayers, washing his or her mouth, and paying homage to the life-giving sun. Offerings may be made during the day, either at a household shrine or in shrines or temples dedicated to certain gods and goddesses. Each caste or subcaste has its own special rites and prayers, and there are certain agricultural observances that resemble the ancient harvest rites of other religious traditions.

Rivers play a central role in Hindu worship. A Hindu who does not live near a river worships in a pond, a lake, a stream, a fountain—wherever there is water. But the ideal is flowing water. All rivers are sacred—as well they might be in a land where the temperature commonly is high and there are long periods of drought. The Ganges is the most sacred of the rivers in Hinduism; Hindus bathe in it for purification.

Hindu temples are usually staffed by one or several priests who perform the sacred ceremonies alone, without a congregation. There is no such thing as communal worship, nor a Sabbath or "Sunday," though there are certain holy days during the year on which people are more likely to perform their sacred duties. Generally speaking, a Hindu will worship wherever and whenever the spirit comes over him or her. The passing Westerner may turn his head in embarrassment, but a Hindu at prayer will often attract a crowd eager to observe the fervor with which he or she prays.

Life-cycle rituals

There is a system of sacred life-cycle rites in Hinduism called the **samskaras,** which include a kind of baptism, an initiation rite, a marriage ceremony, and a death rite. There are anywhere from ten to forty *samskaras,* depending on one's definition of the term.

One of the most beautiful and elaborate *samskaras* is that of marriage, which takes different forms among different castes. In a typical Hindu marriage ceremony, a young couple sits in the street (where the festivities center for five days) while people from their village sit around them, having a party and making ribald remarks about the coming consummation. The young couple are, hopefully, deep in prayer. Normally a bride and groom do not see each other before the ceremony.

samskaras

Hindu sacred life-cycle rituals.

A wedding for members of the Brahman caste, India's highest caste.

Marriages are traditionally arranged by the parents. The ceremony itself takes place before a fire, into which certain symbolic foods are cast. Vows are exchanged, and the respective families pledge mutual love and aid. At the end of the ceremony, the wife leads her husband to a spot where they can see the North Star. She says: "You are steady. May I be as steady in my husband's family." The husband says: "The sky is firm, the earth is firm, and this wife is firm in her husband's family." The wife: "I pay homage to you." The husband: "May you be long-lived." He adds: "I bind your heart and mine with the knot of truth. May your heart be mine. May my heart be yours."

There are equally beautiful ceremonies for other *samskaras,* such as on the day when a child is presumed to be conceived, during pregnancy, at birth, on the child's name day, when the child first takes hard food, at the first cutting of the child's hair, and especially at the time when the child receives the sacred thread that denotes full acceptance into the Hindu community. This last *samskara* is only for those in the upper three classes, especially the Brahmins. This latter ceremony, along with the funeral ceremonies, are probably the most distinctively Hindu.

Sacred cows

Most Westerners find Hindu reverence for the cow incomprehensible. But, for the Hindu, sacred cows symbolize the entire subhuman world. Protection of cows is an expression of people's affinity to all that lives. The cow is referred to as "God Matha" and is treated with the same respect one would give one's own mother. The cow is thus a symbol of divine motherhood, of life, of the entire animal world, of fecundity, and of abundance. Every cow is considered to be a descendant of Kamadhenu, a heavenly cow with the face of a beautiful woman.

There are more than two hundred million cows in India—one for every three people. As one Hindu put it: "We reverence cows. You eat them: the arms and legs, ribs, tail, liver, stomach, testicles, brains, all the other inner organs, the blood, everything except the eyes. What you don't eat, you wear (the skin). And what's left over you use as soap for washing and for fertilizer to make your vegetables grow. You call it practical efficiency. We call it cannibalism. Would you eat your mother?"

On September 4, 1987, Roop Kanwar, an eighteen-year-old woman in the village of Deorala in Rajasthan, burned to death as she sat upright, enclosed in the logs of her husband's funeral pyre. The practice of sati, widow burning, is an ancient one in northwest India, although without sanction in any Hindu text. Condemned by nineteenth-century reformers such as Ram Mohan Roy and prohibited by ordinances beginning in 1829, it has survived in sporadic instances in the last two centuries, one of many graphic illustrations of the manner in which India and Hinduism appear to inhabit multiple time frames.

The nationwide debate generated by the Deorala sati is instructive for those who seek to understand the destiny of Hinduism at the close of the twentieth century. The government of India, as a modernizing secular state under constitutional law, was swift and unanimous in passing a bill providing for life imprisonment or the death sentence for abetment of sati. Vigorous condemnations of this cultural anachronism appeared in the press, along with denunciation of those who would glorify sati by citing scriptures on women's loyalty to their husbands, even to the point of self-sacrifice. But little was said about the thousands of active shrines throughout the subcontinent that commemorate sati events of the past. Some prominent Hindu sectarian leaders even came out in support of "voluntary sati" and "sati dharma." One of their arguments was that the ideal of feminine loyalty demonstrated throughout Hindu mythology, folklore, ritual, and symbolism is upheld by only a few women, just as the ideal of renunciation is maintained by only a few samnyasis. Still others resisted taking a stand on the issue on the grounds of freedom of religious expression guaranteed by the constitution.

A few weeks after Roop Kanwar's death, which some witnesses stated was physically enforced by her male in-laws, a poll was conducted in thirty-two towns and villages in fourteen districts of Rajasthan. A majority (63 percent) of those interviewed were women. Of those interviewed, 86.6 percent knew of the sati cult, 80.7 percent knew of Roop Kanwar, and 63.4 percent approved of the act in her case. Only 3.65 percent of those interviewed felt that the young woman had been forced to commit sati. A number of respondents declared that she had become a goddess (Sati Devi).

—David M. Knipe, "Hinduism," Religious Traditions of the World, edited by H. Byron Earhart (HarperSanFrancisco, 1993), 827.

There was neither non-existence nor existence then; there was neither the realm of space nor the sky which is beyond. What stirred? Where? In whose protection? Was there water, bottomlessly deep?

There was neither death nor immortality then. There was no distinguishing sign of night nor of day. That one breathed, windless, by its own impulse. Other than that there was nothing beyond.

Darkness was hidden by darkness in the beginning; with no distinguishing sign, all this was water. The life force that was covered with emptiness, that one arose through the power of heat.

Desire came upon that one in the beginning; that was the first seed of mind. Poets seeking in their heart with wisdom found the bond of existence in non-existence. . . .

Whence this creation has arisen—perhaps it formed itself, or perhaps it did not—the one who looks down on it, in the highest heaven, only he knows—or perhaps he does not know.

—Rig Vedas, *10.129, Creation Hymn, 1–4, 7.*

A certain wise man, while seeking immortality,

Introspectively beheld the Soul (Atman) face to face.

The childish go after outward pleasures;

They walk into the net of widespread death.

But the wise, knowing immortality,

Seek not the stable among things which are unstable here.

—Katha Upanishad, *4:2.*

OM TAT SAT: "That Is the Real"—this is the triple symbol of the infinite spirit that gave a primordial sanctity to priests, sacred lore, and sacrifice.

OM—knowers of the infinite spirit chant it as they perform acts of sacrifice, charity, and penance prescribed by tradition.

TAT—men who crave freedom utter it as they perform acts of sacrifice, charity, and penance, without concern for reward.

SAT—it means what is real and what is good, Arjuna; the word SAT is also used when an action merits praise.

SAT is steadfastness in sacrifice, in penance, in charity; any action of this order is denoted by SAT.

But oblation, charity, and penance offered without faith are called ASAT, for they have no reality here or in the world after death.

—The Bhagavad-Gita: Krishna's Counsel in Time of War, *ch. 17.22–28.*

Sanskrit symbol for "OM."

Summary

1. Hinduism is open to all forms of belief and all ways of worshiping. It is basically a meditative faith.
2. Hindus can accept all forms of gods, believing that each is an expression of the Ultimate, their Brahman.
3. Hindu life and morality are directed toward final mystical union with Brahman or absorption into Brahman.
4. Hindus believe in reincarnation because it usually takes more than one lifetime to arrive at an awareness of one's true identity, and thus to achieve union with Brahman.
5. Hindus practice yoga in order to be incorporated into Brahman.

For review

1. What are the primary characteristics of Hinduism? Explain.
2. What is Brahman? Why do Hindus have so many gods?
3. What is yoga? What are the different kinds of yoga and why are there different kinds?
4. Explain the Hindu concept of self.
5. What is reincarnation? Explain. Why do Hindus believe in reincarnation? What do they mean by "the eternal cycle of life"?
6. Explain the Hindu concept of the stages of a person's life. What is the highest stage of life according to Hindu belief?
7. What is the caste system? How is it possible for the Indian culture to accept the caste system?
8. What are the Hindu Scriptures? Explain their main divisions.

For discussion

1. Discuss the possibility of reincarnation. Do you know any people who believe in reincarnation?
2. Discuss the Hindu concept of self. How does it compare to how you understand your self?
3. Discuss why Hindus seem to be unconcerned about the situation in life in which they find themselves.
4. Given the Hindu conception of women, discuss why women in India are faithful Hindus, why Hinduism is accepted by some North American women, and the impact of the feminist movement on Hinduism.

For research

1. Do a descriptive oral presentation on the Ganges River in Hindu life and worship.
2. Look up information on the economic conditions in present-day India.
3. Who was Mohandas Gandhi? Why might he have been called "The Great Soul"?
4. Investigate the interest in Hinduism in the United States.
5. Prepare a report on the caste system in India.
6. Find out what you can about the Hindu "holy men," or fakirs.

Word list

Atman

Bhagavad-Gita

Brahma

Brahman

Brahmanas

caste

guru

Hinduism

Kali

Krishna

law of karma

moksha

nirvana

panentheism

reincarnation

Shiva

samskaras

Upanishads

Vedas

Vishnu

yoga

yogi

8 Buddhism

Closely associated with, but distinct from Hinduism is **Buddhism.** Like Christianity and Islam, Buddhism arose in a particular time in a particular place—in India, in the fifth century before the Common Era. It was the result of the spiritual insights of Siddhartha Gautama, who lived from 563 to 486 B.C.E.

Gautama, or, as he became known, **Buddha** (meaning "The Awakened or Enlightened One"), was one of the most remarkable men who ever lived. He was raised in the Hindu tradition and enjoyed the benefits of being the son of the chief of the Sakya clan (he had money, servants, prize horses, beautiful women, and exquisite places to live at his command). At the age of twenty-nine, he started out in search of peace and salvation for himself and wound up bringing it to millions of others. Eventually, he broke with Hindu tradition, rejecting the caste system, the concepts of many gods, the need for many rebirths to attain perfect peace, and unquestioning submission to fate. From his own enlightenment and his preaching to others has come one of the world's great living religions.

Buddhism

A way of life based on the Four Noble Truths and the Eightfold Path.

The Buddha

Siddhartha Gautama, The Awakened or Enlightened One.

Seated Buddha, Polonnaruwa, Sri Lanka.

Today there are over 313 million Buddhists in Asia—primarily in Sri Lanka, Myanmar, Vietnam, Thailand, Korea, Japan, China, and Mongolia. In North America, there are about 558,000 Buddhists, although some of these are "pseudo-Buddhists" who have merely adopted certain Buddhist practices.

During the lifetime of the Buddha, Buddhism presented a reaction against some of the perversions of Hinduism. However, in modern times no antagonism between Hinduism and Buddhism exists. It is interesting to note that although Buddhism arose in India, it has lost much of its distinctiveness as a religious practice in that country. The historical reasons for this include the decline of Buddhist universities and monastic centers following the invasions by Turkish Muslims from the eleventh to the thirteenth centuries and the strong cultural force of Hinduism, which absorbed remaining Buddhist distinctions following the invasions.

Perhaps the best way to describe Buddhism is to say that it "is a faith, a body of philosophy and wisdom, and a group of practices meant to relieve humankind of material, spiritual, and psychological suffering and to resolve the inevitable contradictions of life." Buddhism is not so much concerned with God or the *why* of life as it is with the *how* of humans doing their best to live in this world.

The origin of Buddhism

ascetic

One who dedicates his or her life to the pursuit of contemplative ideals, and practices extreme self-denial for religious reasons.

Having gone through the first two stages of Hindu life and seeing that the promised peace of Jnana Yoga came only to the relative few who mastered it and that misery and discrimination were the lot of many, Gautama went in search of the secret to peace and happiness. For seven years after his twenty-ninth birthday (leaving his wife and child in good care, as Hindu belief demanded), he studied, meditated, fasted, and worked to achieve "the perfect peace." He did not find it. Finally, abandoning the ritualistic practices of yoga and extreme **asceticism**, Gautama set himself to meditation on the causes for evil and the means to happiness.

As legend tells it, Gautama seated himself under a fig tree[1] in the forest and meditated on the meaning of life and the means to happiness and peace. After long hours of serious thought, he became enlightened. He grasped what he called The Four Noble or Sacred Truths of the way to enlightenment. Leaving his meditation spot, he went to tell his companions of his discovery. Convinced of its truth, he spent the rest of his life preaching his way of enlightenment. It is from his experience of being suddenly enlightened that Gautama received the name "the Buddha"—"The Enlightened One."

---

1. This particular fig tree, called "peepul," is now known as the "Bo" tree, from *bodhi,* meaning "enlightenment."

Enlightenment

Was it not his Self, his small, fearful and proud Self, with which he had wrestled for so many years, but which had always conquered him again, which appeared each time again and again, which robbed him of happiness and filled him with fear? Was it not this which had finally died today in the wood by this delightful river? Was it not because of its death that he was now like a child, so full of trust and happiness, without fear?

Siddhartha now realized why he had struggled in vain with this Self when he was a Brahmin and an ascetic. Too much knowledge had hindered him; too many holy verses, too many sacrificial rites, too much mortification of the flesh, too much doing and striving. He had been full of arrogance; he had always been the cleverest, the most eager—always a step ahead of the others, always the learned and intellectual one, always the priest or the sage. His Self had crawled into this priesthood, into this arrogance, into this intellectuality. It sat there tightly and grew, while he thought he was destroying it by fasting and penitence. Now he understood it and realized that the inward voice had been right, that no teacher could have brought him salvation. That was why he had to go into the world, to lose himself in power, women and money; that was why he had to be a merchant, a dice player, a drinker and a man of property, until the priest and Samana in him were dead. That was why he had to undergo those horrible years, suffer nausea, learn the lesson of the madness of an empty, futile life till the end, till he reached bitter despair, so that Siddhartha the pleasure-monger and Siddhartha the man of property could die. He had died and a new Siddhartha had awakened from his sleep. He also would grow old and die. Siddhartha was transitory, all forms were transitory, but today he was young, he was a child—the new Siddhartha—and he was very happy.

These thoughts passed through his mind. Smiling, he listened to his stomach, listened thankfully to a humming bee. Happily he looked into the flowing river. Never had a river attracted him as much as this one. Never had he found the voice and appearance of flowing water so beautiful. It seemed to him as if the river had something special to tell him, something which he did not know, something which still awaited him. Siddhartha had wanted to drown himself in this river; the old, tired, despairing Siddhartha was today drowned in it. The new Siddhartha felt a deep love for this flowing water and decided that he would not leave it again so quickly.

—Hermann Hesse, Siddhartha (New York: New Directions, 1951), 99–100.

"Was it not his Self, his small, fearful and proud Self. . . which robbed him of happiness and filled him with fear? Was it not because of its death that he was now like a child, so full of trust and happiness, without fear?"

Youngster fascinated by the size of a Buddha statue, Sukothai, Thailand.

The "Way" of Buddha

What distinguishes Buddhism from Hinduism, from which it sprang? For one thing, it was founded by a man; it was not the result of an accumulation of centuries of prehistoric religious growth. For another, it rejected the wheel of birth idea in favor of going to the very heart of every person's search for nirvana. It rejected the idea of several deities as outside helpers in people's search for happiness and urged them to look within themselves, thereby ridding themselves of unhappiness. It rejected the complexities of Hinduism for the simplicity of search for self.

Buddha had tried the many "true" ways of Hinduism. He found that they did not lead *him* to better awareness of his goal or bring him any closer to it. He found that his path lay not in conformity to the set practices of yoga or in abandoning himself to the fates as prescribed by the cherishing or unfriendly gods, but in himself. He came to realize that happiness lay within each person and his or her capacities, and not in the various and uncertain revelations of many gods.

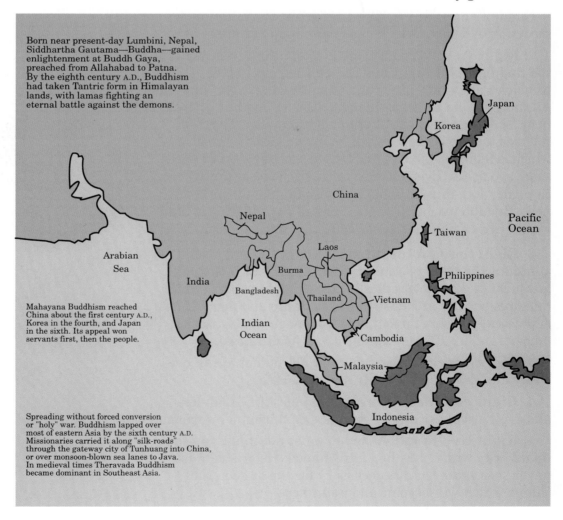

Born near present-day Lumbini, Nepal, Siddhartha Gautama—Buddha—gained enlightenment at Buddh Gaya, preached from Allahabad to Patna. By the eighth century A.D., Buddhism had taken Tantric form in Himalayan lands, with lamas fighting an eternal battle against the demons.

Mahayana Buddhism reached China about the first century A.D., Korea in the fourth, and Japan in the sixth. Its appeal won servants first, then the people.

Spreading without forced conversion or "holy" war. Buddhism lapped over most of eastern Asia by the sixth century A.D. Missionaries carried it along "silk-roads" through the gateway city of Tunhuang into China, or over monsoon-blown sea lanes to Java. In medieval times Theravada Buddhism became dominant in Southeast Asia.

The Four Noble Truths that Buddha discovered were:

1. All things in the world entail sorrow and suffering.

2. The cause of suffering is desire, the craving of the pleasures of life.

3. The end of suffering will come only when the craving for pleasure is ended; one must let go of one's desires.

4. The end of craving will come if a person follows the Eightfold Path to perfection.

Buddha preached that every person has the capacity and the ability to resist those desires and drives which cause a person to impose his or her desires on others and thus cause suffering. He preached that a person should resist and eventually destroy in himself or herself that which causes unhappiness. This is done by accepting the first three truths and following the eight steps in the path to the destruction of desires. They are called steps because, in the Theravada (monastic) tradition, the eight parts of the path depict steps to be followed one after the other. The Mahayana viewpoint says that although they are called steps, each must be cultivated in relation to and along with the others (a less linear approach).

Buddha's eight steps, **The Eightfold Path,** to the destruction of desires which cause unhappiness are:

1. Right views: A person must accept the key elements of the Buddhist philosophy and accept The Four Truths. Three principles are vitally important to cultivating Right View: (1) All things in life are impermanent. (2) Nothing has a permanent "self" (**ego-self**). (3) Nirvana is tranquility. The "self" referred to here is the "ego-self," our own view of ourselves, which is highly subjective and biased according to our personal ego needs. Even our real or true self is constantly changing and, thus, in some way, also ultimately impermanent. Buddha teaches that the cause of our suffering is that we feel attachments to things which are impermanent.

2. Right thought (or intent): Correct thought should not stimulate the three poisons of greed, anger, and foolishness. We ought to develop a radically new thinking process which nurtures positive attitudes free from desire and temptations of physical pleasure (greed), free from anger and irritation (anger), and free from harming others (foolishness).

3. Right speech: A person must not lie nor speak uselessly and never speak badly about others.

4. Right conduct: A person must not kill, steal, lie, abuse others physically or sexually, or consume intoxicants.

5. Right livelihood: A person must not injure another in any way while pursuing a livelihood. He or she must never seek more than is necessary for life or seek those things which will become encumbrances.

The Four Noble Truths

According to Buddha, four principles for living that lead to happiness.

The Eightfold Path

Eight steps or modes of being and acting necessary in the Buddhist way of life.

ego-self

Our own view of ourselves, which is highly subjective and biased according to our personal ego needs.

Theravadad Buddhist monks and laypeople returning from breakfast, Kanduboda Meditation Center, Sri Lanka.

6. Right effort: A person must always do the right thing. He or she must avoid evil thoughts about persons and things. He or she must always seek to do things in the best way.

7. Right mindfulness: Through meditation, a person must arrive at a state of consciousness that lifts him or her above physical desires, enables him or her to see things in their proper perspective, and gives one control over self in all things. Thoughts of loving kindness should prevail.

8. Right concentration: A person must work for the highest form of meditation, contemplation, which enables one to do away with even the minutest cravings and selfish desires, and lifts one to the mystical stage called nirvana.

Buddha's "way" was not easy (nirvana was not just for the asking). For the dedicated Buddhist, the key to attaining nirvana, or perfect happiness, lies in following the eight steps, which are interrelated. For example, if a person does not have right views on what brings happiness, he or she cannot have the right purpose (that is, he or she will have selfish motives), he or she will not have right speech, will not have right conduct, and so on.

Buddhism stresses long hours of thought and prayer to achieve right understanding, and strong self-discipline to rid one's self of avarice, ambition, ill will, malicious talk, lust, and hurt to any living thing. (This is the reasoning behind Buddhist nonviolent doctrines.) It asks people to avoid anything which might interfere with a person's direction toward nirvana.

Compassion

Compassion is a state of calmness; it also involves intelligence and enormous vitality.... True compassion is spacious and wise as well as resourceful. In this type of compassion we do not just blindly launch into a project but we look into situations dispassionately. There is a sense of priorities as to which situations should be handled immediately and which are worth putting off. This type of compassion could be called intelligent love or intelligent affection. We know how to express our affection so that it does not destroy a person but instead helps him to develop. It is more like a dance than a hug....

It is perhaps most important in working with others that we do not develop idiot compassion, which means always trying to be kind. Since this superficial kindness lacks courage and intelligence, it does more harm than good. It is as though a doctor, out of apparent kindness, refuses to treat his patient because the treatment might be painful, or as though a mother cannot bear the discomfort of disciplining her child. Unlike idiot compassion, real compassion is not based on a simple-minded avoidance of pain. Real compassion is uncompromising in its allegiance to basic sanity. People who distort the path—that is, people who are working against the development of basic sanity—should be cut through on the spot if need be. That is extremely important. There is no room for idiot compassion. We should try to cut through as much self-deception as possible in order to teach others as well as ourselves. So the final cop-out of a bodhisattva is when, having already achieved everything else, he is unable to go beyond idiot compassion....

According to Buddhism, the human essence is compassion and wisdom. So you do not have to acquire skillful communication from outside yourself; you have it already. It has nothing to do with mystical experience or any kind of higher spiritual ecstasy; it is just the basic working situation. If you have an interest in people's suffering and conflicts, you have that openness constantly. And then you can develop some sense of trust and understanding, so that your openness becomes compassion.

—Chögyam Trungpa, The Heart of the Buddha (Boston: Shambhala, 1991), 17–18, 126, 183.

Buddhist monks

Having found his own path to personal contentment and the means to rid people of suffering, Buddha set about winning others to his way of thinking. He was a powerful, persuasive speaker who combined knowledge with example. In a short time, he had several disciples who followed his direction. They formed themselves into a "brotherhood" of monks who renounced all things in favor of Buddha's way and, following his lead, went out to persuade others to search for peace through The Four Noble Truths.

These original Buddhist monks became the means for the spread of Buddha's ideas and for the continuity of Buddhism. In India and Southeast Asia particularly, Buddhism became essentially a religion for monks. Although other people follow Buddha's way, its perfect expression is found in a monastic way of life. The monks are still—after 2,500 years—the secret of Buddhism. Buddhist monks keep Buddha's ideas alive, his way of life viable, and his memory one of the treasured heritages of the Eastern world. Among many Buddhists, Buddha is not simply a good man and a great religious prophet; he is a divine person. For all Buddhists, he is first and foremost a teacher, one who points the way for others.

Kinds of Buddhism

There have been many offshoots of the original Buddhism, but all have been based on a vigorous simplification of many things inherent in the Hinduism of Buddha's day. Buddhism contains no authority, no ritual, no hidebound tradition, no philosophic niceties to interfere with a person's real experience, no abandonment to fatalism, no supernatural, preternatural, or superstitious practices. (However, many of these things have crept into some forms of Buddhism.)

The principle kinds of Buddhism are Theravada Buddhism, Mahayana Buddhism, and Tantric Buddhism. Zen Buddhism is a school under the branch of Mahayana Buddhism. Buddhism developed along its three main lines in Southeast Asia and in India—where it was born.

One, **Theravada Buddhism,** *calls itself the Way of the Elders. . . . It prevails today in [Sri Lanka, Myanmar], Thailand, Cambodia, and Laos. Theravadins stress the sangha (the brotherhood of monks) as the means of following the* **dhamma** *(the essential quality or character of Buddhism); a monk who succeeds in reaching nirvana becomes an arhat, or saint. At the same time Theravada Buddhism gives the layman a positive role in supporting the sangha, winning merit to better his own karma.*

Theravada Buddhism

A division of Buddhism which stresses the *sangha* (the brotherhood of monks) as the means of following the *dhamma* (the essential quality or character of Buddhism).

dhamma

The essential quality or character of Buddhism.

[The second] division of Buddhism [is] known as Mahayana, the Great Vehicle, because it offers a broader means of gaining the ultimate goal—a goal open both to the pious monk and to any layman. Further, the goal could be not only nirvana but also a godly existence of self-sacrifice and compassion. The ideal saint became not the arhat, but the **bodhisattva**—*he who at the threshold of nirvana postpones his own entry to help others to salvation. . . .* **Mahayana Buddhism**, *once centered in China, now predominates in Korea, Japan and part of Vietnam. . . .*

[A] third branch of Buddhism, **Tantric** *[Mantrayana] sprouted around the sixth century [C.E.] and finds its chief expression in Himalayan lands. It interlaced Mahayana Buddhism with Tantric cults of India that invoked deities by magic and rituals. And it expanded the pantheon with an array of new divinities—personifications of Buddha's thoughts and acts, female counterparts of deities, even demons.*

Each division of Buddhism musters claims that it represents the original or true form. Actually, each developed by stressing specific elements within the early faith. And as Buddhism spread, it articulated its insights in words and symbols that differed from country to country. In Southeast Asia it learned to speak the language of kingship. In Tibet it learned to speak with shamans. In China it picked up the language of the family. But its essence remains the message of Siddhartha Gautama: "Seek in the impersonal for the eternal man, and having sought him out, look inward—thou art Buddha."[2]

In the West, the most widely known form of Buddhism is **Zen Buddhism.** It is an example of a tradition that has managed to successfully convey to the West certain aspects of the Buddha's teaching. Zen is a school, development, or refinement of Mahayana Buddhism begun in China in the sixth century C.E. (and in Japan in the twelfth century C.E.). It emphasizes the search for a glimpse of enlightenment for the student by the most direct means: accepting formal studies and observances only when they form part of the means. Studies and ritual practices, no matter how worthy or important for someone else, are only a means to an end; they are never an end in themselves.

bodhisattva

In Buddhism, one who is on the threshold of nirvana but postpones his or her own entry to help others reach nirvana.

Mahayana Buddhism

A major division of Buddhism which extends the goal of Buddhism to laypersons, as well as to monks, the goal being a godly existence of self-sacrifice and compassion, as well as nirvana.

Tantric [Mantrayana] Buddhism

A division of Buddhism which combined Mahayana Buddhism with Tantric cults of India, includes many deities and spirits.

Zen Buddhism

A school of Mahayana Buddhism which has successfully conveyed to the West certain aspects of the Buddha's teachings; its hallmark is contemplation. It is the form of Buddhism practiced in Japan.

---

2. Dr. Joseph Kitagawa from *Great Religions of the World,* copyright National Geographic Society, 1971, 1978.

Buddhist temple complex in Singapore.

Zen Buddhism is not a new religion in the way that Christianity is different from Judaism or the ancient Egyptian religion was different from the Babylonian search for an answer to the mystery of life. It is a refinement of Buddhism.

All great religious movements tend to shed the complexities, the extravagances, the rigid philosophical, theological, the moral aspects of institutionalized religion. These religious movements are a reaction to entrenched interests. People feeling a need for simplification and meaning *for their lives,* eagerly receive the insights and compelling magnitude of a unique person who can bring them the message they know in their innermost being is correct and relevant. So it was with Jesus, Buddha, and Muhammad. Thus it was with the origin of Zen.

Buddhism had tended to become formalistic, just as had the yoga exercises of Hinduism. The answer to the search for self was found in the ritual rather than in the person. For some people, The Eightfold Path had become a sophisticated form of magic—as long as the action was done, the result was assured. Zen Buddhism was a reaction to this defect which had crept into Buddhism.

Zen Buddhism attempts, by meditation under the guidance of a master teacher, to arrive at the moment of truth—the **satori,** or glimpse of enlightenment (achieved in a flash)—about life. Zen Buddhism teaches that truth does not lie in any particular revelation, wise sayings, person, or particular way. It lies in existence itself. Consequently the Zen Buddhist seeks through serious contemplation on seemingly nonsensical statements (Q. What is the most excellent thing in Zen? A. I sit alone on the great mountain) to arrive at his own understanding of his life. The Zen Buddhists believe that by concerted effort (the founder of Zen, a Buddhist monk named Bodhidharma [about 600 c.e.], contemplated a blank wall for nine years), a person will arrive at his or her own glimpse of enlightenment through a sudden intuition which will shed once and for all the complexities and strivings that keep people in turmoil.

Zen Buddhism attempts to address the spiritual needs of a certain type of seeker, one who is deeply attached to mental concepts. It is a version of Buddhism stripped of the accumulated traditions and rituals of centuries. Its hallmark

satori

Glimpse of enlightenment (achieved in a flash) about life.

is contemplation, which produces an inscrutability, a calmness, an assurance, and a grace that enables a person to face the problems of life because, having become enlightened, he or she no longer worries about life but is seeking the depth of his or her own being where real truth and beauty lie. As the Zen Buddhists say: "One should not think about life; one should live it." "One should not worry about life or death, heavens or hell or gods or magic or rites or sacrifices. One should seek the exaltation of *Samadhi* (deep contemplation) to arrive at nirvana."

Buddhist Scriptures

The Buddhists share with the Hindus the Vedic sources. In addition to these ancient texts, they also have what is known as the **Pali Canon,** or Theravadin Canon, a collection of revered writings, or Scriptures, recorded from oral traditions and codified and standardized in the first century C.E. These Scriptures contain sermons, rules, and essays on philosophy and psychology. They are used not only to train Buddhist monks, but also for meditation by experienced monks, and for pious reading of the layman who is a believer in the Buddha's way. These Scriptures are also called The Tripitaka, or The Three Baskets of Wisdom, because they are divided into three parts (Discipline, Sermon, and Metaphysical). Other materials have been added to the Tripitaka over the years, but these later additions do not merit the same reverence as the originals.

Pali Canon

A collection of revered Buddhist writings recorded from oral traditions and codified and standardized in the first century C.E.; they contain sermons, rules, and essays on philosophy and psychology.

The Path of Teaching in the "Sermon Basket" of the Pali Canon

All that we are is the result of what we have thought: it is founded on our thoughts, it is made up of our thoughts. If a man speaks or acts with an evil thought, pain follows him, as the wheel follows the foot of the ox that draws the carriage.

All that we are is the result of what we have thought: it is founded on our thoughts, it is made up of our thoughts. If a man speaks or acts with a pure thought, happiness follows him, like a shadow that never leaves him.

—Dhammapada 1:1–2.

Few are there among men who arrive at the other shore (become Arhats); the other people here run up and down the shore.

But those who, when the law has been well preached to them, follow the law, will pass across the dominion of death, however difficult to overcome.

A wise man should leave the dark state (of ordinary life), and follow the bright state (of the Bhikshu). After going from his home to a homeless state, he should in his retirement look for enjoyment where there seemed to be no enjoyment. Leaving all pleasures behind, and calling nothing his own, the wise man should purge himself from all the troubles of the mind.

—Dhammapada 6:85–88.

Do not speak harshly to anybody; those who are spoken to will answer thee in the same way. Angry speech is painful, blows for blows will touch thee.

—Dhammapada 10:133.

Even the gods envy those who are awakened [Buddha] and not forgetful, who are given to meditation, who are wise, and who delight in the repose of retirement (from the world). . . .

Not to commit any sin, to do good, and to purify one's mind, that is the teaching of (all) the Awakened.

The Awakened call patience the highest penance, long-suffering the highest Nirvana. . . .

Not to blame, not to strike, to live restrained under the law, to be moderate in eating, to sleep and sit alone, and to dwell on the highest thoughts—this is the teaching of the Awakened.

There is no satisfying lusts, even by a shower of gold pieces; he who knows that lusts have a short taste and cause pain, he is wise.

—Dhammapada 14:181, 183–186.

There is no fire like passion, no capturer like hatred; there is no net (snare) like delusion, no torrent like craving.

—Dhammapada 18:17.

The best of ways is the eightfold; the best of truths the four words; the best of virtues passionlessness; the best of men he who has eyes to see.

—Dhammapada 20:273.

"All created things perish," he who knows and sees this becomes passive in pain; this is the way to purity.

"All created things are grief and pain," he who knows and sees this becomes passive in pain; this is the way that leads to purity.

"All forms are unreal," he who knows and sees this becomes passive in pain; this is the way that leads to purity.

He who does not rouse himself when it is time to rise, who, though young and strong, is full of sloth, whose will and thought are weak, that lazy and idle man will never find the way to knowledge.

—Dhammapada 20:277–280.

Him I call indeed a Brahmanza who calls nothing his own, whether it be before, behind, or between, who is poor, and free from the love of the world.

—Dhammapada 26:421.

—The Sacred Books of the East, Vol. X, The "Dhammapada," *translated by F. Max Müller (India: Motilal Banarsidas, 1965). Taken from* World Scriptures *by Kenneth Kramer. Copyright © 1986 by Paulist Press. Used by permission.*

Summary

1. Buddhism developed out of Siddhartha Gautama's dissatisfaction with traditional Hinduism in his native India.
2. Buddhism stresses that happiness is found in discovering our true selves, not in magical practices or some unknown future.
3. Dedicated Buddhists accept The Four Truths and The Eightfold Path to enlightenment.
4. Buddhism is a religion of meditation/reflection and insight that leads a person to a natural evolution from ego-centered behavior and thought to wise and compassionate behavior and thought.
5. The distinguishing characteristic of Buddhists is that they do not rely upon an outside deity or deities to help them find spiritual fulfillment.

For review

1. In what essential ways does Buddhism differ from Hinduism?
2. Who was Buddha? How did he get the name Buddha?
3. What are Buddha's basic principles of life?
4. How do you react to Buddha's view of the reasons for unhappiness in life? Give reasons for your answer.
5. What do you think are the chief characteristics of Buddhism?
6. Do those who are not monks have any role in Buddhism? Explain.
7. What are the principle expressions of Buddhism? How do they differ?
8. What is contemplation? Do you think it ought to be part of a person's religious life regardless of his religion? Why?
9. What seem to be the essentials of Buddha's "way"? What are the goals of these essentials? What is "nirvana"?
10. Explain Buddha's Eightfold Path, giving examples.
11. Describe Zen Buddhism.
12. How do you account for the popularity of Hinduism and Buddhism among certain people raised in Western cultures?

For discussion

1. Discuss whether Buddhism is a practical form of religion, or way of life, for the average person.
2. Given the basic principles of Buddhism, discuss whether Buddhism is a way of life for the elite only, and, if it is, why it has so many adherents.
3. Discuss why Buddhism and Hinduism are largely confined to the subcontinent of Asia and the Orient.
4. Discuss the similarities between Muhammad and Buddha.

For research

1. Find out what you can about the life of a Buddhist monk.
2. Prepare a report on the effect of Communism (1949–present) on Buddhism in China, Vietnam, and Cambodia.
3. Prepare a report on Buddhism in North America.
4. Complete at least two more readings in Buddhist Scriptures; then report on the content and what you think about them.

Word list

ascetic

bodhisattva

Buddha, The

Buddhism

dhamma

ego-self

Eightfold Path, The

Four Noble Truths, The

Mahayana Buddhism

Pali Canon

satori

Tantric [Mantrayana] Buddhism

Theravada Buddhism

Zen Buddhism

9 The Religions of China and Japan

In recent years, stories about China and Japan have increasingly made the news in Western newspapers and news magazines. In spite of this fact, however, the heritage and culture of China, and to a lesser extent, Japan, have remained a mystery to most non-Orientals. Interest in and concern about China and Japan have waxed and waned through centuries since Marco Polo "opened" the East to Western eyes in the fourteenth century C.E.

Since World War II, which ended in 1945, Japan has become rather well known, but China, due chiefly to the Communist takeover in 1949, has remained virtually unknown. Both, however, are still lands of mystery to most Westerners because the heritage and culture of China and Japan are so foreign to Western ways and patterns of thought. Chinese and Japanese ways, however, can be partially understood if a person studies the origin of the culture and heritage of each, and the philosophy of life that has shaped their responses to the mystery of life.

Fushimi–Inan Shrine, Kyoto, Japan.

The Oriental response to mystery

China has been civilized for over 6,000 years. For at least 5,000 years, it has been governed by a succession of dynasties, or ruling families or groups. Those dynasties developed a highly sophisticated system of agriculture, economics, and engineering geared to the preservation and development of the Chinese people.

Japan, according to legend, was organized into an empire by a certain Jimmu, a lineal descendent of the sun goddess, about 660 B.C.E. Between the sixth and eighth centuries C.E., Japan came under the strong cultural influence of the Chinese. It was during this time that Japan was introduced to Chinese Buddhism.

China and Japan, like other lands, have a religious heritage whose origins go back to prehistoric times. That heritage has left a legacy of myths, legends, gods, rituals, and tendencies to the practice of magic. Like other lands, China and Japan have gone through periods of reorganization and reinterpretation of these multiple religious fragments.

The great religions of the West, and to some extent Hinduism (India being midway between the West and the Far East), have tended to find their principle of organization in the concept of God. The Chinese and Japanese religions, however, have tended to find their principle of organization in the concept of harmony with the divine in nature. Judaism, Christianity, and Islam stress God and God's plan for the world. Eastern religions stress people and their ability to fit into the world.

The two principal responses to the mystery of life in China and Japan, Confucianism and Taoism (dowism), combine with Buddhism, and in Japan with Shintoism, to give China and Japan their moral and spiritual base.

It is difficult to tell how many people in China are still practicing Confucianism, Taoism, and Buddhism, because the Chinese Communist government tried systematically to suppress religious practice in mainland China.[1] Despite such persecution, however, religion has remained alive in China. In the Republic of China (Taiwan), there are about eight million Buddhists/Taoists and about 720,000 Christians. In a population of 125 million in Japan, there are around 109 million Shintoists and 96.25 million Buddhists, but there is some overlap in these figures; there are also 1.5 million Christians and a few Muslims.

---

1. In 1976, Mao Tse-Tung, China's revolutionary leader, died. Since that time, the Chinese Communist government has relaxed the harsh measures aimed at wiping out all religion.

Of the four principal responses to the mystery of life in China and Japan, Confucianism and Taoism are unique to China and offer a new aspect to the responses to the mystery of life people have found most useful.

The Oriental philosophy of life

Before a person can look at Confucianism and Taoism separately, he or she must become acquainted with the fundamental Chinese life-outlook underlying both. For the Chinese mind, all of life has a pattern: the eternal interplay between yang and yin. **Yang** is a general term referring to any active or positive principle. **Yin** is a general term referring to any receptive or negative principle. The interplay between activity–receptivity is what produces everything we know. Neither can exist without the other. Just as male is not complete without female, or water has no form without a container, or a sound cannot be distinguished unless there is sufficient silence for it to be heard in, so nothing in life can exist without its corresponding opposite.

"Big" has no meaning except by comparison with something "small," "bright" has no meaning except by comparison with something "dark," a man cannot be a "husband" without a "wife," and "life" itself cannot be appreciated without a proper appreciation for "death"—hence, the importance of ancestor worship, or constant remembrance of the dead, in traditional Chinese daily life. Life constantly brings the various opposites together in creative combination: rain and shine, good and evil, light and darkness, war and peace, life and death. The eternal pattern swirls endlessly on, a continuing interplay of yang and yin. This philosophy exists even in Chinese medicine, as exemplified in acupuncture.

The Chinese have kept this understanding before them from time immemorial by the traditional symbolic drawing. It shows the two opposites, yang and yin, eternally pursuing each other in a harmonious way. There is opposition, but not conflict; there is order-in-tension; there is balance, but not stalemate.

This drawing symbolizes the way life should be lived. No one can hope for all pleasure and no pain, or all life and no death, or all happiness and no waiting, or all agreement and no disagreement. The art of living is to combine harmoniously the yang and yin of one's own life. One can never stop in life and think he or she has it made. There are always adjustments that have to be made because of the changing circumstances of one's life.

yang

A general term referring to any active or positive principle.

yin

A general term referring to any receptive or negative principle.

Gold-plated bronze man unearthed in China in 1987. Han mythology has it that this elf-like, winged man is an immortal who directs the dead to heaven. The Han dynasty existed from 206 B.C.E. to 220 C.E.

If "harmonious interplay between yang and yin" is the goal of one's life (in other words, if life has no goal outside itself, but is an ongoing process), then the question is how to achieve it? How does the individual person—and how does society as a whole—unite all the opposites of life in a harmonious rather than a discordant way?

Traditional Chinese culture produced two major answers to this question—Confucianism and Taoism. Indeed, these two systematic answers complement each other; neither alone seems to have been able to hold Chinese culture together, but the two seem to have balanced each other. The interplay between these two answers seems to be another example of yang and yin in Chinese life. Confucianism stresses tradition, Taoism stresses spontaneity. Confucianism stresses being rational, Taoism stresses being intuitive. Because these emphases are not opposed but complementary, many Chinese have chosen to be both Confucianists and Taoists at the same time.

In recent decades, of course, China has become rather Westernized—especially since the Communist party took power. It is not yet clear to outsiders how greatly traditional Chinese culture has been transformed by Marxist philosophy. All we know in a general way is that Marxism is being expressed in distinctively Chinese ways. The teachings of Confucius are still taught in many Chinese schools, but they are given a Marxist interpretation.

Confucianism

Confucianism gets its name from Confucius (the Latinized form of ***Kung-Fu-tzu***, which means "Kung the Teacher"), who was born around 551 B.C.E. Very little is known about his early home life, except that he was not well-to-do. His father died before Confucius was three, and he grew up with his mother, living in poverty. As he grew up, he earned a living by doing manual labor and, thereby, came to know the life of the common people.

Confucianism

A moral/ethical system developed by the Chinese philosopher Confucius, which emphasizes patience and moral acting.

Kung-Fu-tzu

Confucius, "Kung the Teacher."

At the age of fifteen, he began to take studies seriously, and he delved into the Chinese traditions and classics of his time. He became a civil servant in various low-level government positions but gave this up in his early twenties to become a tutor, in which work he found his place. His reputation as an honest and wise man grew. He seems to have entered politics off and on, but he was always too honest to get far in the political world. However, he never quit trying: he believed that thoughtful men should not retire from the world but should try to put their good ideas into social action. He died in 479 B.C.E. at the age of seventy-three, after having spent the last few years of his life teaching and editing the classic traditional literature known in his day. It is worth noting that Confucius was active in China at the same time Buddha was active in India and Israelite scholars were editing the Jewish Scriptures in exile in Babylon.

It is through his teaching and editing that his influence grew. His many disciples continued to spread his teachings, until centuries later Kung-Fu-tzu was a household word and his many sayings had become proverbs.

Confucius lived in a time when China was being torn apart by constant civil wars. Mass slaughters of 60,000, and even on one occasion 400,000, have been recorded as having taken place in those times. The traditions that had held people together were breaking down as individual clans, led by powerful warlords, claimed the right to establish their own rule.

Conflict was in the air the people breathed, and Confucius feared that all of China could become one vast riot area. Seeing the need to restore order, he thought about how that could be done. What he realized was that order on a large scale began on a small scale. First there had to be order in the family, and then between families, and so on.

Confucius's way to civil order

Confucius did not try to establish new principles for restoring civil peace. Rather, utilizing the Chinese respect for tradition, he took the best of the Chinese traditions and edited them into a systematic whole. He then urged that this treatment of the traditions be taught to the people.

Wherever Confucius's disciples gained influence, they undertook the transformation of local societies. "Moral ideas were driven into the people by every possible means, ... in temples, theaters, homes, toys, proverbs, schools, history, and stories—until they became habits in daily life."[2]

The main outlines of Confucius's teaching can be summarized in five principal terms:

1. *Jen* (humaneness)

Jen was the virtue of virtues, the foundation of all that would follow. It means basically a respect for one's own dignity as a human being and a corresponding respect for other persons. It means loving another as you love yourself.

2. *Chun-tzu* (being the ideal person)

Chun-tzu means taking the abstract quality of *Jen* and putting it into habitual action. It means more than etiquette and politeness. It means making the right attitude so much a part of oneself that it flows out into action no matter what the circumstances.

3. *Li* (the right pattern)

Li has two related meanings: first, doing things the right way, and second, using the correct ritual when doing them. In our own culture, we have similar features to which these can be compared. For example, "doing things the right way" means not being too informal in impersonal situations. For instance, when taking an employment test in a room with hundreds of other applicants, one does not show the instructor one's baby pictures.

---

2. Chiang Monlin, *Tides from the West* (New Haven: Yale University Press, 1947), 9.

"Using the correct ritual" means completing all the required formalities, such as putting one's last name first, first name last, and so on, on the form.

In order to reconstruct society, Confucius stated five general categories of "doing things the right way." He described them in detail and then encouraged appropriate rituals for expressing them:

a. Using the right name for the right thing
b. Choosing the mean between two extremes
c. Living the five basic relations correctly:
- The father–son relationship
- The older brother–younger brother relationship
- The husband–wife relationship
- The older friend–younger friend relationship
- The ruler–subject relationship
d. Devotion to the family
e. Respect for age

Living the five basic relationships correctly, devotion to the family, and respect for the aged (including reverence for ancestors) are hallmarks of the Chinese character.

Appropriate to the five basic relations are ten attitudes: kindness in the father and filial piety in the son, gentility in the older brother and respect in the younger brother, righteous behavior in the husband and obedience in the wife, humane consideration in the older friend and deference in the younger friend, and benevolence in rulers and loyalty in subjects.

4. *Té* (government by moral power)

In his many sayings on *Té*, Confucius taught that the only way to establish a stable government that people would respect in the long run was to base it, not on military might, but on the power of good example and the obviously sincere intent to serve the welfare of the people. While a tyrannical government can repress the people into outward submission for a time, it is really building up hidden resentment, which will one day work against it. The governments that last and are effective are those that win the spontaneous consent of the people.

5. *Wen* (cultivation of the peaceful arts)

Confucius encouraged people to admire musicians, artists, poets, and teachers more than soldiers. If people's ideals are directed toward the good and beautiful things of life, they will not be easily inclined to war, which destroys these things.

Diety in Thian Hock Keng Temple (Temple of Heavenly Happiness).

Confucius emphasized the correct way to live in this life. He did this by laying out in a rational step-by-step order the best of Chinese tradition and exhorting that it be systematically taught to all the people. He was a pious man who believed in a heavenly world, but he did not focus upon the heavenly side of things. His focus was on this world. He took religious piety for granted but did not explicitly delve into the supernatural side of things.

Three hundred years after Confucius's death, Confucianism became the state religion of China. In 130 B.C.E., it became also the basic training for government officials, maintaining its influence even up to the twentieth century.

Tolerance in Eastern religions

One of the things that is difficult for westerners to understand about eastern religions is that in general they are very tolerant of divergent views. The name Catholic came to Christianity early on in its history as the result of the development of heresies or divergent views. Actually it was the Emperor Constantine who insisted on uniformity in the [Christian] Church's teachings, calling the Council of Nicea to set forth "catholic" doctrine, that is, an interpretation that would be upheld universally throughout the Church. Eastern religions rarely insist on such a normative interpretation, and in some cases allow their members to embrace more than one faith. To these religions, if one belief is good, two is even better.

The place of Taoism among Chinese religions is a further indication of this eclectic approach.

In China one does not find some dedicated to Confucianism and others to Taoism, so much as one sees each person making use of several religions, usually for different purposes or on different occasions. In China there are actually three religions common among its people. The two native religions of Confucianism and Taoism are practiced, as well as Buddhism, brought from India by Bodhidharma and other missionary-monks. There religions do not seem to compete; rather they complement one another. In the days prior to the communist revolution, it was common that the young would be educated in the principles of Confucianism, married in a Taoist ceremony, and buried at a service led by a Buddhist monk.

—Lucius Boraks, CFX, Religions of the East *(Kansas City, MO: Sheed and Ward, 1988), 69. Used by permission of Sheed and Ward.*

Taoism

Taoism

A religious system of China which teaches the importance of union with and balance in nature.

Tao

The nameless, formless eternal principle that governs the universe, or the Path, or Way, that the universe (nature) follows; as used in Taoism, it means roughly "The Way Life Is."

Lao-Tzu

Legendary author of the *Tao Te Ching* ("The Way and Its Power"), from which Taoism evolved.

Tao Te Ching

"The Way and Its Power," the foundational book of Taoism.

Taoism derives its name from the Chinese word **Tao** (pronounced "Dow"), which means "path," or "way." Tao is the nameless, formless eternal principle that governs the universe, or the Path, or Way, that the universe (nature) follows. As used in this religious system, it means roughly "The Way Life Is."

Taoism arose as a counterbalance to the heavily rational and traditional emphasis of Confucius's approach to life. Confucius, in effect, had laid out detailed blueprints about The Way Life Ought to Be; many people felt that equal weight should be given to The Way Life Is.

According to tradition, Taoism was born about 500 B.C.E., when an old man named **Lao-Tzu** (meaning "The Grand Old Teacher") was riding a water buffalo into Tibet to become a hermit. He was stopped by a border guard who asked him to put his wisdom into a book so it would not be forever lost. This he did, in the book the **Tao Te Ching** ("The Way and Its Power"). Then he disappeared across the border and was never heard from again.

Many Taoist legends tell anecdotes of Lao-Tzu meeting with Confucius and their having debates. Most scholars, however, think that Lao-Tzu is a legendary figure and agree that the beginnings of Taoism cannot be traced with certainty any farther back than about two centuries after Confucius's time, when his teachings had been around long enough to merit a widespread reaction.

Taoism has since split into three branches: (1) Religious Taoism, a popular form of Taoism; (2) an **esoteric** form of mysticism, which never became popular, and (3) Philosophical Taoism, a philosophy of intuitive respect for the "Natural Way Things Have of Working Themselves Out." In this latter form, it has greatly influenced Chinese art, culture, thinking, and religion. It is this form that we will consider.

The basic principle of Taoism is **wu wei** (translated roughly as "let go" or "let it happen"). Taoists believe that there is in everything a natural tendency to act harmoniously with the rest of the universe. Rain and shine, night and day, pleasure and pain—all things tend to balance out—unless people put artificial obstacles in the way.

esoteric

Meant for only the select few who have special knowledge, not common or ordinary, not simple.

wu wei

Taoism principle translated roughly as "let go" or "let it happen"; act in harmony with the nature of what one is dealing with.

Kamakochi, Japan.

Sometimes human plans are shortsighted: human beings attempt to gain a momentary advantage over nature by working "against the grain" of things. When they do this, they upset the balance of nature and their plans collapse. For example, a man who is in a hurry may run too fast for his physical condition; his momentary burst of speed is compensated for by an exhaustion that overtakes him before he can finish his journey. As a result, he winds up arriving later than if he had paced himself at a comfortable speed, letting his body carry him and set its own pace rather than attempting to force his body by sheer will-power. Or a busy housewife may work herself into a nervous breakdown if she anxiously rushes from job to job instead of letting the work carry her along. Or a sculptor may cause his statue to break if he chisels into the stone arbitrarily rather than by studying the grain of the material and carving in accord with it.

In other words, the principle of *wu wei* does not mean human beings should be inactive do-nothings. It means they should act in such harmony with the nature of what they are dealing with that it almost seems the work is doing itself. Thus, there is no need for an excessive number of blueprint directions from the outside in order to do something; the true directions come from the inner nature of what is to be done.

Taoism, rightly understood, applies not only to the fine arts but to every aspect of the art of living. In politics, for example, the *Tao Te Ching* says,

> *A leader is best*
>
> *When people barely know he exists. . . .*
>
> *Of a good leader, who talks little,*
>
> *When his work is done, his aim fulfilled,*
>
> *They will all say, "We did this ourselves."*

Here again, those (in this case the rulers) who live according to Tao—who let The Way It Is be their principle of action—are active, but they act "with the grain" of their people. They help them fulfill their plans; they do not arbitrarily dictate their own plans to them.

The art of "letting go" or "letting it happen" is not an easy one to learn. By over-concentrating on external rules, people can become self-conscious and defeat their own purposes—like baseball batters who work themselves into a slump by concentrating excessively on their swing and forgetting about the ball. The way out of their slump is the principle of *wu wei*—they should be absorbed in *what* they are doing, not worrying about *how* they are doing. They should allow themselves to see the motion of the ball; they should swing comfortably and naturally.

Actually, "natural hanging-looseness" can be carried to lazy extremes just as much as "rational calculation of one's moves" can lead to the opposite extreme of self-consciousness.

While Confucianism lends itself to the second extreme, Taoism can be oversimplified to the first. That is why Confucianism and Taoism together operate as a yang-yin pair to keep the Chinese mentality in balance. Each needs the principles of the other within itself in order not to go to extremes.

Because they trust the inner "Isness" of things, Taoists see no reason for a God above nature, a Lord to direct it and give it an "Oughtness" from the outside. For them, such a God would be contrary to The Way It Is. In some popular forms of Taoism, there may be many gods, but these are not the God Above All in the Western sense.

Hence, many Taoists find the God of Judaism, Christianity, and Islam unintelligible. Not only does that God seem to be a super-Confucianist making people's decisions for them, but that God seems to be a rival to the harmonious order of nature itself.

Furthermore, God (as the Western mind conceives God) seems to be all yang and no yin: all good and no evil; all activity and no receptivity. In the Western understanding of the struggle between God and the devil (who is not pure evil but is represented as having been made good in his nature but having made himself evil in his own will), Western religions foresee the ultimate triumph of God. But the Oriental mind cannot conceive of an end to the eternal conflict, with yang winning out over yin; that would destroy the harmony of the whole universe. It would be contrary to The Way It Is.

Perhaps it is the yang-yin philosophy pervading Eastern thought that leads Westerners to consider the Chinese and Japanese people inscrutable. It is perhaps also the reason that Eastern people consider Westerners naive. In any case, people of both East and West are basically religious. Both have their own answers to the mystery of life.

The Chinese religious sense

In spite of the fact that Confucianism and Taoism seem to be primarily "secularist" religions and deal fundamentally with how to live a happy or meaningful life, most of the Chinese people who are not Muslim or Christian are not pure secularists. They do have beliefs and practices that are distinctly religious in the strictest sense. They have their gods (literally hundreds of them), their forms of worship, their temples, their shrines, their hymns and stories, their belief in an afterlife, and practices Western people might call magic (but the Chinese would call liturgy, if they used that term).

This particular religious aspect of Chinese life is a mixture of Confucianism, Taoism, Buddhism, and folk, or popular, religion. It is characterized by deep reverence, ancestor worship, formal religious ceremonies, ritual practices to particular gods, and religious festivals, the chief of which is the celebration of the Chinese New Year. They also have Scriptures made up of stories and legends preserved from ancient oral traditions and the wise sayings of Confucius, Lao-Tzu, the Buddhist masters, and unnamed commentaries on Chinese life and worship.

The religions of Japan

Japan, a tiny island nation off the coast of China and only a few miles from Korea, has nearly 125 million people packed into 143,751 square miles of land, four fifths of which is mountains or hills. Its most famous city, Tokyo, is one of the largest cities in the world, with about twelve million people. Japan is the most densely populated country in the world, with over 870 people per square mile—compared to the United States, which has sixty-eight people per square mile.

Japan is a country of contrasts and contradictions. It is highly developed technologically, yet its culture is extremely traditional. The Japanese are home-loving, family-oriented people, yet they are among the most traveled in the world. Many women in Japan are totally subservient to the men, yet they have complete control over the way money is used in the family. The highly educated, scientific-minded people still send messages to the nature gods in the form of small pieces of paper tied to trees—"just in case."

Fushimi–Inan Shrine, Kyoto, Japan.

Like any people, the Japanese people can be understood only in terms of their culture. It is deeply religious, expressing an interrelatedness in all things, a sense of the spiritual in all aspects of life, and an inherently religious element in even the smallest action seemingly unrelated to what others call religion.

The most widely practiced religion in Japan can best be called **Shinto/Buddhism.** Although each is a religion distinct in itself, most Japanese people practice a combination of both Shinto and Buddhism.

Shinto/Buddhism

The most widely practiced religion in Japan, a combination of Shinto and Buddhism.

Shinto is the native religion of Japan and has its origins in the prehistoric period. The early Japanese, seeing the world around them animated by spiritual powers, revered nature. When they were still hunters and gatherers, their religious ceremonies focused on fertility. Once they turned to agriculture and began to settle in villages, their religious ceremonies focused on agricultural festivals, revering the dead, and honoring the leaders of the ruling class, who were thought to be descendants of the deities. It was only in the seventh century C.E., when Buddhism, Confucianism, and Taoism began to predominate, that Shinto started to define itself.

The word *Shinto* means "the way of the **kami**." For the early Japanese, the *kami*, although they could inhabit human beings, were basically the forces of nature. "Among the objects or phenomena designated from ancient times as kami are the qualities of growth, fertility, and production; natural phenomena, such as wind and thunder; natural objects, such as the sun, mountains, rivers, trees and rocks; some animals; and ancestral spirits."[3] At first the *kami* were worshiped in natural settings, for example, on the top of a hill. Eventually, however, shrines were built in which to worship them. Belief in the *kami* is common among the Japanese today, and accounts for the fact that most of them practice some form of nature worship, believe in an untold number of gods or spirits, and practice a highly developed form of ancestor worship, manifested by their elaborate burial services and care for their graves.

Shinto

A Japanese form of the Chinese *shin tao,* meaning "the way of the kami"; the native religion of Japan.

kami

For the early Japanese, the forces of nature; related to nature worship and ancestor worship in Japan today.

Shinto gods.

3. Dr. Sokyo Ono, *Shinto: The Kami Way* (Tokyo, Japan: Charles E. Tuttle Company, Inc., 1962), 7.

Shinto

In Shinto all life is lived in communion and in accord with the mind of the kami, which afford the devout constant protection. Daily life is regarded as "service to the kami," that is, as matsuri, a term generally associated with only gala occasions and elaborate processions, but which has its deeper meaning of service and worship.

Shinto rites and ceremonies commemorate life: ordinary daily life as well as the major events in the life of the individual, community, and nation. Ceremonies may be observed on such occasions in the home or in some public place, but primarily they are observed in shrines.

Shrine rites and ceremonies are intended to ward off or ameliorate any misfortune and secure or augment the co-operation of the kami in promoting the happiness and peace of the individual and the community. They include prayer for divine protection, communion with the kami, praise of the kami's virtue, comfort for the kami's mind, reports to the kami on the affairs of daily life, and pledges offering the whole of life to the kami. Therefore, the ceremonies are performed on the assumption that a profession of faith in the kami has been made, offerings good and beautiful have been presented, the mind and body have been purified, sincerity has been fulfilled, conduct has been courteous and proper, the evil heart, selfish desire, strife, dispute, hatred and the like have been dissolved, conciliation has been practiced, and a feeling of goodwill, cooperation and affection has been realized among the people.

The ceremonies vary greatly in complexity from the simple, individual acts of worship in front of a home altar or a local sanctuary, and the morning and evening presentation of offerings by priests, to the annual festivals which in some cases include great processions with much paraphernalia and hundreds or even thousands of people participating. Generally speaking, the larger and more important shrines have more elaborate and magnificent functions, but there are exceptions.

All ceremonies, except the simple act of worship performed by an individual before a shrine, involve four elements: purification (harai), an offering (shinsen), prayer (norito), and a symbolic feast (naorai). These may be observed either simply or elaborately, depending upon the occasion. It is a distinctive feature of Shinto that kami-worship is expressed not only from the depth of one's heart, but in a concrete act of religious ritual.

Purification Purification is for the purpose of removing all pollution, unrighteousness, and evil which may hinder life according to the kami-way and the efficacy of worship. Purification may be performed by the worshippers or by priests. . . .

Offerings The minimum ritual requirement for the kami is a periodic presentation of offerings. Ideally this should be done daily. In some cases it is performed twice a day. If this simple act is neglected, it is believed that the kami, particularly the ancestral spirits, will be unhappy and that misfortune will be experienced often by individuals who are remiss in observing this duty. Although there are many small wayside shrines or shrines located in remote, inaccessible areas, which appear to be neglected, there are probably a very few shrines that are not cared for sometime during the year, either by a priest or some devout resident.

In shrines of any great importance, the offerings are quite elaborate and much detailed attention goes into their preparation, especially at the time of the annual festival. But whether the shrine is large or small the manner of preparing offerings is probably prescribed in considerable detail in the shrine records. . . .

Prayers The ceremonial prayers that are read, or rather recited, at shrines by the priest are in classical Japanese, which was intelligible when it was the prevailing language, but is not understood today by people unless they have made a special study of the subject. In ancient times, a great many historical and other important records were written in beautiful, rhythmic poems in order to facilitate their transmission to posterity. Prayers were also composed in this style in order that the mystic feeling embodied in the manner of addressing the kami, which had been inherited from great antiquity, might be transmitted intact to future generations. This was especially necessary because the new, short and to Japanese ears somewhat harsh Chinese words without melody, which had been introduced from the mainland and had modified the Japanese language, were not deemed suitable to preserve the meaning and spirit of ancient ceremonies. . . .

Sacred Feast At the end of any Shinto ceremony, except when only the simple act of worship is performed before a shrine, whether it be in a home or shrine, or for an individual, group, wedding, or grand festival, there is a sacred feast, called naorai, which means "to eat together with the kami." In the case of the worshippers, this consists of formally drinking a sip of rice wine served by a priest or one of the girl attendants. In the case of a shrine festival the priests, prominent laymen, and special guests gather in the priests' quarters or some other place and, after partaking solemnly of a few sips of rice wine, enjoy a relaxing and even hilarious meal at which much more wine is consumed.

—Dr. Sokyo Ono, Shinto: The Kami Way (Tokyo, Japan: Charles E. Tuttle Company, Inc., 1962), 50–57.

The Buddhism practiced in Japan is, as we said, an import from China. Its most widely known form is Zen (from the Chinese *Ch'an,* meaning "religious meditation"), which has uniquely Japanese characteristics.

Modern Japanese Zen consists of two sects, Rinzai and Soto. . . . Both were effectively systematized and transferred to Japan by approximately 1200. . . .

For both Rinzai and Soto the core of the method is sitting meditation (**zazen**)*. . . . Zazen is simply sitting, eyes open and fixed on a spot on a wall in front of you. Individuals so engaged are doing nothing more than observing the universe, including their own thoughts, without comment. While it may seem rather unnatural to sit in a single spot for hours on end, this practice is perfectly consistent with Zen "theory" when it is observed that Zen suggests experiencing reality directly. The state of consciousness associated with Zen is thus one in which dualistic distinctions are dropped, so that the mind ceases its clutching at experience. Clearly, this is best accomplished by quietude—by simply being aware of whatever is happening. To use a cliche,* zazen *is the attempt to "live in the now" while simultaneously eliminating the person who is doing the living.*

Accordingly, one sits solely for the sake of doing so; sitting has no other purpose. To do zazen *with some goal in mind, to do it for some particular reason, such as becoming a buddha, is to miss the point entirely. When not trying to fit the world into our conceptual order, when not trying to experience experience, when not consumed with the illusion of the ego, there is simply nothing else to be done. In other words, monks sit, having seen to other responsibilities, there is no reason to do anything else. . . .*

A second method, the **koan,** *is also used by both Soto and Rinzai, though the latter puts far greater stress (and faith) upon it. The word literally means "public document," though it is often translated as "problem." The latter is closer to the mark idiomatically, in that it suggests the actual use of the term. The* koan *is a story or anecdote of some type, often in the form of a dialogue between a master and student, or a question followed by an answer. Each* koan *contains in it some insight into Zen which the student is expected to grasp.*

The koan *is often "studied" in conjunction with* zazen, *so that the two practices merge. Its* raison d'etre *is identical to that of* zazen *alone: to lead the student to* satori. . . .

The koan *exists to hammer upon the walls of logic and convention until they collapse. The basic premise is to confront the student with a story or question which is utterly incomprehensible. Viewed from the perspective of ordinary consciousness fixed upon dualistic thinking, the* koan *is nothing more than mindless gibberish. It is this very ab-*

zazen

A meditation technique used by Zen Buddhists in Japan.

koan

Zen paradox—arresting question which tends to halt one's "thinking about things," to create doubt and anguish in order to awaken a deeper level of the mind beyond the discursive intellect.

roshi

A master "certified" to "teach" Zen.

haiku

A form of Japanese poetry known for its simplicity.

bodhisattva

In Shintoism, the human form of a Shinto god.

surdity that opens the mind, that slowly evokes the possibility of doubting the world of dualism. In other words, the koan *is like an attorney cross-examining a witness. By constant questioning, even badgering, the questioner begins to expose the basic contradictions of the witness's position. Finally, the level of doubt about this position reaches a critical level and the entire edifice collapses. By employment of the* koan, *the* **roshi** *leads the student to a similar collapse of faith. As Heinrich Dumoulin explains it,*

> *The essence of the* koan *is to be rationally unresolvable and thus to point to what is arational. The* koan *urges us to abandon our rational thought structures and step beyond our usual state of consciousness in order to press into new and unknown dimensions. [Zen Buddhism: A History (India and China) (New York: Macmillan, 1988), 246.][4]*

Zen Buddhism is the most widely known form of Japanese Buddhism because it was "imported" from Japan to the United States during the late 1960s and early 1970s. It answered a spiritual need of many people of the time that was brought on by the activist responses to the mystery of life preached by many Western religious figures. It offered specific techniques for meditation, required periods of silence and repose, and called for self-discipline and temporary removal from the hectic pace of life. Its better-known disciplines involved judo, karate, flower arranging, calligraphy (the art of fine handwriting or printing), the composing of **haiku,** and the tea ceremony. They all became part of the U.S. scene as many North Americans turned to the Orient for its wisdom.

As we have said, however, the predominant religion in Japan itself is Shinto/Buddhist because most Japanese combine the two into one way of responding to life's mystery. They have incorporated the Shinto gods into the Buddhist deity system, theology, and worship services, and the Buddhist deities were adopted by the Shintoists—the Buddhas and the **bodhisattvas** were, for the Shintoists, human forms of the Shinto gods.

Both religions have been highly influenced by Confucian and Taoist doctrines. This accounts for the manners and morals characteristic of the family life, social world, and political structure of Japan.

Western religions have gained some ground among the Japanese, and Western ways have influenced Japanese thinking, but by and large, the Japanese have clung to their ancient religions and practice them with a fervor that is the envy of other religious people.

---

4. Benjamin and Amy Radcliff, *Understanding Zen* (Rutland, Vt: Charles E. Tuttle Company, Inc., 1993), 107–111.

The Master said, He who rules by moral force (té) is like the pole-star, which remains in its place while all the lesser stars do homage to it.

The Master said, If out of the three hundred **Songs** *I had to take one phrase to cover all my teaching, I would say "Let there be no evil in your thoughts."*

—The Analects of Confucius, Book II, 1–2.

The world knows beauty as being beautiful,

Just because there is ugliness.

The world knows good as being good,

Just because there is bad.

Therefore being and non-being produce each other,

Difficult and easy complement each other,

Long and short form each other,

High and low incline to each other.

Therefore the sage engages in non-action,

And teaches without words.

All things are done,

But he did not initiate them.

Creating but not possessing,

Doing but not depending,

He achieves but does not dwell on the achievement.

Just by not dwelling on it,

He never loses it.

—Tao Te Ching, 2.

The Great Tao flows everywhere.

It may go left or right.

All things depend on it for life,

and it does not turn away from them.

It accomplishes its task,

but does not claim credit for it.

It clothes and feeds all things

but does not claim to be master over them.

Always without desires, it may be called The Small.

All things come to it and it does not master them;

it may be called The Great.

Therefore (the sage) never strives himself for the great,

and thereby the great is achieved.

—Tao Te Ching, 34.

"Since the object of your coming is the Dharma," said I, "refrain from thinking of anything and keep your mind blank. I will then teach you." When he had done this for a considerable time, I said, "When you are thinking of neither good nor evil, what is at that particular moment, Venerable Sir, your real nature (literally, original face)?"

As soon as he heard this he at once became enlightened.

—Sutra spoken by the Sixth Patriarch on the High Seat of "The Treasure of the Law," chapter 1.

Summary

1. Oriental religions are generally concerned with ordering life to achieve happiness.
2. Oriental religions include many gods and many forms of early religious development.
3. Most people in China and Japan combine two or more religions in their way of life.
4. The two principle Chinese responses to the mystery of life are Confucianism and Taoism. The principle Japanese response is Shinto/Buddhism.
5. The religions of both China and Japan call for great self-discipline, meditation, and the acceptance of life as it is.

For review

1. What seems to be the basic difference between the East and the West as far as the response to the mystery of life is concerned?
2. Explain the history and nature of Confucianism.
3. Summarize the history and nature of Taoism.
4. Illustrate the Chinese "principle of life."
5. How would you characterize the Chinese religious sense?
6. What are the *kami* in the Shinto religion?
7. What seems to be the predominant Japanese religion? Explain.
8. Why do the Chinese and the Japanese have such respect for family life?

For discussion

1. Discuss your perceptions of Chinese and Japanese people. On what are those perceptions based? Do you think your perceptions are accurate?
2. Discuss whether the principles of Confucius would apply to people living under any form of government.
3. Discuss why the Chinese and Japanese seem to emphasize proper, formal social relationships..

For research

1. How is Marco Polo's venture into Asia a metaphor for East-West relations?
2. Make a chart on the early history of China.
3. Prepare a report on the early history of Japan.
4. Read and analyze some Japanese art and poetry.
5. Find out what you can about the origins of judo and karate.
6. How did the revolution of 1949 in China affect the status of religion there?
7. Prepare a report on the Western religions in Japan.

Word list

bodhisattva	*koan*	Shinto/Buddhism	yang
Confucianism	Kung-Fu-tzu	Tao	yin
esoteric	Lao-Tzu	Taoism	*zazen*
haiku	*roshi*	Tao Te Ching	
kami	Shinto	*wu wei*	

Part Three

The Question of Atheism

All beliefs on which you bet your life are fundamentally religious beliefs, and atheism can be as much a religion as theism.

—H.M. Kallen

10 The Absence of God

In one sense, atheism is not a new phenomenon. In ancient days, people who could not accept certain gods were called a-theists—people "without gods." For example, in the days of early Christianity in Rome, Christians were thought to be atheists because they would not worship the Roman gods. And during the Enlightenment, some philosophers were considered atheists because they did not accept the prevailing understanding of God.

Atheism, in the sense of denying the existence of God, is a relatively new phenomenon, however. It is only in recent times in the Western world that a sizable number of people have come to reject the idea of a God (in contrast to rejecting a particular idea of God in the past). Karen Armstrong, in her book *A History of God,* points out that it wasn't until the very end of the eighteenth century in the West that some would come to deny the existence of God, for the following reasons:

> *From birth and baptism to death and burial in the churchyard, religion dominated the life of every single man and woman. Every activity of the day, which was punctuated with church bells summoning the faithful to prayer, was saturated with religious beliefs and institutions: they dominated professional and public life—even the guilds and universities were religious organizations. . . . Even if an exceptional man could have achieved the objectivity necessary to question the nature of religion and the existence of God, he would have found no support in either the philosophy or the science of the time. Until there had formed a body of coherent reasons, each of which was based on another cluster of scientific verifications, nobody could deny the existence of a God whose religion shaped and dominated the moral, emotional, aesthetic and political life of Europe.[1]*

---

1. Karen Armstrong, *A History of God* (New York: Alfred A. Knopf, 1993), 286–287.

Atheism today

Atheism is usually not a religion in the way we have been speaking about it in this book. It is a religion, however, in the broader sense of the word, that is, as a person's response to the mystery of life. Although atheists don't have a "God" response, they are as fervent in their belief as any person who gives a God response.

There are many forms of atheism. There are, however, two basic categories: philosophical atheists and atheists-in-practice.

Philosophical atheists

A **philosophical atheist,** strictly speaking, is a person who rejects the assumption that there is a God or Supreme Being (a-theist). In popular understanding, however, a religious person who does not see God as personal is, nevertheless, not an atheist. Therefore, those whose answer to the mystery of life is an Ultimate Force or an Unknown are not atheists. For example, the Buddha would be considered by some as an atheist because he chose not to comment on the question of God and emphasized right living and personal enlightenment. However, in the popular understanding, the Buddha would not be an atheist.

A **materialist** is a kind of philosophical atheist, one who believes that nothing spiritual exists. Such a person believes that only matter or forms of matter exist. Therefore, that rules out the possibility of a God.

Materialists realize, of course, that there are many things about people which cannot be located or defined physically—for example, they believe in "truth" and "love" and they realize that a surgeon cannot cut a man open and extricate an organ named "truth" or a tissue called "love." But they believe that such "spiritual" things are in reality *expressions* of matter. As an example of this point of view, one might consider a dance or a song. The dance is not the body, but it is artistic motions of the body; the song is not the vocal cords, but it is the vocal sound arranged artistically. You cannot operate on the body and amputate a dance, nor can you label any particular organ the song. The dance and the song are not physical things, they are *expressions* of physical things, yet they are not spiritual "things" existing in their own right. Following this line of reasoning, materialists say that there is no spiritual substance called a soul or spirit or called God—there is only matter and its various expressions.

philosophical atheist

One who rejects the assumption that there is a God or Supreme Being.

materialist

A philosophical atheist who believes that nothing spiritual exists.

atheist-in-practice

A person who has given no thought to the question of God, or one who displays a disregard for the question.

agnostic

A person who believes one cannot know whether or not there is a God, Supreme Being, Ultimate Force, or Existence.

Atheists-in-practice

An **atheist-in-practice** is one who is an atheist "of convenience," or one who, for one reason or another, has given no thought to the question of God, or one who displays a disregard for the question. Some people who say they believe in God are atheists-in-practice because their lives show no evidence of their belief. They celebrate only this life's triumphs. Their vision is limited to what life has to offer, and their hope is circumscribed by their own death.

Further distinctions

Not all atheists are materialists, since some persons who do not believe in a God still believe that people have a mind or even a soul or spirit or life-force that is more than material.

An **agnostic** is a person who believes one cannot know whether or not there is a God, Supreme Being, Ultimate Force, or Existence.

Most atheists, agnostics, and materialists are sincere, thoughtful people just like those who profess some kind of religious belief based on the acceptance of a God as the answer to the mystery of life. Some, however, are more or less indifferent—they couldn't care less whether there is a God or not. Others are sociological atheists or agnostics—they grew up in a society that was atheist or agnostic.

Reasons some do not believe in a God

It is impossible, of course, to discuss the particular thoughts of every individual atheist. But it is possible to chart the thinking that can be found among many atheists for their denial of the existence of God. Not every one of them thinks all these thoughts, but most atheists think some of them. (Many God-oriented people have thoughts like these also, but instead of looking outside of God for answers to their problems with God, they tend to search more deeply into their religious heritage.)

Among the reasons given by many atheists for their denial of God's existence are these:

1. The concept of God perceived as a threat to people's independence

Modern psychology has revealed that a person does not truly become an adult psychologically until he or she is no longer dependent upon what his or her parents or parent-substitutes think. Some persons may be in their thirties or forties, but they still haven't established an identity separate from another or others—they are always looking over their shoulder for someone older or bolder to tell them what to think or do.

For many people who are not yet adults psychologically, "God" seems to function in their lives as an invisible father-image, a person who has their lives so well planned for them that they are constantly insecure about doing the wrong thing. They scrupulously fear "God's" judgment and punishments, which they imagine are ready to leap out at them from behind every corner.

When some thoughtful atheists observe others whose "God" keeps them so unfree, they say that they don't want anything to do with that "God." They notice that many people obey the moral law, not because things are in themselves right or wrong, but because they fear the punishment of God. The concept of a rewarding or punishing God seems to be an infantile need for directions from a super-parent, and an escape from real adult responsibility.

2. The problem of myth

Scholars have become able to "crack the code" of many ancient myths. We now recognize these myths as symbolic stories. For example, in many ancient religions the sacredness of laws is guaranteed by presenting them as having come from God or the gods in a miraculous manner. This encourages responsibility and obedience to those laws. So, in the Judeo-Christian tradition, the Ten Commandments

demythologize

(1) To translate an ultimate divine truth from mythical language into literal, scientific language, (2) to remove all traces of alleged "myth" from a religious system.

are pictured as being carved in stone by God on Mount Sinai amidst lightning and thunder.

Today, many people look for the meaning in these myths without taking every detail of the myths literally. Thus, while they may not literally believe that the social code of Moses' desert people was inscribed on stone tablets by lightning bolts, they recognize that the sacredness of law is enshrined in such a poetic story. This process is commonly referred to as "**demythologizing**," one meaning of which is to translate an ultimate divine truth from mythical language into literal, scientific language.

Another meaning of demythologizing is to remove all traces of alleged "myth" from a religious system. Atheists do this when they demythologize not only legends like those concerning how human laws got started, but also the very concept of God. They say that the notion of a super-person ruling the universe is really only a poetic way of saying that *persons* should rule things; things should not rule persons. In a world where nature seemed to rule, people needed an imaginary super-person, or super-persons to control nature. In today's world where people, through science, are learning to harness nature, some people think they can rely on themselves and not a mystical super-power. Therefore, they proclaim that such a concept of God has outlived its usefulness and now "God is dead."

3. Historical selectivity

As the old saying goes, "There are three sides to every story: my side, your side, and the truth." We all know how different people who were present at the same event will tend to describe it differently, especially if their advantage is in one way or another connected with the event. (One has only to watch or read about the most recent UN debates over the latest international incident.)

We have always realized this about history—that it is written differently according to who writes it—but until recently many people thought Jewish and Christian biblical history was exempt from this general condition. Jewish and Christian Scripture studies popularized during the twentieth century, however, have shown that "God's inspiration of the Bible" can no longer be interpreted as some kind of "hot line" whereby God dictated exactly what was to be written. We know that the Bible contains historical facts, but they are interpreted from the religious point of view of the Jewish people and sometimes exaggerated or embellished and legendized or told in the form of epic poetry in order to emphasize the sacred meaning of the event.

Many modern people have become very skeptical about historical objectivity in general, and some people are skeptical about any historical arguments offered to prove the existence of God or to prove that God intervened in history with a self-revelation.

4. Unresolved theological problems

Some persons are atheists because they find that the concept of God raises theological problems to which they personally can see no solution. One such problem is that of divine causality and human freedom. Some people ask: How can people be truly free if the source of their actions is really God?

Another problem for some people is that of providence versus the natural laws of the universe. Why should God make natural laws to run the universe if God is always going to be interrupting them in answer to prayer? Or if God already has the answer to someone's prayer "programmed into" the laws of the universe from the beginning, then why pray for what's already going to happen?

Sometimes atheism is the result of "a proof mentality." Seeing no "proof"—that is, physical, tangible evidence—that God exists, this kind of atheist says there is no God. Having concluded that there cannot be a God, this kind of atheist looks for answers to the mystery of life elsewhere.

5. The existence of evil

If a good God exists, why is there so much evil in the world? This serious question bothers many sensitive people. Looking at life to see if they can discern the hand of a Person/God behind it all, they are stumped by what they see. On the one hand, they see evils that have natural causes (sometimes with a little help from human beings, or at least poor judgment): earthquakes, hurricanes, tornadoes, floods, fires. On the other hand, they see evils that are caused intentionally by humans: family quarrels, international wars, daily murder and robbery, violence in their neighborhoods, abused children and spouses, broken hearts and wounded bodies. "Where is the hand of God in all this?" they ask. "Either there's no God or else God is powerless. One way or the other, God is not worth taking into account." Unable to reconcile the existence of pain, suffering, and death in "innocent" people with belief in a good God, they refuse to believe there is a God because "if there were, God would not allow such evil to exist."

6. Failure of religious people and communities to live up to their beliefs

Most believers in God have developed their faith within a religious or Church community. Although they believe the existence and nature of God can be proved from reason, they in their own lives have not reasoned this out but have accepted it because the Church they belong to seemed believable to them.

Likewise, many atheists disbelieve in God, not because of philosophical arguments, but because the Churches they see do not convince them. A community which says God established it to spread love on earth is not believable to people who say they see the Church members showing little or no love within their ranks.

Again, a Church or other religion which says it stands for human progress is laughed at by many atheists if the group appears to use out-of-date techniques, ideas, and political methods within its own institutions. A community which says God loves the poor, but does nothing as a community to assist poor people, is a blasphemy in the eyes of many humanitarian atheists who love their fellow human beings and who see the "God" of religious groups as the Super-Defender of the status quo. This is especially so if the Church has expensive buildings, its leaders are wealthy, and the group supports political regimes which favor the wealthy class over the suffering poor.

Under this heading we should also take note of those who use as an argument against God the many instances of violence and war which have been committed in the name of religion in the course of history. Logically, of course, this is not an argument against the existence of God, but many people use it as such.

Memorial to the Dead at Yad Vashem Holocaust Memorial, Jerusalem.

When God is not the answer . . .

Out of the Nazi death camps and the violence of the Second World War came a voice, more numb than mad, asking in a hushed whisper rather than a crazed shout, "Where is God?" In his autobiography, Elie Wiesel, who survived the unspeakable suffering of the death camps in which his family perished, tells of a Polish rabbi who, in the dark, hopeless world of the prison camps that the Nazis had constructed for the forced labor and ultimate liquidation of the Jews, was driven to despair, to a loss of faith. The rabbi asked, "Where is the divine Mercy? Where is God? How can I believe, how could anyone believe, in this merciful God?"*

The death camps were not alone in obscuring the light. German soldiers experienced a similar emptiness. **Last Letters from Stalingrad** *is a poignant collection of letters from German soldiers facing death in the Battle of Stalingrad. Cut off from any course of retreat by Russian forces and left by the German high command to perish or surrender, the soldiers were afforded, in January of 1943, what was to be their last chance to send letters home. One letter from a son facing death, to his father, a Christian pastor, illuminates the way in which senseless suffering and violence can result in a loss of meaning.*

> *In Stalingrad, to put the question of God's existence means to deny it. I must tell you this, father, and . . . I regret my words doubly, because they will be my last. . . . You are a pastor, father, and in one's last letter one says only what is true or what one believes might be true. I have searched for God in every crater, in every destroyed house, on every corner, in every friend, in my fox hole, and in the sky. God did not show himself, even though my heart cried for him.*
>
> *The houses were destroyed, the men as brave or as cowardly as myself, on earth there was hunger and murder, from the sky came bombs and fire, only God was not there. . . . And if there should be a God, he is only with you in the hymnals and the prayers, in the pious sayings of the priests and pastors, in the ringing bells and the fragrance of the incense, but not in Stalingrad.***

* Elie Wiesel, Night *(New York: Avon Books, 1969), 87.*

** Last Letters from Stalingrad, *trans. by Franz Schneider and Charles Gullans (New York: New American Library, 1965), 65–66.*

—*Roger Schmidt,* Exploring Religion, *2nd. ed. (Belmont, CA: Wadsworth Publishing Company, 1988), 468.*

Watching the Vietnam War during the mid-1960s on the nightly news inspired me to perform my patriotic duty and join the army. There, I was trained as a light weapons infantryman and a paratrooper. I was ordered to the front lines of battle in South Vietnam in September 1966 and fought until January 1968. I extended my tour of duty for the special privilege of an early honorable discharge.

My Vietnam War experiences began in the fall of 1966 fighting the South Vietnamese communists—the Viet Cong. After my first month in Vietnam, I became an atheist. . . . No compassionate God, I thought, would permit all this killing to happen. After witnessing the dead and wounded during my first "firefight," I looked up and said, "You sadistic God! You're not worthy of my worship."

Medical evacuation by helicopter "dust-off" was a comfort to many soldiers in the jungles. When soldiers incurred critical wounds, they could expect to be returned home to the United States. Otherwise, they could be assured of arriving at a hospital operating table and being treated with professional care, usually in about thirty minutes. However, when ambushed and outnumbered by an enemy force with superior firepower, the fear of dying strikes one's intellect and emotions to the point of crippling panic.

This happened to me near a hamlet northwest of Saigon. I, along with five other men, was assigned to night duty at an outpost about a half-mile from company perimeters. We carried only our M-16 rifles, grenades, Claymore mines, and a two-way radio to protect us. That night we were surprised by an assault group of Viet Cong guerilla fighters. Three dead young American soldiers were silhouetted by the moon's reflections inside our outpost bunker. The radio man sputtered, "Oh, Lord! Oh, Lord! Help us!" My response to him was to stop praying. I exclaimed, "To hell with God! You help us! You radio back for mortar and artillery fire support!" Fortunately, he regained his composure and radioed the forward observers for fire support to be directed at our map coordinates. Common sense dictated that staying alive was more important than wasting precious time praying. Consequently, he saved our lives.

The next morning, I was thrilled to see the men from my company. Fortunately, I didn't sustain any personal injuries from the night assault. However, the assaults of the next morning struck me personally when a surviving soldier said to me, "See, Paulsen, God answers prayers." I replied, "I'm . . . glad that **someone** *was an atheist in a foxhole!" He laughed because he thought I was joking, and I had to allow him to believe that I was—I had to keep my atheism to myself.*

—*Philip K. Paulsen, "I Was an Atheist in a Foxhole,"* The Humanist *(Sept. / Oct. 1989): 28.*

7. Closed-mindedness of "true-believers"

Some atheists react against certain features of some God-centered religions. They reject ideas of God or habits and practices of current religions or of "religious people" that they feel go contrary to the thrust of society or to the discoveries of modern science, psychology, politics, and economics. The reaction is caused, on the one hand, by the existence of religions that do in fact contradict modern knowledge, and on the other, by ignorance of the development of religious understanding in response to modern knowledge.

In the face of new scientific discoveries and the questions they raise, some atheists say, a person who wishes to retain his or her religious faith can do so in one of two ways: (1) open his or her mind to the discoveries, let the questions speak themselves in his or her mind, and reinterpret what has been inherited from religion in a way that makes sense, or (2) close his or her mind to the discoveries, squelch questions before they are bothersome, and think that any kind of reinterpretation is a form of blasphemy.

Some atheists believe that the first way is a "nice try" that can't be kept up for any length of time because a completely honest reinterpretation could only lead (so they say) to atheism. They believe that the only way a person can retain religious faith is to adopt the second way, that of closed-mindedness, of refusing to consider the evidence. There are enough religious believers of this type around to convince them that religious faith creates a closed mind. Thus, these atheists believe people must make an either-or choice between science and religion. Having misconceptions about what modern religious understanding consists in, they look outside of "religion" for the answers to the mystery of life.

8. Vested interests

Many nonbelievers feel that religious faith (which to them is a form of closed-mindedness) could not be maintained by ignorance alone, but must also be the result of selfish leadership in a religion or Church. They believe that persons in power maintain a system which promotes their own position of authority, using moral fear to control people and make them conform. This is especially true for cult-type groups, some of whom may even use this control to acquire the savings and income of cult members.

Conclusion

There are, of course, other reasons for choosing atheism, such as repressed religious feelings, neglect of religious practices, traumatic religious experiences, dislike of or hatred for certain religious persons or things, superstition, peer-group pressure, or social fashion. For the most part, people with these motives are not convinced atheists; they are "emotional" atheists. For them the denial of God fulfills some psychological need, like getting even with God or someone who represents God, punishing themselves for not being more religious, or fear that if they say they believe in God or show any sincere conviction that God exists, they will be laughed at or considered "different."

For the most part, true atheists live in God-oriented societies as individuals seeking answers to life's mystery in their own ways, seldom banding together to form any community of believers. They have only one common denominator: belief that there is no God. Atheism, like religious faith, is a way of looking at the world, human experience, and the mystery of life. For some people, it is the only way. They are as secure in their faith as many religious people are in theirs.

Summary

1. Atheism is a response to the mystery of life, a no-God response.
2. There are various kinds of atheists and various ways to describe atheists: philosophical atheists, materialists, atheists-in-practice, emotional atheists, sociological atheists.
3. An agnostic believes one cannot know whether or not there is a God, Supreme Being, Ultimate Force, or Existence.
4. Some atheists reject the idea that there is a God because they can find no physical proof that there is a God. Others are disappointed or disenchanted with the religious faith and actions of established religions.

For review

1. What is the difference between a philosophical atheist and an agnostic?
2. What is the difference between a materialist and an atheist-in-practice?
3. What are some of the reasons that some people reject the idea of God?
4. Is it correct to say that atheists and agnostics are really religious? Why? Why not?

For discussion

1. Debatewhether or not it is realistic to blame God for the faults of some God-oriented people.
2. Propose some reasons that some religious people attack people who do not believe in God.
3. Discuss why some atheists work so hard against religion and/or religious institutions.
4. The First Amendment of the Constitution of the United States states: "Congress shall make no law respecting the establishment of religion, or prohibiting the free exercise thereof. . . ." What does this mean? Do you think this is a good idea? Explain. Is making laws forbidding prayer in the public schools "prohibiting the free exercise of" religion? What have the U.S. Courts said about these issues? Exchange your thoughts with your classmates in an open forum.
5. Discuss what aspects in established religions discourage people from practicing religion.
6. Discuss the following quotation from Voltaire. Do you think it is true? If it is, what effect does it have on world affairs? Might it apply to people in general and not simply to people in power? Explain.

   Most of the great men of this world live as if they were atheists. Every man who has lived with his eyes open knows that the knowledge of God, his presence, and his justice, has not the slightest influence over the wars, the treaties, the objects of ambition, interest or pleasure, in the pursuit of which they are wholly occupied.

For research

Karl Marx and Friedrich Engels, the "fathers" of modern communism, said, "Religion is the sigh of the oppressed creature, the feeling of a heartless world, just as it is the spirit of unspiritual conditions. It is the opium of the people." What do you think they meant? Do some research on the origins of communism; try to determine why it has been called "atheistic" communism.

Word list

agnostic
atheist-in-practice
demythologize
materialist
philosophical atheist

Appendix

Places and dates associated with the origin of the prinicpal expressions of religious awareness

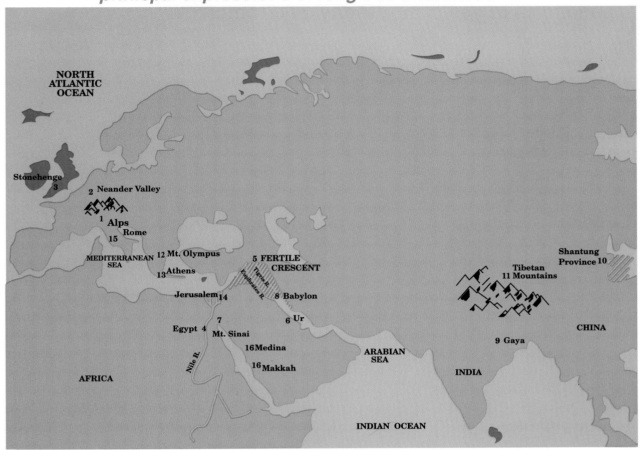

1. 180,000–50,000 B.C.E.: totems (bear shrines) caves.
2. 50,000–10,000 B.C.E.: cave paintings.
3. 5000–200 B.C.E.: stone arrangements for sacred worship places.
4. 3100 B.C.E.: Egyptian religion flourishes.
5. 3000 B.C.E.: Babylonian religion flourishes.
6. 1900 B.C.E.: Biblical "Abraham" migrates to Promised Land.
7. 1285 B.C.E.: Moses establishes the covenant with the LORD after the Exodus.
8. 587–536 B.C.E.: Babylonian Exile of the Jewish people.
9. 500 B.C.E. (roughly): Buddha becomes "awakened" under the Bo tree.
10. 500 B.C.E. (roughly): Conficius edits the Chinese classics.
11. 500 B.C.E. (roughly): Legendary Lao-Tzu is said to write *Tao Te Ching* before crossing Tibetan border.
12. 900 B.C.E.: Greek gods "established on Mount Olympus."
13. 500–300 B.C.E.: Golden Age of Greek philosophers.
14. 29 C.E.: Jesus of Nazareth crucified near Jerusalem.
15. 1st century C.E.: St. Peter establishes focus of Christianity at Rome.
16. 622 C.E.: Muhammad flees from Makkah to Medina.

The faithful of yesterday, today, and tomorrow

Adherents in millions and as a % of world population

Religion	1900	%	1980	%	2000	%
Christian	558	34.4	1,433	32.8	2,020	32.3
Roman Catholic	272	16.8	809	18.5	1,169	18.7
Protestant and Anglican	153	9.4	345	7.9	440	7.0
Eastern Orthodox	121	7.5	124	2.8	153	2.4
Other	12	.7	155	3.6	258	4.1
Non-religious and atheist	3	.2	911	20.8	1,334	21.3
Muslim	200	12.4	723	16.5	1,201	19.2
Hindu	203	12.5	583	13.3	859	13.7
Buddhist	127	7.8	274	6.3	359	5.7
Chinese Folk Religion	380	23.5	198	4.5	158	2.5
Tribal and Shamanist	118	7.3	103	2.4	110	1.8
"New Religions"	6	.4	96	2.2	138	2.2
Jewish	12	.8	17	.4	20	.3
Other*	13	.8	36	.8	81	1.0
World population	**1,620**		**4,374**		**6,260**	

Due to rounding off, percents may not equal 100.
• including Sikh, Confucian, Shinto, Baha'i, Jain, Spiritist, Parsi
Source: World Christian Encyclopedia

MAJOR WORLD RELIGIONS

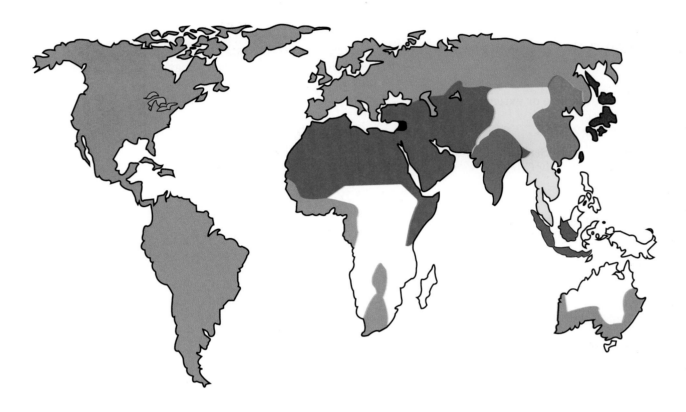

This map gives a general idea of the areas where the world's major religions have exerted their strongest direct influences.

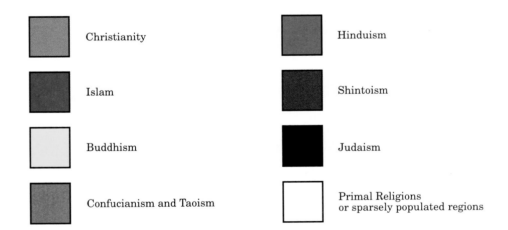

Christianity		Hinduism	
Islam		Shintoism	
Buddhism		Judaism	
Confucianism and Taoism		Primal Religions or sparsely populated regions	

Word List

Abraham

Patriarch of the Hebrew people.

accretions

Additions; growth in size or extent.

Acts of the Apostles

A book in the Christian Scriptures which tells the story of the early Christians.

Adonai

A Jewish name for God which means "my Lord."

agnostic

A person who believes one cannot know whether or not there is a God, Supreme Being, Ultimate Force, or Existence.

Allah

The God, in Islam.

amalgam

A union of items into a whole; a combination or mixture.

angel

A messenger from God, usually considered a spiritual being.

anthropologist

One who studies the science of human beings, especially their origin, nature, and destiny.

apostles

Twelve men who followed Jesus and (with the exception of Judas, who was replaced) became leaders of groups of early Christians.

archaeologist

A scientist who studies the material remains of past human life and activities.

areligious

Without religion.

artifacts

Usually handmade objects representing a particular culture or stage of technological development.

ascetic

One who dedicates his or her life to the pursuit of contemplative ideals, and practices extreme self-denial for religious reasons.

astrology

The study of the stars or heavenly bodies to see if favorable conditions existed for undertaking an action.

atheist-in-practice

A person who has given no thought to the question of God, or one who displays a disregard for the question.

Atman

The true self or soul of each individual, the soul being divine and eternal and beyond the ego or personality.

auguring

Foretelling, especially from omens.

Babylonian Exile

The capture of the Jewish leadership and exile of this group into the Babylonian empire from 587 to 536 B.C.E.

Babylonian religion

An ancient polytheistic religion which originated in the Fertile Crescent and which reflected a dark outlook on life.

baptism

Initiation into the Christian community by water (immersion, pouring over the head, or sprinkling) and the words, "I baptize you in the name of the Father and of the Son and of the Holy Spirit."

Bhagavad Gita

A book of Hindu Scripture containing the story of Lord Krishna, who is the source of the manifestations of Vishnu.

Bible

The book of sacred writings for Christians, which includes the Hebrew Scriptures (Old Testament) and the Christian Scriptures (New Testament); the Bible is a collection of many smaller books.

bodhisattva

In Buddhism, one who is on the threshold of nirvana but postpones his or her own entry to help others reach nirvana; in Shintoism, the human form of a Shinto god.

Brahma

The Hindu god who is the Creator.

Brahman

For Hindus, the transpersonal ultimate divine reality (or the Absolute, or the Godhead), primal source of the universe and ultimate goal of all beings.

Brahmanas

A collection of writings for priests containing directions for sacrifice.

Buddha, The

Siddhartha Gautama, The Awakened or Enlightened One.

Buddhism

A way of life based on The Four Noble Truths and The Eightfold Path.

capricious

Impulsive

caste

A division in Hindu society based on one's position in life, determined by birth into that group.

Catholic

The word *catholic* means "universal"; *Catholic* (as in Church) refers to the Christian Church centered in Rome under the authority of a pope.

celibate

Unmarried, abstains from sexual intimacy.

charismatic

Having extraordinary or supernatural power or charm; persuasive.

Christ

A Greek term roughly equivalent to "messiah"; used by Christians to refer to Jesus.

Christian feast days

Days of Christian celebration to recall God's saving actions in Jesus.

Christian Scriptures

The New Testament of the Christian Bible.

Christianity

Religions based on a belief in Jesus and his teachings.

Christmas Day

The Christian celebration of the birth of Jesus.

Confucianism

A moral/ethical system developed by the Chinese philosopher Confucius, which emphasizes patience and moral acting.

covenant

A sacred agreement, contract, testament between two parties.

crucifixion

Execution by being nailed to or hung on a cross; the manner of Jesus' death.

culture

A people's expression of who they are and what they believe about themselves and the world in which they live, the sum of their art, literature, music, dance, folklore, and religion.

deity

A god or goddess; sometimes refers to an impersonal god.

demythologize

(1) To translate an ultimate divine truth from mythical language into literal, scientific language, (2) to remove all traces of alleged "myth" from a religious system.

dhamma

The essential quality or character of Buddhism.

divination

The attempt to tell the future or to discover hidden knowledge by magical means.

doxology

A prayer of praise to God.

early Egyptian religion

An ancient and serene polytheistic religion of Egypt centered around two important gods: Re and Osiris.

Easter Sunday

The Christian celebration of the resurrection of Jesus.

Eastern religions

Those religions that arose and are practiced in India, China, and Japan, and are practiced in Southeast Asia and the Far East.

economic system

The network of services by which a group of people obtain food, water, shelter, and other material necessities.

ecumenical movement

The promotion of a worldwide Christian unity or cooperation.

ego-self

Our own view of ourselves, which is highly subjective and biased according to our personal ego needs.

Eightfold Path, The

Eight steps or modes of being and acting necessary in the Buddhist way of life.

El Shaddai

The clan-god of Abraham and Sarah; "God Almighty."

esoteric

Meant for only the select few who have special knowledge; not common or ordinary, not simple.

Exodus

The escape of the Jewish people from captivity in Egypt and their journey through the Sinai desert on the way to the Promised Land of Canaan (Israel); also the name of the second book of the Jewish Bible.

formula

A set form of words for use in a ceremony or ritual.

Four Noble Truths, The

According to Buddha, four principles for living that lead to happiness.

Genesis

First book of the Jewish Bible.

God the Father

The first person of the Trinity, as understood by Christians.

Gospel

One of four books in the Christian Scriptures which deal with the life and teachings of Jesus; literally, the word means "good news."

Great Schism

The division of the Christian Church into the Roman Catholic Church and the Eastern Orthodox Church.

Greek religion

A humanized religion of Greece in which the gods were supermen and superwomen and which dealt with the meaning of life.

guru

A spiritual director, teacher, or guide, in the Hindu tradition.

Habiru

A name referring to a social group in the ancient Middle East who lived on the fringe of society, at times referring to roving bands, mercenaries, and foreign slaves. It may be that the Hebrews emerged from one such group.

Hadith

A collection of Muhammad's words, sayings, explanations, and examples to help the believer follow the Quran.

haiku

A form of Japanese poetry known for its simplicity.

hajj

The Muslim obligation to make a pilgrimage to the Ka'ba in Makkah.

Hammurabi

The king who codified known existing laws in the eighteenth century B.C.E.

Hanukkah

The Jewish Festival of Lights or Feast of Dedication celebrated in December.

Hebrew

A name for the Jewish people and their language.

Hegira

Muhammad's flight from Makkah to Yathrib (Medina).

hierarchy

A ranking system based on an agreed upon classification.

Hinduism

The basic religion of India, marked by contemplation and self-denial for religious reasons.

Holy Spirit

The third person of the Trinity, God's Spirit, as understood by Christians.

horoscope

A chart based on the movement of the stars which is used to attempt to foretell the future.

human society

The organization of people into political and social groups to provide the necessities of life.

icon

A religious image common to Eastern Christianity which is painted to a conventional model and has high symbolic significance.

Imam

The leader of prayer in a mosque.

incantation

A spell or verbal charm used as part of a ritual of magic.

infantilism

The living of religion on the level of children.

Isaac

Son of Abraham and Sarah.

Ishmael

Son of Abraham by the servant woman Hagar.

Islam

The religion of Muslims.

Israeli

A native or inhabitant of the republic of Israel.

Israelites

The Jewish people, at one time named after Israel, also known as Jacob, son of Isaac and Rebekah, grandson of Abraham and Sarah.

Jacob

Son of Isaac and Rebekah, grandson of Abraham and Sarah.

Jesus

The person on whom Christians base their faith; considered human and divine by most Christians; the second person of the Trinity, as understood by Christians.

Jewish Bible

Scriptures of the Jewish people.

Jews

Those who belong through descent or conversion to a continuation of the ancient Jewish people.

jihad

Islamic holy war to spread Muslim rule.

jinn

Sprites or spirits (sometimes described as similar to elves or fairies) capable of taking on human forms and of influencing human beings for good or evil; spiritual beings between humans and angels.

Judaism

The religion of the Jewish people characterized by belief in one God and the living out of God's law as expressed in the Jewish Scriptures.

Ka'ba

The rectangular sacred shrine of Islam located in the courtyard of the Great Mosque in Makkah.

Kali

The Hindu goddess who destroys evil.

kami

For the early Japanese, the forces of nature; related to nature worship and ancestor worship in Japan today.

koan

Zen paradox—arresting question which tends to halt one's "thinking about things," to create doubt and anguish in order to awaken a deeper level of the mind beyond the discursive intellect.

Krishna

A popular and important incarnation of Vishnu in Hinduism.

Kung–Fu–tzu

Confucius, "Kung the Teacher."

Lao-Tzu

Legendary author of the *Tao Te Ching* ("The Way and Its Power"), from which Taoism evolved.

law of karma

The moral law of cause and effect; the Hindu connection between how one acts and the consequences for those actions.

linguist

One who studies languages.

liturgy

An action associated with religious worship and practice; public acts of worship.

Lord's Supper

Celebration (in some Christian Churches, remembrance) of the last meal Jesus had with his friends, in which he blessed and shared bread and wine and asked them to do this in memory of him.

magic

The use of devices, such as spells and charms, believed to have supernatural powers.

Mahayana Buddhism

A major division of Buddhism which extends the goal of Buddhism to laypersons, as well as to monks, the goal being a godly existence of self-sacrifice and compassion, as well as nirvana.

Makkah

The holy city of Islam, located in Saudi Arabia; in the West, often spelled *Mecca*.

materialist

A philosophical atheist who believes that nothing spiritual exists.

messiah

Someone sent by God to lead the Jewish people to their days of glory.

Messianic Age

A "Golden Age" with a royal ruler who would be an ideal person to rule an ideal people.

minaret

Muslim tower with balconies used for the announcement of prayers.

minister

A person officially charged with performing religious functions in a Christian Church; may be ordained and/or appointed.

moksha

Release from the endless cycle of rebirth.

monotheism

Religion based on belief in only one God.

moral or ethical code

A system of rules or principles or laws regarding right conduct.

mores

Customs of a group that are morally binding.

Moses

Leader and prophet of the Hebrew slaves who escaped from Egypt.

mosque

The Muslim house of prayer and worship.

Muhammad

The last of God's prophets or messengers, according to Islam.

mummification

Process of embalming and preservation of the dead practiced in ancient Egypt.

Muslim

An adherent or believer in Islam.

mystery

The unknown and unknowable dimension of reality that lies behind and beyond ordinary human experience.

myth

A story or tradition with a loose historical basis which serves to unfold part of the worldview of a group of people or explain a practice or belief or a natural event.

nirvana

In Hinduism, a state in which a person is united with his or her deepest self, Brahman.

Orthodox

The word *orthodox* literally means "right worship"; *Orthodox* refers to the Christian Church of the East which separated from the Roman Church in 1054 C.E.

Pali Canon

A collection of revered Buddhist writings recorded from oral traditions and codified and standardized in the first century C.E.; they contain sermons, rules, and essays on philosophy and psychology.

panentheism

Belief that the whole of reality is in God.

patriarchs and matriarchs

The famous ancestors of a people.

Pentecost

The Jewish festival of Shavu'ot, commemorating the giving of the Ten Commandments by God to Moses; the Christian feast celebrated fifty days after Easter, which celebrates the gift of the Holy Spirit to the first Christians.

Pesah or Passover

The Jewish spring festival recalling the Exodus; includes the seder meal.

philosophical atheist

One who rejects the assumption that there is a God or Supreme Being.

philosophy

The pursuit of wisdom; a search for a general understanding of reality.

placate

To appease or soothe someone or some power.

political system

The network of government to ensure the provision of necessities in an orderly and equitable manner.

polygamy

Religious practice that allows a man to take more than one wife.

polytheism

Religion based on a belief in many gods.

postulate

Propose; put forward a plan or intention.

prehistory

The time before written records.

preliterate

Before the use of writing.

priest

Common term for an ordained leader of the community in some Christian Churches: Orthodox, Catholic, Anglican (Episcopalian).

primitive

Early ancestral type.

prophet

Among the Jews, one who called the people back to the covenant and who led the people in their understanding of God; in Islam, Muhammad is the greatest prophet and Jesus is considered also to be a great prophet.

propitiation

An attempt to appease or pacify someone or some power.

Protestant

The term encompasses a large number of Christian Churches which formed at the time of the Reformers (sixteenth century) and thereafter; used to describe most Christian denominations which are not Catholic or Orthodox.

Purim

A Jewish winter feast which recalls the biblical story of Esther.

Quran

The holy writings of Islam; alternative spelling: *Qur'an*. Koran is the previously used English form of the Arabic word meaning "book," or "reading."

rabbi

A teacher of the Jewish Torah and other written and oral traditions.

Ramadan

The Muslim obligation to fast during the ninth lunar month in the Arabian calendar.

redemption

A "buying back," a return to a relationship with God after individual or corporate sin.

reincarnation

Rebirth into a higher or lower form of life according to how well or how poorly a previous life was lived.

religion

The response a person gives to the mystery of life; a response to the mystery of life that is organized, ritualized, and agreed upon by a group of people.

religious system

A response to the mystery of life adhered to by a group, and expressed by means of formulas, rituals, and a moral or ethical code.

resurrection

A rising from the dead; belief in the resurrection of Jesus is common among Christians.

revelation

That which God has disclosed to people about God, human beings, the meaning of life and death, and the world as a whole.

rite

A prescribed form for words or actions in a ceremony.

Rite

A division of a Christian Church using a particular liturgy.

ritual

The ordered words and actions of a religious ceremony.

Rosh Hashanah

Jewish celebration of the new year.

roshi

A master "certified" to "teach" Zen.

Sabbath

A day of worship and rest; in Judaism, from sundown on Friday to sundown on Saturday; in most Christian Churches, Sunday.

sacrament

A sign or symbol which expresses the Holy as understood by members of a particular religion; for Christians, a sacrament is a visible sign of the action of Jesus in their lives.

salat

The duty of Muslim men to pray, including the obligatory five times daily.

samskaras

Hindu sacred life-cycle rituals.

Sarah

Wife of Abraham and matriarch of the Hebrew people.

satellite gods

Secondary or minor gods, often in the service of a major god.

satori

Glimpse of enlightenment (achieved in a flash) about life.

Second Vatican Council

The official gathering of Catholic bishops (1962–1965), at which representatives of many other religions were present as observers.

secular

Nonreligious; worldly or temporal.

seder

The Jewish ritual meal of Passover.

seer

A wise person and/or one who foretells future events.

shahada

Islamic public profession of acceptance of Allah as the One God and Muhammad as the messenger of God.

shaman

A religious or magic practitioner who, on behalf of a group, with the aid of guardian spirits, enters into a trance-like state to make contact with the powers of the spirit world.

Shavu'ot

The Jewish feast celebrated on the fiftieth day after Passover; the Feast of Weeks or Pentecost.

Shema

The Jewish doxology which expresses the essence of that faith.

Shinto

A Japanese form of the Chinese *shin tao*, meaning "the way of the *kami*"; the native religion of Japan.

Shinto/Buddhism

The most widely practiced religion in Japan, a combination of Shinto and Buddhism.

Shiva

The Hindu god who is the Destroyer.

sin

An act or attitude which goes against the wishes or law of the God or gods; in Judaism, missing the mark or failing to follow the Torah.

Sinai

The peninsula extension of the continent of Asia between the Red Sea and the Mediterranean; also the name of the desert on that peninsula and a mountain from which, Jews believe, the Law was given to Moses.

Sukkot

The Jewish autumn harvest celebration; Feast of Booths or Feast of Tabernacles.

synagogue

In Judaism, a special building for worship and instruction.

syncretism

An attempted reconciliation or fusion of opposing beliefs or practices.

taboo

A positively forbidden action.

Talmud

A collection of Jewish laws and traditions; a compilation of Jewish doctrine and discipline based and built on the Torah.

Tantric [Mantrayana] Buddhism

A division of Buddhism which combined Mahayana Buddhism with Tantric cults of India, includes many deities and spirits.

Tao

The nameless, formless eternal principle that governs the universe, or the Path, or Way, that the universe (nature) follows; as used in Taoism, it means roughly "The Way Life Is."

Taoism

A religious system of China which teaches the importance of union with and balance in nature.

Tao Te Ching

"The Way and Its Power," the foundational book of Taoism.

theology

The study of religious faith, faith in general, and religious experience.

Theravada Buddhism

A division of Buddhism which stresses the *sangha* (the brotherhood of monks) as the means of following the *dhamma* (the essential quality or character of Buddhism).

Torah

The Law and teachings of the Jewish Scriptures; the first five books of those Scriptures: Genesis, Exodus, Leviticus, Numbers, and Deuteronomy.

totem

A spiritual force in an object (usually animal or plant) affecting the life of an individual or a group.

transcultural

Spanning more than one culture or social group; passing from one culture to another.

Trinitarian

Characterized by belief in one God in three persons; in general, the Christian understanding of God.

Upanishads

A collection of philosophical and mystical texts dealing with Atman and Brahman; they are appended to the Vedas and are a major part of the Hindu Scriptures considered to have divine origin.

Vedas

Four collections of religious material containing prayers, ritual, liturgy, hymns, and spells and charms of a popular nature.

Vishnu

The Hindu god who is the Preserver.

Western religions

Those religions that arose in the Middle East and are practiced in the Western world and in the Muslim countries: Judaism, Christianity, Islam.

worship

Religious ritual of adoration of forces, a deity, or deities.

wu wei

Taoism principle translated roughly as "let go" or "let it happen"; act in harmony with the nature of what one is dealing with.

yang

A general term referring to any active or positive principle.

yin

A general term referring to any receptive or negative principle.

yoga

A system of physical and mental discipline designed to achieve a spiritual purpose.

yogi

Practitioner of yoga.

Yom Kippur

The Jewish Day of Atonement.

zakat

The Muslim obligation to give alms for the care of the poor and needy.

zazen

A meditation technique used by Zen Buddhists in Japan.

Zealots

A militant faction within Judaism in the first century C.E.

Zen Buddhism

A school of Mahayana Buddhism which has successfully conveyed to the West certain aspects of the Buddha's teachings; its hallmark is contemplation. It is the form of Buddhism practiced in Japan.

Index

Photo Credits

Cover—Robert Fried (top right, center), Richard B. Levine (bottom left)

Editorial Development Associates—84, 108
Robert Fried—2–3, 13, 16, 21, 44, 45, 62, 78, 85, 87, 98-99, 106, 115, 117, 129, 134, 135, 144, 147,
    148, 155, 156, 158, 170, 177, 180
Luke Golobitsh—1, 8, 14, 28, 119, 128, 132, 140, 143, 173
Jean-Claude LeJeune—124, 131, 138
Richard B. Levine—6, 48, 109, 160, 163, 164, 168
Richard T. Nowitz—32, 36, 50, 60, 64, 66, 67, 69, 103
Gene Plaisted/The Crosiers—41, 72, 75, 81, 83, 90
Frances M. Roberts— 54, 59, 65, 95, 105, 111, 152
James L. Shaffer—18, 80

Maps by Mike Cooper